P9-CEI-848

MAY 2 5 2006

OUR
CONSTITUTION

"Citizenship is every person's highest calling."

Ambassador Walter H. Annenberg

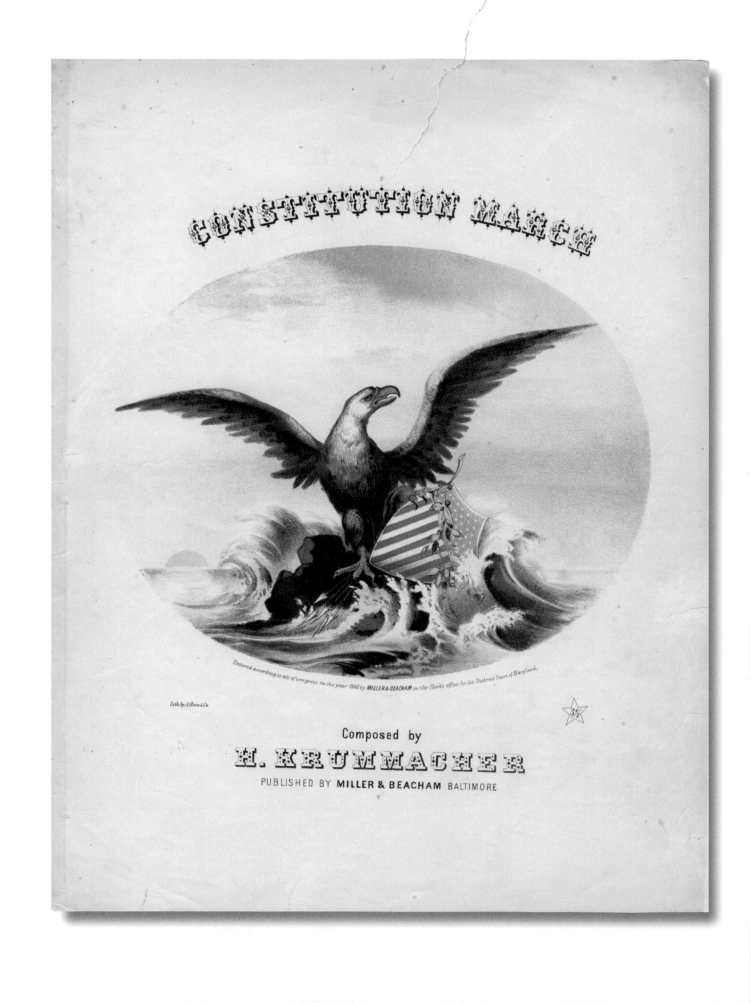

CONSTITUTION MARCH

Entered according to act of congress in the year 1860 by MILLER & BEACHAM in the Clerks office for the District Court of Maryland.

Lith. by A.Hoen & Co.

3½

Composed by

H. KRUMMACHER

PUBLISHED BY **MILLER & BEACHAM** BALTIMORE

OUR CONSTITUTION

Donald A. Ritchie
& JusticeLearning.org

CARVER PUBLIC LIBRARY

THE ANNENBERG FOUNDATION TRUST AT SUNNYLANDS

THE ANNENBERG
PUBLIC POLICY CENTER
OF THE UNIVERSITY OF PENNSYLVANIA

OXFORD
UNIVERSITY PRESS

Oxford University Press, Inc. publishes works that further
Oxford University's objective of excellence
in research, scholarship, and education.

Oxford New York
Auckland   Cape Town   Dar es Salaam   Hong Kong   Karachi
Kuala Lumpur   Madrid   Melbourne   Mexico City   Nairobi
New Delhi   Shanghai   Taipei   Toronto

With offices in
Argentina   Austria   Brazil   Chile   Czech Republic   France   Greece
Guatemala   Hungary   Italy   Japan Poland   Portugal   Singapore
South Korea   Switzerland   Thailand   Turkey   Ukraine   Vietnam

© 2006 by the Trustees of the University of Pennsylvania
Published by Oxford University Press, Inc.
198 Madison Avenue, New York, New York 10016
www.oup.com

Oxford is a registered trademark of Oxford University Press

All rights reserved. No part of this publication may be reproduced,
stored in a retrieval system, or transmitted, in any form or by any means,
electronic, mechanical, photocopying, recording, or otherwise,
without the prior permission of Oxford University Press.

Library of Congress Cataloging-in-Publication Data
Ritchie, Donald A.
Our Constitution/Donald A.
Ritchie.— 1st ed.
p. cm.
ISBN-13: 978-0-19-522385-9
ISBN-10: 0-19-522385-3
1. Constitutional law—United States—Popular works. 2. Constitutions—United
States. I. Title.
KF4550.Z9R57 2005
342.7302—dc22

2005031885

Printing number: 9 8 7 6 5 4 3 2

Printed in the United States of America
on acid-free paper

Design: Nora Wertz

Frontis: Constitution March, composed by Hans Krummacher (Baltimore, 1860).

Contents

THE U.S. CONSTITUTION

Introduction

What does our Constitution mean to you, and why should you bother studying it? When it comes to your rights and liberties, it would be dangerous to be indifferent. True, the U.S. Constitution has stood the test of time for more than two hundred years, preserving our rights, preventing despotism, and adjusting to the needs of an ever-growing nation. Yet despite its appearance of strength and stability, time and again constitutional rights and liberties have been imperiled and might have crumbled if taken for granted.

The U.S. Constitution has never been perfect. Like all laws, constitutions involve compromises. The original Constitution was a remarkable document, wise in construction and broad and balanced in powers, but it contained serious flaws. The First Congress addressed a flaw of omission by hastily adding the Bill of Rights to the Constitution. A decade later Congress quickly repaired problems that had surfaced with the electoral college. The Constitution's most damaging compromise was its tolerance of slavery, an issue that eventually led to a constitutional breakdown and terrible Civil War. Out of that war came amendments to the Constitution

On December 13, 1952, military personnel escorted the Constitution with pomp and ceremony to the National Archives for permanent display. The Constitution had previously been housed in a number of locations, including the Department of State and the Library of Congress.

abolishing slavery and guaranteeing the equal protection of the law to all citizens, regardless of race.

There were other unresolved issues that required additional amendments. Women struggled for a century to achieve political equality with men by gaining the right to vote. Young men between the ages of eighteen and twenty-one were subject to the military draft without having the right to elect the leaders who might send them into combat. States charged poll taxes that prevented poor people from casting ballots. Some issues were more structural, but still had significant consequences for every citizen because they involved national leadership: the long delay between a Presidential election and the inauguration; the ability of Presidents to run for an unlimited number of terms; the succession to the Presidency and Vice Presidency if the incumbent became ill, died, or resigned.

Beyond amendments, our lives have been influenced by thousands of laws enacted in Congress, by executive orders signed by Presidents, and by judicial decisions of the Supreme Court. These affect your education, your wages and hours, your taxes, and your pensions. The continuing debates over how to interpret the Constitution influence your freedom to worship, to read what you want, to speak your mind, and to protest injustices. They involve your life, liberty, and property, everything that you consider valuable. For these reasons, it is in your interest to know your constitutional rights. You will have the opportunity to choose your leaders—and perhaps to become one yourself. That carries with it a civic responsibility to understand how government works, to know its powers and its limits, and the meaning of a constitution written in the name of "we the people."

— 1 —

Why Was the Constitution Necessary?

I doubt . . . whether any Convention we can obtain, maybe able to make a better constitution; for, when you assemble a number of men, to have the advantage of their joint wisdom, you inevitably assemble with those men all their prejudices, their passions, their errors of opinion, their local interests, and their selfish views. From such an assembly can a perfect production be expected? It therefore astonishes me, Sir, to find this system approaching so near to perfection as it does.

—Benjamin Franklin, addressing the
Constitutional Convention on September 17, 1787

Do you have a right to hold opinions that differ from others around you? Can you write and publish what you think? Can you worship as you believe? Can you protest to your government if you disapprove of its policies? Can the government search and seize your property? Can you be arrested and held without trial? Can the government treat you differently than it treats other people? As a citizen, you must know your constitutional rights in order to assert them.

Every society sets rules to live by. Our Constitution established the United States government and determined its relationship with the peo-

In the rotunda where the National Archives displays the Constitution, this mural by Barry Faulkner depicts the delegates to the Constitutional Convention. Dressed in a cape at the right of the mural, George Washington cuts an imposing figure, just as he did in life.

ple and the individual states. As constitutions go, it is remarkably short and durable. Most state constitutions are hefty documents, and the proposed constitution of the European Union runs to 60,000 words. The original text of the U.S. Constitution, by comparison, came to only 4,200 words, and all its amendments, made over the course of two hundred years, added just another 3,000 words. Despite its brevity, the Constitution has continued to satisfy the needs of a nation that has grown enormously in territory and population, and has seen a vast expansion in both its international and domestic responsibilities.

In existence for more than two centuries, the Constitution has been amended infrequently. In order to win the campaign to ratify the Constitution, the supporters of the new government promised to add a bill of rights, guaranteeing certain basic protections to the people. Congress proposed the first ten amendments, known as the Bill of Rights, almost as soon as the new government began. Although thousands of amendments have been proposed since then, only seventeen other amendments have been ratified. This means that the basic structure, functions, and powers of the federal government remain essentially the same as when the framers drafted them, giving the United States a bedrock of continuity and stability.

Because we live under these rules, it is essential that we know what they are, why they were established, how they have been implemented, and how they directly affect us. The Constitution not only designed a government but also placed limits on it to prevent arbitrary rule. Particularly through its amendments, the Constitution guarantees every American fundamental rights and protection of life, liberty, and property.

Our Constitution created an effective national government, one that balances expansive powers with specific limits. By contrast to its sturdy endurance, the first American government established under the Articles of Confederation in March 1781 showed signs of weakness and disorder within a few years after it was organized. That first national government depended upon the states for revenue but could not compel their cooperation. Surrounded by lands controlled by Great Britain, France, and Spain, Congress under the Articles of Confederation had trouble funding its own army. Its weaknesses troubled many of the leaders of the young republic. In 1787, they gathered in Philadelphia to form a more perfect union.

The road to the Philadelphia convention started two years earlier at Mount Vernon, the Virginia estate of General George Washington. The hero of the American Revolution brought together representatives from Virginia and Maryland to settle navigation rights on the Potomac River, which ran between them. Following that gathering, the Virginia Assembly called for a larger conference to deal with trade among all thirteen states. Only five states bothered to send delegates to the meeting in Annapolis, Maryland, the following year. Although disappointed by the turnout, the delegates who had gathered were persuaded by a New Yorker, Alexander Hamilton, to call for a full constitutional convention

Before George Washington presided over the Constitutional Convention, he had served as a delegate to the Continental Congress and as commander in chief of the Continental Army during the American Revolution.

to tackle the serious weaknesses in their union. They requested that the Confederation Congress issue formal invitations to the states to appoint delegates to meet in Philadelphia.

This Constitutional Convention drew fifty-five delegates from all but one of the states. Rhode Island, fearing national interference in its own state economic initiatives, stayed away. Those who decided to come to Philadelphia gained prestige when General Washington agreed not only to serve as a delegate but also as the convention's presiding officer.

In May 1787, the delegates convened in Philadelphia's Independence Hall, where the Declaration of Independence had been adopted in 1776. The Confederation Congress had also met there until 1783, when American soldiers marched on Philadelphia to demand their unpaid salaries. Unable to raise sufficient funds either to provide for the military, or to protect itself, Congress hastily departed. The Confederation Congress met in several locations before it settled in New York City.

At his Mount Vernon plantation, George Washington hosted a 1785 conference between delegates from Maryland and Virginia to allocate navigation rights on the Potomac River. The success of the Mount Vernon conference encouraged other efforts to strengthen relations between the states.

The inability of Congress to handle the soldiers' protest demonstrated the powerlessness of America's first national government. Real power rested with the individual states. The Articles of Confederation established a single legislature but no executive or judiciary branch. In that Congress, all the states had an equal vote, regardless of size. Delegates from seven states had to be present in order to conduct business. To amend the Articles required the unanimous agreement of all the states. These requirements made it difficult to get much done.

What the Articles of Confederation created was less a nation than a "league of friendship" among the thirteen states. The national government could make treaties and declare war, but it could not raise taxes or require the states to provide the funds that it requested. Nor could it stop the states from imposing taxes on each other's exports. The weak national government was in no position to prevent the American economy from sinking into depression.

In Massachusetts, during the winter of 1786, deeply indebted farmers whose land was being foreclosed refused to pay their state taxes, shut down the local courts, and seized a government arsenal. Troops from Massachusetts put down the farmers' revolt—known as Shays's Rebellion after its leader, Daniel Shays—while the Confederation Congress stood helpless in the crisis. "From the high ground we stood upon," General Washington despaired in a May 18, 1786, letter to John Jay, "to be so fallen! So lost! It is really mortifying." To national leaders, including Washington, the need for a stronger central government grew

Delegates to the Constitutional Convention met in the Pennsylvania State House, now known as Independence Hall (below), in 1787, in the same room (right) where the Declaration of Independence had been signed eleven years earlier.

increasingly evident. Yet Americans had only recently rebelled against a tyrannical government, and remained suspicious of a concentration of government power.

This was the dilemma facing the delegates who gathered in Philadelphia. Fortunately, they were well educated and experienced in law and government. Eight of them had signed the Declaration of Independence. A third had served in the Continental Army during the American Revolution. Most had been members of the Continental Congress or the Congress under the Articles of Confederation. They ranged from young men, including James Madison and Alexander Hamilton, who were still in their thirties, to the eighty-year-old Benjamin Franklin. They were merchants, planters, and professionals who had a personal interest in creating and preserving a stable society. Some of them had read widely in history and philosophy and had studied other forms of government, from republics to monarchies.

The delegates did not intend to produce the type of "pure democracy" that existed in the ancient Greek city states, where citizens voted on everything. Instead, during their debates several of the delegates warned against the "excesses of democracy," with its "turbulence and follies," and "dangerous leveling spirit." They were more impressed with the ancient Roman republic, where representatives of both the aristocracy and the people had a say in passing laws.

As British subjects by birth, all the delegates shared in the British legal tradition dating back to the writing of the Magna Carta (the Great Charter) in 1215, which stated that all people have rights that even a king has to respect. The delegates to the Constitutional Convention were also influenced by the ideas of philosophers from the European Enlightenment, the eighteenth-century intellectual movement that emphasized rational thought. These philosophers had defined ideal governments as ones in which power was separated between executive, legislative, and judicial branches that could check and balance each other.

As North Americans, the delegates had the additional example of the Iroquois Confederation, in which five Native American tribes in New York State governed themselves independently but also sent their chiefs to a Great Council to make decisions on larger issues of war and peace affecting the five tribes.

In writing a constitution the delegates departed from the practice in Great Britain, where the government was established not by a single document but rather by the entire body of British common law, the rulings of judges and parliamentary legislation. The delegates were instead continuing a colonial tradition that dated back to the Mayflower Compact of 1620, and other colonial charters. These systems had accustomed Americans to the idea of a single document serving as a contract between the people and their government.

When the delegates convened, Virginia's Governor Edmund Randolph offered a bold proposal that they not simply revise the Articles of Confederation but create an entirely new form of national government. Randolph introduced the Virginia Plan, which outlined a Congress with two bodies: a House of Representatives and a Senate. The new government would also have a separate executive branch, headed by a president, who would be both chief executive and commander in chief of the armed forces. The plan also called for an independent judiciary.

Although Randolph introduced the Virginia Plan, its actual author was James Madison, a young Virginian who served in the Confederation Congress and knew its weaknesses firsthand. Much of what we know today about the Constitutional Convention we owe to Madison, who kept detailed notes of the secret sessions. In an effort to avoid public pressures that might hinder their ability to reach a consensus, the delegates had barred the doors and windows and conducted all their business away from public view. The official minutes of the convention recorded little of the debate between the delegates. But Madison took a seat in front of the chamber, where he could hear the presiding officer and members on both sides, and he diligently kept a daily journal that summarized the members' arguments. His notes reveal the shared sentiments and disagreements among the delegates, the alternative proposals they considered, and the compromises they reached. Not published until after his death, Madison's notes have become an essential source for jurists who ponder the founders' intent for each provision of the Constitution.

The Virginia Plan envisioned a republic based on popular consent. Elected officials would represent the people, although the people could vote directly only for members of the House of Representatives. State legislatures would elect senators. Members of an Electoral College, cho-

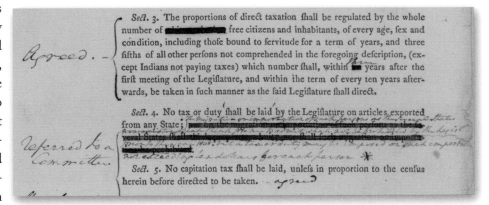

In handwritten revisions on a printed draft of the Constitution, George Washington recorded the compromises that the delegates reached over slavery. These included a ban on the importation of slaves after 1808, and requiring the return of fugitive slaves to their owners.

Often called the Father of the Constitution, James Madison was born in 1751 and raised on a plantation in Orange County, Virginia. He graduated from the College of New Jersey (later Princeton University) during the American Revolution, but his fragile health kept him from military service. Madison instead involved himself in public affairs by helping to write Virginia's first constitution. He served in both the Continental Congress and the Confederation Congress, and was a delegate to the Annapolis Convention. Having lost faith in the government formed under the Articles of Confederation, he actively promoted the Constitutional Convention and took the lead in drafting the Virginia Plan, which offered the basic structure of the new government. After winning Virginia's ratification of the Constitution, Madison was elected to the House of Representatives during the First Congress. There he led the Federalists and sponsored the Bill of Rights.

Madison grew troubled over the policies of Presidents George Washington and John Adams. He joined with Thomas Jefferson in founding the Democratic-Republican Party in opposition to the Federalists. When Jefferson became President in 1801 he named Madison as his secretary of state. Later Madison succeeded Jefferson, serving as President from 1809 to 1817. During his administration, the United States declared war on Great Britain. In August 1814, British troops invaded Washington, D.C., and burned the Capitol and White House, forcing Madison to flee to safety. America's pride was salvaged by the later victory of its troops at New Orleans. Madison devoted his last years as President to rebuilding the capital and the national economy. At the time of his death in 1836, James Madison was the last surviving delegate to the Constitutional Convention.

sen by the people, would elect the President. The Virginia Plan provided that each state would have representation in the House and Senate that reflected the size of their populations. This was the desire of the larger states, which blamed the Articles of Confederation's weakness on the equal representation of the states. Because every state had one vote under the old system, the smaller states, representing a minority of the population, could block the will of the majority.

The smaller states refused to accept any plan that sacrificed their equality. They countered with a plan, introduced by William Patterson of New Jersey, that would have preserved the government structure under the Articles of Confederation. The convention voted to reject the New Jersey Plan in favor of the Virginia Plan, granting the larger states the most members in both houses of the new Congress. But the smaller states would not tolerate inequality, and they continued to fight for their rights. The convention reached an impasse, just as it planned to take a few days off to celebrate the Fourth of July. It appointed a special committee to try to work out the disagreement during the recess. Chaired by Roger Sherman of Connecticut, the committee split the difference between the two factions. It proposed that the larger House of Representatives reflect the size of each state's population, while the states would have equal representation in the Senate. This became known as the Connecticut Compromise, or the Great Compromise. The delegates accepted the compromise and, as an additional assurance to the smaller states, wrote into the Constitution that no state would lose its equality in the Senate without its consent (which, of course, no state would give). Through this compromise, the Constitution went on to create a single nation from a confederation of states. Yet, the states remained as permanent and integral parts of the new federal system.

The absence of anyone representing Rhode Island served as a reminder to the other delegates that it would be folly for them to require unanimity in any new form of government. They provided that the Constitution could be ratified by the vote of nine of the thirteen states. Nor would unanimity be needed for future amendments. Instead, the approval of two-thirds of both houses of Congress and three-quarters of the states would be required to ratify an amendment.

From May until September 1787, the delegates deliberated over all aspects of the new government. They worked out its structure and listed the specific powers of each branch. However, they left considerable flexibility in implementing those powers, by giving Congress the power to make all laws "necessary and proper" for carrying out its explicit powers. The great difficulty in framing a government, as James Madison pointed out in *The Federalist*, the papers written to support ratification of the Constitution, was first to "enable the government to control the governed; and in the next place, oblige it to control itself." Assuming that human nature would always be the same, and that powerful leaders would inevitably try to amass greater power, the Constitution divided power among the branches of government and created a system of checks and balances. Madison reasoned that "ambition must be made to counteract ambition."

On September 17, 1787, most of the delegates signed the new Constitution. A few of them, notably Virginia's George Mason, declined to add their signatures on the grounds that the Constitution lacked a bill of rights that would identify and protect the rights of citizens. The weary delegates had voted down a bill of rights on the grounds that the state constitutions already protected the people's liberties. Otherwise, the signers had good reason to feel satisfied with their accomplishment. The elderly Benjamin Franklin pointed out at the end of their deliberations that the back of the chair where General Washington sat while presiding had a half-sun carved upon it. Often during the debates he had "looked at that behind the president without being able to tell whether it was rising or setting," he said. "But now at length I have the happiness to know that it is a rising and not a setting sun."

Afterward, some of the delegates traveled directly to New York City to serve in the Confederation Congress. They presented the Constitution to the Congress, which transmitted it to the states for ratification. Proponents of the Constitution identified themselves as Federalists. Its skeptics became known as Anti-Federalists. The opponents feared the Constitution would create a powerful central government that would overwhelm the states and would run contrary to the democratic spirit of the American Revolution. They were particularly agitated over the Constitution's lack of a bill of rights.

Unlike the idealistic Declaration of Independence, which had declared that "all men are created equal . . . [and] endowed by their Creator with certain unalienable rights," the Constitution made little reference to religion, except to prohibit any religious test as a qualification for candidates for federal office. It did, however, date its completion "in the year of our Lord one thousand seven hundred and eighty-seven," as was customary at the time. The Constitution was a pragmatic document that sought to balance the varied interests of the large and small states, the mass of people and the wealthier elite, and those who supported and those who opposed human slavery.

Slavery seemed to many Americans contradictory to their Revolution's principles of freedom and equality. The northern states had already begun to abolish slavery at the time of the Constitutional Convention, but the southern states were growing more dependent on slave labor. At the convention, southern delegates insisted that the Constitution not interfere with slavery. Northerners agreed, both because they considered slavery a state matter, and because they felt that the southern states would never enter the Union without such a guarantee.

The framers did not use the word "slave" in the Constitution, but referred instead to "other persons" when addressing issues related to slavery and the slave population. The Constitution prohibited Congress from ending the importation of slaves before 1808. It also provided that slaves be counted as three-fifths of a person to determine taxation and

AGAINST RATIFICATION OF THE CONSTITUTION

George Mason had never left his native Virginia until he traveled to Philadelphia as a delegate to the Constitutional Convention. He preferred to remain at his comfortable home, Gunston Hall, but went to the convention because he favored a stronger national government. Born on a Virginia plantation in 1725, Mason was a planter and also treasurer of the Ohio Company, which sold land to settlers moving westward. To assist his work with the Ohio Company, he read each of the colonial charters. This experience proved handy in 1776, when he joined with Virginia patriots in writing the state's Declaration of Rights and its first constitution.

Mason served as a delegate to the conference held at Mount Vernon in 1785, and became one of Virginia's delegates to the Constitutional Convention in 1787. At first he worked closely with his fellow Virginia delegate, James Madison, but soon their thinking diverged and Mason grew disillusioned. Mason feared the Constitution gave too much authority to the President over Congress, and too much power to the national government over the states. When Mason lost a motion to add a bill of rights he told the delegates that he would rather "chop off his right hand than put it to the constitution as it now stands." Back in Virginia, he fought against ratification. Not even Congress's enactment of the Bill of Rights appeased Mason. He died in 1792, suspicious of the Constitution to the end.

As president of the Constitutional Convention, George Washington sat in a chair emblazoned with a half sun. When the convention finished its work, the elderly delegate Benjamin Franklin declared himself satisfied that it was a rising sun rather than a setting one.

The architect Pierre L'Enfant designed the banquet pavilion for New York City residents celebrating the ratification of the Constitution in 1788. L'Enfant later designed the new capital of Washington, D.C.

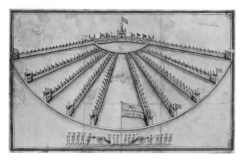

representation in Congress. (At the time, slaves accounted for about 20 percent of the U.S. population, mostly concentrated in the South.)

During the ratification of the Constitution, the most inflammatory issue was not its toleration of slavery but its lack of a bill of rights. Thomas Jefferson, who had drafted the Declaration of Independence, was away serving as the American minister to France. Jefferson admired the delegates' work, but he wrote to his friend James Madison that "a bill of rights is what the people are entitled to against every government on earth . . . and what no just government should refuse." Many other Americans shared Jefferson's concern about the protection of their rights.

In order to win ratification, the authors of the Constitution needed to explain and defend their handiwork to the people. Under the joint pen name of Publius (Latin for "the public" or "the people"), James Madison, Alexander Hamilton, and John Jay wrote a brilliant series of essays published in newspapers throughout the states in 1788. These essays have been reprinted in book form in many editions since then, and are known today as *The Federalist.* They explained how the new government would work, and sought to calm people's apprehensions about it. In one of his essays, Madison discussed the failure of past republics when one faction grew so strong that it dominated and suppressed all others. Madison predicted that the American republic would survive because of its size and its continued growth. In a large republic, no single faction would predominate, he reasoned. This would prevent a powerful majority from suppressing the rights of the minority. As Americans moved westward into new territories, they would form new states that would join the Union and add even more groups into the equation. The arguments put forth by the authors of *The Federalist* carried great weight, and they still inform us about the thinking of the framers of the Constitution.

On December 7, 1787, Delaware became the first state to ratify the Constitution, and other states quickly followed. The fiercest battles took place in the larger states. In Virginia, Revolutionary War patriots such as Patrick Henry and Richard Henry Lee opposed the Constitution, while Washington and Madison argued in its favor. To gain support, Madison pledged that the new government would move speedily to adopt a bill of rights. On June 25, 1788, after four months of debate, the Virginia convention voted 89 to 79 for ratification. On July 26, New York concluded an equally divisive debate and approved the Constitution by the narrow margin of 30 to 27. North Carolina's convention voted against ratification, however, and Rhode Island never called a convention. Still, eleven of the thirteen states had ratified the Constitution, which was two more than required. North Carolina eventually joined the Union in 1789, and Rhode Island in 1790.

Among its last acts, the outgoing Confederation Congress set the first Wednesday in January of 1789 as the date for the first Presidential election. The Electoral College would cast its ballots on the first Wednesday in February, and the new government would begin on the first Wednesday in March. But on March 4, 1789, neither the House nor the Senate could establish a quorum. Both had to wait until April, when enough members

The Secretary of the Constitutional Convention made this record of the delegates' votes on the new Constitution on September 15, 1787. The states had one vote each, so even though a few of the individual delegates dissented, the vote to agree to the new Constitution, as the Secretary noted, was unanimous.

arrived to conduct the business of implementing the new Constitution. Many of the delegates to the Constitutional Convention were elected as members of the First Congress, including James Madison, who served in the House of Representatives.

Representative Madison, true to his word, introduced a bill of rights. Congress crafted his proposals into twelve amendments. The states ratified ten of them, which became known as the Bill of Rights. Two hundred years later, in 1992, the states ratified the eleventh of these original amendments, which dealt with congressional pay increases. (The unratified twelfth amendment would have set the number of people to be represented in each congressional district at fifty thousand, a number so low that the House of Representatives would by now have grown to many thousands of members.)

Over the following centuries, Congress continued to enact all laws "necessary and proper" to carry out the powers enumerated in the Constitution. Presidents vastly expanded their power in competition with Congress. The Supreme Court became the final arbiter of whether acts of Congress or Presidential actions were constitutional. Beginning with the case of *Marbury* v. *Madison* (1804), the Supreme Court asserted its right to declare laws unconstitutional—a power that is implied but not specified in the Constitution. In the case of *McCulloch* v. *Maryland* (1819), Chief Justice John Marshall observed that the Constitution provided only the "great outlines" of government. The brevity of the document suggested that its authors expected judges to interpret its meaning, and anticipated flexibility in its implementation.

THE FEDERALIST NO. 10: GROWTH WILL STRENGTHEN THE REPUBLIC

At the time that the Constitution was written, people worried that past republics had worked best in small governments such as city-states. James Madison saw different possibilities and argued in The Federalist *that the American republic would grow stronger as it expanded because it would be harder for any one group to dominate it.*

The smaller the society, the fewer probably will be the distinct parties and interests composing it; the fewer the distinct parties and interests, the more frequently will a majority be found of the same party; and the smaller the number of individuals composing a majority, and the smaller the compass within which they are placed, the more easily will they concert and execute their plans of oppression. Extend the sphere, and you take in a greater variety of parties and interests; you make it less probable that a majority of the whole will have a common motive to invade the rights of other citizens; or if such a common motive exists, it will be more difficult for all who feel it to discover their own strength, and to act in unison with each other. Besides other impediments, it may be remarked that, where there is a consciousness of unjust or dishonorable purposes, communication is always checked by distrust in proportion to the number whose concurrence is necessary.

Hence, it clearly appears, that the same advantage which a republic has over a democracy, in controlling the effects of faction, is enjoyed by a large over a small republic—is enjoyed by the Union over the States composing it.

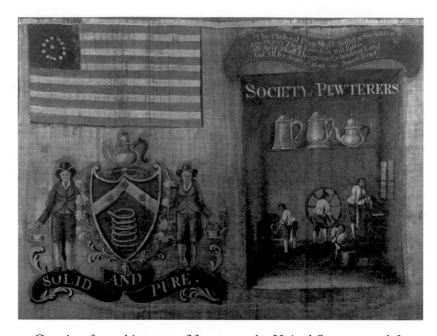

Members of the Society of Pewterers, craftsmen who fashioned plates, bowls, pitchers, and other items from pewter, carried this flag when they marched in a "federal procession" in support of the Constitution on July 23, 1788. Three days later New York ratified the Constitution.

Growing from thirteen to fifty states, the United States spread from the Atlantic to the Pacific Ocean, with a larger population, a more complex economy, and a mightier military than the authors of the Constitution could possibly have imagined. Yet the Constitution remains essentially the same document they drafted during the summer of 1787. The Constitution's succinctness helped it to survive largely intact, forcing Presidents, Congress, and the courts to find new applications periodically to meet changing circumstances and cope with new problems. Understanding the Constitution requires careful reading of the original document and its amendments, taking into consideration what we know about its framers' intent, and the ways in which generations of judges have construed its language to make it work.

2

What Kind of Government Did the Constitution Create?

Constitutions should consist only of general provisions: The reason is, that they must necessarily be permanent, and that they cannot calculate for the possible changes of things.

—Alexander Hamilton,
addressing the New York ratification convention
on June 28, 1788

Visitors to the U.S. Capitol often expect to find the President's office there. They assume—incorrectly—that the entire government leadership must work under the Capitol's recognizable dome. There is a President's Room in the Capitol, but it is simply a ceremonial room that was set aside a century ago. Back when the President's term ended on the same day as the Congress, on March 4, Presidents would use the room to sign or veto the last bills enacted at the end of a session. After 1933, when the Twentieth Amendment set different dates for the end of Presidential and congressional terms, Presidents rarely used the President's Room. Instead, the President works across town, in the West Wing of the White House. The Supreme Court did once occupy a chamber in the Capitol Building, until 1935 when the separate Supreme Court building was opened across the street from the Capitol. The three branches come together now only occasionally, for an inauguration or a State of the Union message. Otherwise, they operate out of separate buildings in largely separate spheres.

Monarchs ruled the nations of the world when the U.S. Constitution was written in 1787. Some monarchies, such as the one that ruled Great Britain, also had parliaments in which the people and the aristocracy were represented. As parliamentary systems developed, they combined legislative and executive functions, with the prime minister and other cabinet members serving as members of Parliament. This differs sharply from the separation of powers established in our Constitution.

The delegates to the Constitutional Convention often referred to the English philosopher John Locke's *Two Treatises on Government*, written in 1690 just after England's Glorious Revolution of 1688 had strengthened Parliament's hand against the king. Locke argued that all people

The seventeenth century English philosopher John Locke believed that government needed to operate under some restraints. His writings made a strong impression on the delegates to the Constitutional Convention.

were born with certain "natural rights" to life, liberty, and property, which governments existed to protect. Locke believed that a government should be seen as the agent of the people, not their ruler, and therefore should operate under some restraints. An equally influential book was *The Spirit of the Laws,* written in 1748 by the French philosopher the Baron de Montesquieu. Writing while France was still under the rule of an all-powerful monarchy, Montesquieu admired the British system that separated the powers of the monarch, the parliament, and the judiciary. In Britain, the king served as the head of state, performing ceremonial functions and commanding the military, while the prime minister functioned as the head of government, providing political and legislative leadership. Because the Americans had rebelled against Great Britain, the delegates modified Montesquieu's political theories into something that differed from the British parliamentary system. They created entirely separate executive, legislative, and judicial branches of government, making sure that no single branch would hold exclusive power, but each would check and balance the others. With power so divided, the independent branches must reach some common agreement for the federal government to act harmoniously.

Under the system of government the framers of the Constitution created, the President of the United States combines the monarch's role as head of state with the prime minister's role as head of government. The President serves as chief executive and commander in chief of the military. The President appoints the heads of the executive offices of the government and, with the officers he appoints, is responsible for administering the laws of the land. The President proposes legislation, and vetoes or approves bills that Congress enacts, but depends entirely on the legislature for all the funds necessary for operating the government. While the American Presidency has grown steadily more powerful, particularly in matters of diplomacy and military policy, the Constitution's division of powers has caused Presidents to contend with Congresses that have often disagreed with their policies and attempted to steer a different course.

As the only federal official elected by the entire population, Presidents feel they have a mandate from the people to lead in the manner they see fit and to establish the policies on which they campaigned. Presidents are elected separately from members of Congress. Their administrations do not fall if their party loses the legislative majority, unlike a prime minister whose party loses a working majority in Parliament. Often, American Presidents have had to cope with opposition party majorities in one or both houses of Congress. Democrats, for instance, lost their majorities in Congress two years into Bill Clinton's Presidency, in 1994, and for the next six years he faced Republican majorities in both the House and Senate. When Presidents are on the ballot, their "coattails" may help some fellow party members win election, which will encourage them to support the President's legislative agenda. The President's party leaders also do their best to ensure legislative victories.

Nonetheless, members of Congress feel that they are elected to represent the people of their states and districts. They often campaign on different issues than the President, even when they are members of the same party, and they often serve through several Presidential administrations. Members of Congress therefore resist being a "rubber stamp" for the President and act according to their own principles, and in the interests of their own constituents. Personal ambition plays a role as well, as some members of Congress may see themselves as candidates for the Presidency in future elections.

The different perspectives of the White House and the Capitol often create tensions between the branches. Presidents have the constitutional right to name cabinet officers, agency heads, diplomats, and federal judges, but these nominations must be confirmed by the U.S. Senate. Over the past two centuries, the Senate has confirmed all but a very small percentage of the executive branch nominations—on the assumption that Presidents deserve to work with people of their own choosing. But the statistics change dramatically for judicial nominations—on the grounds that the judiciary is an independent branch of the government, and that all federal judges hold lifetime appointments. Since the administration of George Washington, the Senate has blocked a third of all Supreme Court nominations. Senators also point out that the Constitution refers to Presidents seeking the "advice and consent" of the

Beginning in 1810 the U.S. Senate met in this elaborately decorated chamber in the Capitol. But with the addition of many new states over the next half century, the Senate outgrew the space. It moved to its current chamber in 1859.

Senate, and note that Presidents are much more likely to seek their consent than their advice. Senators therefore insist on scrutinizing all nominations and rejecting those they consider unfit.

Foreign policy has provided another major arena for struggle between the executive and legislative branches. Presidents conduct the foreign policy of the United States, but Congress appropriates the necessary funds and senators hold hearings in which they interrogate State Department officials about policy developments. The Senate also has the constitutional power to reject or approve by a two-thirds margin treaties that the President's administration has negotiated. In the late nineteenth century, the Senate rejected a number of significant treaties, causing Secretary of State John Hay to compare a treaty entering the Senate to a bull entering the ring. "One thing is certain," said Hay, "neither will leave alive."

The most tragic confrontation between a President and the Senate took place after the First World War, when President Woodrow Wilson went to Paris to negotiate the Treaty of Versailles that ended the war and created a League of Nations to preserve the peace. Republicans by then had won the majority in the Senate, but Wilson took no Republican senators with him on that mission. Suspicious of the Democratic President's treaty, and unwilling to see the United States enter the League, Republican senators sought to amend the treaty. But Wilson fought any changes and refused to authorize Democratic senators to reach a compromise with the Republicans. Wilson took his case directly to the American people, warning that without the League of Nations the world would face another war within a generation. On his national speaking tour, Wilson suffered a paralytic stroke and could offer no further leadership. The Senate then rejected the Treaty of Versailles and the United States never joined the League of Nations. A generation later, after the world had plunged into the Second World War, President Franklin D. Roosevelt learned from Wilson's mistakes and made sure that prominent senators of both parties were involved in negotiating the treaty that created the United Nations, which the Senate overwhelmingly approved.

Although the Constitution gives Congress the sole power to declare war, Congress has not passed a declaration of war since World War II. Subsequent military missions overseas were authorized by congressional resolutions, some in support of United Nations efforts. In 1964, following a confrontation between American and North Vietnamese naval vessels in the Gulf of Tonkin, President Lyndon B. Johnson asked Congress to enact a resolution authorizing him to use military force in response to North Vietnamese military action. The Senate and House passed the Gulf of Tonkin Resolution with only two dissenting votes. Members of Congress saw their vote as an act of solidarity with the President at a critical moment, but none anticipated that he would use it as the equivalent of a declaration of war. Yet that was exactly how Johnson used the resolution when he sent large numbers of American combat troops to fight in Vietnam. Congress later repealed the Gulf of Tonkin Resolution, but it had no effect on American military policy. Johnson's successor as

President Woodrow Wilson (left) arrived in Paris on December 14, 1918, to head the American delegation to the peace conference that ended World War I and created the League of Nations. He was accompanied on a triumphant procession through Paris by French President Raymond Poincaré.

President, Richard Nixon, insisted that the Gulf of Tonkin Resolution had not been necessary and that his powers as commander in chief were enough to continue the war effort.

As a result of the Vietnam War, Congress passed the War Powers Resolution in 1973, over President Nixon's veto. The resolution required Presidents to notify Congress within set time periods when they sent American troops into combat, and it permitted Congress to vote to withdraw troops from combat. The War Powers Resolution has proved difficult to implement, however, and neither Presidents nor Congress invoked it when the United States became involved in the Persian Gulf War in 1991 or the Iraq War in 2002.

The Constitution requires the President to give Congress a periodic report on the state of the union. Presidents have used the State of the Union message as a vehicle for recommending legislation to be enacted, and have therefore become the chief legislator as well as the chief executive. Presidents George Washington and John Adams delivered their State of Union addresses in person. Thomas Jefferson thought this practice too closely resembled the pomp of the monarch's messages to the British Parliament. Jefferson chose to send his message to be read aloud by clerks in the Senate and House. Other Presidents followed Jefferson's lead until 1913, when Woodrow Wilson revived the practice of delivering the message in person.

Throughout each session of Congress, Presidents meet regularly with the legislative leaders of the major parties, and will often contact individual legislators to win their support on key measures. The modern White House also maintains a congressional liaison staff that shepherds nominees through the Senate confirmation process and works with the leadership of the President's party to develop legislative strategies.

Presidents have complained that Congress attempts to "micromanage" the executive branch by specifically instructing agencies how to administer the laws. Congress has objected when Presidents have withheld documents

"So long as I have a mind to think, a tongue to speak, and a heart to love my country, I shall deny that the Constitution confers any arbitrary power on any President, or empowers any President to convert George Washington's America into Caesar's Rome."

— North Carolina Senator Sam Ervin, addressing students at the University of North Carolina at Chapel Hill in 1973

Although the United States had technological advantages in the Vietnam War, troops had to fight under difficult ground conditions. Growing dissatisfaction with the war led Congress to pass the War Powers Act in 1973.

In his first Inaugural Address, delivered at the depth of the Great Depression, on March 4, 1933, Franklin D. Roosevelt spoke for those who believe that the U.S. Constitution is an elastic document, designed to grow with the times and to confer extraordinary authority in times of crisis. This is what he said:

If I read the temper of our people correctly, we now realize as we have never realized before our interdependence on each other; that we cannot merely take but we must give as well; that if we are to go forward, we must move as a trained and loyal army willing to sacrifice for the good of a common discipline, because without such discipline no progress is made, no leadership becomes effective. We are, I know, ready and willing to submit our lives and property to such discipline, because it makes possible a leadership which aims at a larger good. This I propose to offer, pledging that the larger purposes will bind upon us all as a sacred obligation with a unity of duty hitherto evoked only in time of armed strife. . . .

Action in this image and to this end is feasible under the form of government which we have inherited from our ancestors. Our Constitution is so simple and practical that it is possible always to meet extraordinary needs by changes in emphasis and arrangement without loss of essential form. That is why our constitutional system has proved itself the most superbly enduring political mechanism the modern world has produced. It has met every stress of vast expansion of territory, or foreign wars, or bitter internal strife, or world relations.

It is to be hoped that the normal balance of Executive and legislative authority may be wholly adequate to meet the unprecedented task before us. But it may be that an unprecedented demand and need for undelayed action may call for temporary departure from that normal balance of public procedure.

it sought (a practice known as executive privilege), and when agencies have administered the laws in a different manner than the legislation specified. Congressional committees therefore hold oversight hearings, calling cabinet secretaries and other officials to explain and justify their departments' actions. When John F. Kennedy served in the House and the Senate, he believed that the real power in the American political system resided in the Oval Office. It was only after he was elected President and faced a skeptical Congress that he realized how much power resided on Capitol Hill. While an individual member has limited authority, the Congress as a whole can be a formidable opponent to any President's plans.

Yet, the Congress itself is divided into two very different bodies, the Senate and House of Representatives. Although the Senate has the exclusive power to confirm nominations and approve treaties, the two bodies participate equally in all legislation and appropriations. The Constitution permits each house to set its own rules, and as a result they have grown distinctly different. The larger House, where membership reflects the population of each state, has set rules that permit the majority to prevail, so long as it stays united. Members of the House operate under rules that limit how long they can speak and reduce their opportunities to block legislation from coming to a vote. The House operates under a hierarchy headed by the Speaker, who is elected by the majority party, and a Rules Committee, most of whose members are chosen by the Speaker. When the House leadership is ready to hold a debate and vote on a bill, the House Rules Committee determines how long the debate will last and how many amendments will be considered. Members of the House gain influence through their seniority, which requires them to win reelection and move up through their party's ranks until they chair a sub-committee or full committee.

By contrast to the majority-run House, the smaller Senate has set rules that give greater voice to the minority. In the Senate, all states are equally represented, meaning that California, with 34 million residents (and fifty-three representatives in the House) has two senators, as does Wyoming, with a half million residents (and one representative). The majority of all the senators therefore represent a minority of the population. For certain actions, the Constitution requires the approval of a "supermajority" of senators, such as the two-thirds vote needed to overturn a Presidential veto, to approve a treaty, or to convict a federal official who has been impeached by the House.

Senate rules add another supermajority requirement: it takes a vote of three-fifths of the Senate (currently sixty out of one hundred) to invoke cloture, closing a debate and calling for a vote. Unlike the House, which sets limits on the length of all speeches, senators can engage in "unlimited debate." They can speak for as long as they feel necessary and can use the rules of the Senate to prevent a vote from occurring. This practice is called a filibuster, a name that comes from the Dutch word for "pirate," for those who seize the Senate floor and hold it against all others to prevent a vote from being taken. Only if sixty senators agree can the majority leadership cut off debate and force a vote. Bills that sail through the House with little amendment, therefore, can be subject to delay and revision in the Senate.

Playing Mr. Smith in the 1939 Hollywood film Mr. Smith Goes to Washington, *actor Jimmy Stewart (right) reacts with dismay over messages showing that the public opposes his filibuster. Looking on is the treacherous senior senator from his state, who has manipulated public opinion against him.*

A CALL FOR A LIMITED GOVERNMENT

In contrast to those who view the Constitution as expansive, there are others who see the role of the federal government as far more confined and insist that all powers not expressed in the Constitution belong to the states. Tom A. Coburn, a medical doctor who was elected first to the House of Representatives and then to the U.S. Senate from Oklahoma, campaigned on arguments that he expressed in his 2003 book Breach of Trust: How Washington Turns Outsiders into Insiders:

In 1791, the framers clarified the Constitution's intent to limit the role of the federal government with the Tenth Amendment, which reads, 'The powers not delegated to the United States by the Constitution, nor prohibited by it to the States, are reserved to the States respectively, or to the people.' In other words, Congress's role is limited to providing for the common defense, regulating interstate commerce, providing for the general welfare, and levying taxes. All other powers are reserved for the states. . . .

Still, most members of Congress are either ignorant of or indifferent to Congress's constitutional guidelines and the warnings in history that should caution us against consolidating too much power in a large central government. The courts themselves have overreached and undermined the founders' design for limited government. I always found it ironic when my Republican colleagues would deliver passionate speeches criticizing the judicial branch for not respecting the Constitution when they were gladly joining their colleagues in the legislative branch in violating the very same document. The next time a member of Congress criticizes the Supreme Court for not respecting the Constitution they should be prepared to offer legislation rescinding about half of the federal budget that is used for purposes never envisioned by our founders.

CARVER PUBLIC LIBRARY

Not until 1917 did the Senate establish the cloture rule to cut off filibusters. When the rule was first established, it took a two-thirds vote to establish cloture, which proved almost impossible to achieve. Over the next forty-six years, the Senate was able to invoke cloture only five times. The most significant cloture vote occurred on June 10, 1964. After fifty-five days of debate, supporters of the Civil Rights Act of 1964, which banned racial discrimination in all public facilities, mustered the necessary two-thirds of the Senate to cut off debate. Nine days later the Senate overwhelmingly approved the bill. Because the filibuster had so often been used to protect segregation, senators who favored civil rights had generally refrained from using the filibuster as a tactic. After segregation was illegal, however, the filibuster became a more universally employed tactic. In 1975, liberal Democrats led a movement to make cloture easier to establish, reducing the needed number of senators from two-thirds to three-fifths. Despite that change, the filibuster has continued to distinguish the Senate from the House, the rules of which prohibit such tactics.

Committees in both the House and Senate hold hearings on prospective legislation, collecting information and listening to testimony, before they vote on a bill that will be reported to the full House or Senate for debate, amendment, and passage. Both the Senate and House must pass legislation in exactly the same form in order for it to be sent to the President for approval before it becomes law. Frequently, the two houses will pass different versions of the same piece of legislation. To resolve their differences they appoint members of each house to serve on a conference committee. Once the conference committee reaches agreement, it reports back to the Senate and House, which must accept or reject the conference report, but cannot amend it any further. The practical result of this complicated process is that legislation almost never passes in its original form, but is revised constantly until a sufficiently broad consensus can be reached. This helps to make sure that legislation benefits and appeals to large portions of the country rather than favoring one region or interest over the others.

To become law, the bill must still go to the White House. The President can approve and sign the bill or can veto—reject—the bill. It takes a two-thirds vote of both the House and Senate to overturn a Presidential veto. If Congress adjourns within ten days after sending a bill to the President, the President can decide not to act on it, neither signing nor formally vetoing it. This is called a pocket veto, which kills the bill, as Congress is out of session and cannot vote to overturn the veto. Presidents will often use the threat of a veto to convince Congress to pass a bill more to their liking. Presidents whose own party controls the majority in Congress will veto bills far less frequently than Presidents who face opposition majorities. Gerald Ford, who had spent decades in Congress as the Republican leader of the House, issued many vetoes during his Presidency to establish more legislative control over a Congress with large Democratic majorities.

Convinced that he was looking out for their interest, many people hung portraits of President Franklin D. Roosevelt in their homes during the Great Depression. Such heartfelt public support helped Roosevelt's New Deal legislation win speedy enactment in Congress.

In times of national emergency, the President can call the Congress into special session. This was a critical feature during the nineteenth century, when Congress met for just a few months each year, but it became unnecessary in the twentieth century, when Congress began meeting year round. During wartime and periods of economic crisis, Congress has tended to give the President much more room to act, passing legislation quickly and with less second guessing. This was especially true during the First and Second World Wars and during the First Hundred Days of Franklin D. Roosevelt's New Deal in 1933. The nation had been plunged into a deep depression that had caused many banks to fail, businesses to close, and workers to lose their jobs, a crisis so severe that members of both parties felt the urgency to approve the President's legislative proposals to restore economic order. During that period, members of Congress found themselves voting for bills on which they had held no hearings and sometimes had no chance to read in advance.

Once the struggles between Congress and the President have ended and the bill becomes law, it is still subject to judicial review. Even the legislative initiatives of Roosevelt's New Deal, which had overwhelming public and Congressional support, were reviewed by the Supreme Court, which struck down many of its major programs as unconstitutional. In

The House of Representatives adjourns at the end of the 75th Congress (1937–1939). Democrats, who sat to the right of the center aisle, held the largest majority in congressional history, with 334 seats compared to 88 Republicans and 13 independents.

one of the most significant of the New Deal cases, the Supreme Court rejected the National Recovery Administration, which set production levels and wages for various industries, on the grounds that Congress had improperly delegated its own constitutional powers over commerce to an executive branch agency. Many other Presidents were frustrated by court rulings that ran contrary to objectives. This is why Presidents take such care in making judicial appointments, and why the Senate so often resists Presidential choices.

Other than creating the Supreme Court, the Constitution said less about the judiciary than any other branch of the government. The Constitution left it to Congress to set the number of justices on the Supreme Court and to create the lower federal courts. Congress did this with the Judiciary Act of 1789. Over the next two centuries the federal judiciary has grown larger, more influential, and more controversial. The U.S. Constitution stands as the "supreme law of the land," as it identifies itself in Article VI, which puts federal law above state law, and federal court decisions over state court decisions, when they are in conflict. (Although federal law is supreme, state constitutions and courts are free to recognize rights beyond those included in the federal Constitution.)

Some federal judges have taken a more active approach to the law than others, striking down federal and state laws as unconstitutional. This puts the burden back on the state and federal legislatures to end programs or to pass new laws that will gain the courts' approval. Some judges believe in interpreting the Constitution broadly to meet new developments in society, and therefore refer to a "living Constitution." Others insist that they cannot go beyond the "original intent" of the founders in applying the Constitution to current situations. Both approaches weigh the accumulated court rulings and precedents and attempt to maintain some consistency in how the laws are interpreted. Sometimes the courts will dramatically reverse earlier rulings, declaring them to have been in error. This was especially notable in 1954 when the Supreme Court unanimously declared school segregation unconstitutional, sixty years after a previous court had upheld racial segregation.

Most cases dealing with federal laws are heard in the lower federal courts and only a few cases reach the U.S. Supreme Court each term. Once a case reaches the Supreme Court through the appeals process, the Court can review, uphold, or overturn the decisions of other federal judges. The lower federal courts then must tailor their rulings to meet the standards set by the Supreme Court's decisions.

In addition to the three branches, the federal government has also created a number of independent regulatory commissions that straddle the division of powers, performing quasi-administra-

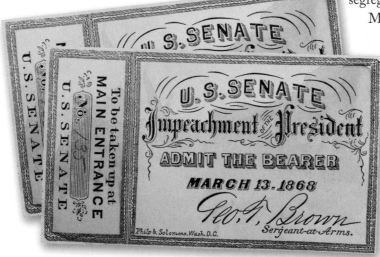

So many people wanted to watch the 1868 impeachment trial of President Andrew Johnson that the Senate for the first time issued tickets for admission to its galleries. The trial lasted from March until May.

tive, legislative, and judicial functions. Beginning with the Interstate Commerce Commission in 1887 and continuing with the Federal Trade Commission in 1914, Securities and Exchange Commission in 1934, and later agencies, these commissions combine executive, legislative, and judicial functions in an effort to resolve complex economic issues outside of the political arena. Congress created these agencies under the commerce clause, which grants Congress the right to oversee interstate commerce, a justification that the federal courts have accepted as constitutional. The commissions are not entirely "independent," however, as their members are appointed by the President, confirmed by the Senate, and subject to scrutiny by the courts.

This complex system of independence and interdependence among the branches of government also includes a system to punish those who act improperly and violate their offices. Each house of Congress is authorized to discipline its own members, whether censuring (or condemning) them by a majority vote or expelling them by a two-thirds vote. The Constitution also authorizes the House of Representatives to impeach, a form of indictment, any judge or executive officer for "high crimes and misdemeanors." A majority vote is required for the House to impeach. In order for an impeached officer or judge to be convicted, the Senate must hold a trial and cast a two-thirds vote. If this happens, the person is removed from office. The Vice President presides over such trials, except when a President has been impeached, in which case the chief justice of the United States presides.

Impeachment is a rare occurrence. Most executive branch officials accused of crimes either resign or are fired before impeachment proceedings can begin, but federal judges serve lifetime appointments and cannot be fired. In the 1990s, three federal judges were impeached and removed from the bench for crimes ranging from tax evasion to bribery. There have been three impeachment efforts against Presidents. In 1868 and 1998, the House impeached Presidents Andrew Johnson and Bill Clinton. Both were acquitted in the Senate. In 1974, President Richard Nixon resigned in the face of an impeachment that would likely have led to conviction in the Senate.

Impeachment stands as a reminder that no federal official, even the President, is above the law and all can be brought to justice. The American constitutional system is often cumbersome and slow. It has frustrated Presidents and legislators alike. Yet, while the federal government has grown much larger, the basic powers and responsibilities of its three branches have changed very little since the Constitution was first implemented in 1789. In times of crisis, the branches of government pull together to meet a common threat. In ordinary times, they pull back to check and balance each other. No single branch has been able to amass total power and the government remains the agent of the people who elect it.

"It should be remembered, as an axiom of eternal truth in politics, that whatever power in any government is independent, is absolute also."

— Thomas Jefferson,
letter to Spencer Roane,
September 6, 1819

3

What Rights Does the Constitution Protect?

"The First Amendment does not speak equivocally. It prohibits any law 'abridging the freedom of speech, or of the press.' It must be taken as a command of the broadest scope that explicit language, read in the context of a liberty-loving society, will allow."

—Justice Hugo L. Black,
majority opinion in
Bridges v. *California* (1941)

Newspapers have gained possession of highly classified government documents that shed an unfavorable light on an ongoing war. Should they be allowed to publish what they found? A poor man has been arrested on a criminal charge but cannot afford a lawyer. Should he stand trial without the benefit of legal counsel? Facing reapportionment, the representatives of rural districts in a state legislature argue that because their districts cover so much more territory than city districts, it should not matter that they have fewer residents than the urban districts. Is that fair to the city dwellers? Home owners confront a local government that requires them to sell their property and move to make way for economic development. Do the needs of the community outweigh those of the individual property owners? These are real issues that involve fundamental constitutional rights. The decisions made in these and many other cases of human rights, liberty, and equality have significantly affected the lives of every American citizen.

Yet, surveys show that alarming numbers of Americans are unaware of the full extent of their constitutional rights. Some people readily admit that they do not know what rights are included in the Constitution and its first ten amendments, the Bill of Rights. Other Americans have expressed the opinion that the Constitution went too far in granting such rights as free speech and free press and that society should be able to restrict opinions and behavior with which the majority disapproves. These are perilous attitudes, because those who remain unaware or unappreciative of their rights run the risk of losing them.

In reading the original U.S. Constitution, one finds very few specific rights mentioned, and those that are deal primarily with legal practices. Article I, section 9 protects the right of "habeas corpus" (a Latin term meaning "you may have the body"). To keep suspects from lingering

James Madison took the most complete set of minutes of the debates of the Constitutional Convention, but kept them secret until his death. "It has always been my intention that they should, some day or other, see the light," he said, although he considered it wiser that they appear posthumously.

indefinitely in prison, habeas corpus literally commands a jailer to produce the person jailed. This means that a prisoner has the right to challenge wrongful imprisonment, and the right to a speedy trial before a civilian court. The same section of the Constitution outlaws "bills of attainder," the practice by which some governments convict citizens using legislation rather than a jury trial. It forbids "ex post facto" laws (Latin for "after the fact"), making something a crime after an action had been committed. It also bans any religious requirements for candidates for public office. Beyond these few prohibitions, the Constitution of 1787 remained silent on citizens' specific rights.

When the Constitution was submitted to the states, the absence of a bill of rights generated more controversy than any other aspect of the document and nearly derailed its ratification. Most of the delegates to the Constitutional Convention felt it was unnecessary to spell out people's rights in the national Constitution. They argued that the state constitutions already protected those rights. A few dissenters among the delegates refused to sign the document because it lacked a guarantee of individual rights. When James Madison campaigned for the Constitution's ratification in Virginia, he encountered such intense popular dismay over the missing bill of rights that he pledged to support amendments to the Constitution as soon as the new government got under way. Elected to the House of Representatives, he kept his word.

"The Constitution is a charter of negative liberties; it tells the federal government or the state to let people alone; it does not require the federal government or the state to provide services, even so elementary a service as maintaining law and order."

— Judge Richard A. Posner,
Bowers v. *DeVito* (1982)

Madison studied all of the two hundred amendments the states proposed during their debates over ratification of the Constitution. He pared these down to nineteen, which he introduced in the new Congress in 1789. Some of the other members protested that it seemed too soon to change the new Constitution, which had barely gotten started and had yet to prove itself. Yet, Madison felt committed to honoring the pledges that he and other supporters of the Constitution had made during the ratification campaign.

The House and Senate remolded Madison's proposals into twelve amendments. The states swiftly ratified ten but allowed the other two to languish. Two centuries later, in response to public complaints over a large pay increase that Congress voted for itself, the states revived and ratified one of Madison's amendments not included in the Bill of Rights. This amendment prohibits any raise in congressional salaries from going into effect until after the next election, giving the voters a chance to express their approval or disapproval at the polls. That left only one of the original twelve amendments unratified. This one would have pegged the number of people in a congressional district at fifty thousand. If that amendment had been approved, the U.S. House of Representatives would now contain several thousand members, rather than 435. The national population has grown far greater than the first members of Congress ever anticipated.

Ratified in 1791, the first ten amendments are collectively known as the Bill of Rights. Some of their provisions date back to the English Bill of Rights of 1689, which included freedom to petition the government and freedom of assembly, as well as prohibitions against cruel and unusual punishment and against taxation without representation. Having long considered themselves British subjects, Americans claimed all the rights of "freeborn Englishmen." The first state constitutions limited government from performing arbitrary acts that would deprive people of their freedom of speech, their freedom of religion, their right to bear arms, and their right to assemble peacefully and to petition the government.

Madison thought that the greatest danger to individual liberties came from the states, so he originally drafted the First Amendment to read: "No state shall violate . . ." In its final version it became: "Congress shall make no law . . ."

For many years, the courts interpreted the Bill of Rights as applying only to the federal government, not to the states. Added just after the Civil War, the Fourteenth Amendment seemed to extend the Bill of Rights to the states by prohibiting the states from abridging people's "privileges or immunities" or depriving them of life, liberty, or property without due process of law. It further guaranteed "equal protection of the laws." But, for decades after

This chimney ornament depicted George III as the defender of the Magna Carta and the British Bill of Rights. By contrast, leaders of the American Revolution argued that the king had violated these charters.

This draft of the Bill of Rights was printed for use in Congress and amended during its debates. Congress eventually sent twelve amendments to the states, which ratified ten of them in 1791.

the Fourteenth Amendment was ratified in 1868, the federal courts interpreted it narrowly. Not until the 1920s did the courts begin to apply the provisions of the Bill of Rights, one by one, to the states. (Although, it has not yet been used to apply the Second and the Seventh Amendments.) Liberal justices have argued that the Fourteenth Amendment "incorporates" the Bill of Rights, or extends the rights guaranteed to the state level. Conservative justices have been more skeptical of this argument and more restrained in their application of the Bill of Rights to the states.

The most sweeping provisions of the Bill of Rights are contained in the First Amendment. It embodies a host of fundamental rights, from freedom of religion, speech, and the press, to the right to assemble and to petition the government with complaints. In just a few words the First Amendment captures the essence of being an American.

The First Amendment bars the federal government from formally recognizing any religion as the official state religion, no matter how many citizens follow that faith. At the same time, it guarantees all citizens the right to exercise their individual religious beliefs. When the first state governments were established, some tried to recognize a particular church or Protestant Christianity in general as an established religion, and barred non-Christians from holding public office. Some states taxed religious minorities differently than others. The First Amendment followed Thomas Jefferson's advice that a "wall of separation" be erected between church and state. Jefferson believed that the separation of church and state would protect government and organized religion from each other. Under the First Amendment, the government cannot favor one religion over others, aid any religions, or stop people from exercising their religious beliefs.

To improve morality, various groups have frequently advocated religious practices in the public sphere. For instance, some states required that all public school students begin the day by reciting a prayer. The New York State legislature drafted what it considered a neutral prayer that made no references to any specific religion, but in the 1962 case of *Engel* v. *Vitale* the Supreme Court struck down the practice on the grounds that it was not "part of the business of government to compose official prayers." Similar disputes later developed over the placing of the Ten Commandments in courtrooms and on other public property. In two narrow decisions in 2005 the Supreme Court split the difference, concluding that displaying the Ten Commandments on government property was only unconstitutional if it seemed that government was promoting religion. The Court ruled against displaying the Commandments in a Kentucky courthouse, where their religious content was emphasized, but let a monument to the Commandments stand on the grounds of the Texas capitol as an acceptable tribute to the nation's religious history.

The right of free speech has been just as controversial as the separation of church and state, because it involves freedom of expression, freedom of thought, and freedom to criticize the government. One person's free speech may be offensive to another. The government has acted to restrict speech in radio and television broadcasting if it involves obscenity. During wartime, the government has also suppressed speech that it considers subversive, such as urging citizens to refuse to be drafted into military service. During the First World War, the Supreme Court concluded that the government could restrict such speech if it demonstrated that the speech posed a "clear and present danger" to the nation. In his opinion in *Schenck* v. *United States* (1919), Justice Oliver Wendell Holmes Jr. used the example of someone falsely crying "fire" in a crowded theater—simply to cause a panic and injure people—as an example of speech not protected by the Constitution.

Free speech sometimes involves symbolic action. The courts ruled that when protesters burn an American flag, the act is a legitimate extension of their right of free speech, no matter how much it offends people's patriotism. In the case of *Buckley* v. *Valeo* (1976) the Supreme Court also extended the concept of "speech" to political campaign contributions. It ruled out any limit on the amount of money that candidates can contribute

The Supreme Court ruled in the case of Van Orden v. Perry *(2005) that a monument to the Ten Commandments on the grounds of the Texas state capitol did not violate the First Amendment because it had stood there unchallenged for forty years and that it reflected the state's "cultural heritage" rather than an effort to "advance religion."*

to their own campaigns as an infringement of their right to free speech.

An important corollary to free expression is freedom of the press. Newspapers have fiercely criticized government leaders and their policies since the Presidency of George Washington. The news media has developed into an unofficial "fourth branch of the government" that provides additional checks and balances by scrutinizing what government is doing and exposing corruption. One significant restraint on reporting for many years was the threat of libel suits brought by the public officials whom the media criticized. Then, in the case of *New York Times Co.* v. *Sullivan* (1964), the Supreme Court ruled that the media could not be convicted of libeling public officials, unless their accusers could prove malicious intent, not simply criticism or inaccuracies. This ruling substantially reduced the media's liability for libel, which enabled reporters to question and criticize government officials more freely.

A teacher continues a daily practice of reading passages from the Bible to her class in 1962, despite the Supreme Court's ruling against religious practices in public schools in Engel *v.* Vitale *earlier that year. The court ruled that prayer in schools was a violation of the separation of church and state.*

During the Vietnam War the *New York Times, Washington Post,* and other newspapers obtained and published still classified government documents, known as the Pentagon Papers. These documents detailed the history of how the United States entered the war. President Richard Nixon asked the courts to issue injunctions to stop the papers from publishing any more of these documents, an action called prior restraint. The Nixon administration argued that release of the documents would gravely harm national security. Yet, when the administration cited specific examples of such vital secrets, the newspapers were able to demonstrate that the information was already publicly available through other sources. The most damaging revelation in the Pentagon Papers was not classified information but evidence of the government's poor decision-making. Through the course of the trial, it became apparent that the administration's primary motivation for suppressing publication was to avoid the perception of weakness in allowing the material to leak out. In the case of New York Times v. *United States* (1971), the Supreme Court ruled in favor of the newspapers, responding that the government had failed to show a "compelling interest" in restricting the right of a free press. "The press was to serve the governed, not the governors," wrote Justice Hugo Black for the majority of the Court.

The First Amendment also protects people's freedom to gather peacefully and to petition the government with their requests. These rights permitted the picketing and other protests during the civil rights and antiwar movements of the 1950s and 1960s, so long as they remained nonviolent. Americans have also made much use of the right to sign petitions. In the nineteenth century, antislavery groups sent

In August 1963 civil rights supporters from around the nation gathered for a March on Washington. They demanded an end to racial segregation and inequality. Among those marching together, from left to right, are Roy Wilkins of the NAACP (second from left with striped tie), A. Philip Randolph of the Brotherhood of Sleeping Car Porters, and Walter Reuther of the United Auto Workers.

Congress countless petitions demanding an end to the slave trade, and to other aspects of human slavery. Women's groups also used petitions as a tactic in their long campaign to win the right to vote.

The Second Amendment guarantees the rights of citizens to "bear arms," or own guns. Writing in *The Federalist*, Madison assured Americans that they need not fear the new government because of "the advantage of being armed, which you possess over the people of almost every other nation." The amendment couples the right of individuals to own guns with the responsibility of forming state militias, to be called on in times of emergency. Today these militias are known as the National Guard. Congress and the courts have reasoned that the Second Amendment does not limit the federal government from enacting certain forms of gun control, such as requiring registration and a waiting period when purchasing firearms, prohibiting children and convicts from owning guns, or declaring certain weapons illegal.

The next six amendments in the Bill of Rights deal with legal rights. They protect one's home from being taken over by the military—outlawing a practice that the British had employed during the American Revolution, when they quartered military troops in private homes. They further protect people's homes, as well as their persons, papers, and other property, against unreasonable search and seizure by the authorities. The Fourth Amendment requires that police first obtain search warrants when hunting for incriminating evidence. It does not define "unreasonable," however, and left the term for the courts to determine. In the twentieth century, electronic eavesdropping was deemed a violation of the Fourth Amendment, so that authorities must obtain legal permission to conduct wiretapping in criminal investigations. The Fourth Amendment assumes that people have a right to privacy and has been cited in many instances where people believe their privacy has been violated.

The Fifth Amendment safeguards the rights of anyone accused of a crime. It prohibits defendants from being tried again twice for the same crime if they have already been acquitted (a practice called "double jeopardy"). Nor can people be forced to give damaging testimony against themselves ("self-incrimination"). Such rights protect the innocent as well as the guilty, and some critics have complained that they hamper law enforcement. In the 1940s and 1950s, when congressional committees conducted investigations into Communist subversion and espionage, many witnesses "took the Fifth." They refused to testify whether they had been members of the Communist Party or to name others who might have been involved. Government employees, including teachers, were fired from their jobs if they cited the Fifth Amendment when they declined to answer questions. The Supreme Court later in *Watkins* v. *United States* (1957) ruled that witnesses before congressional committees retained all their constitutional protections, including that against self-incrimination.

The *Watkins* ruling came too late for the popular writer Dashiell Hammett, whose crime novels included *The Maltese Falcon* (1930) and *The Thin Man* (1934). During the Great Depression, in 1937, Hammett had joined the Communist Party and was the trustee of a bail fund established by the Civil Rights Congress, later identified as a Communist-dominated organization. Called to testify before the House Un-American Activities Committee in 1947, Hammett was asked to "name names" of those who had contributed money to the fund. He refused to provide information that might jeopardize people's reputations and careers. Despite his prominence, Hammett was convicted of contempt of Congress for not answering these questions, and spent six months in a federal prison in 1951.

TAKING THE FIFTH

During the Cold War, when congressional investigators were trying to root out subversives in the government, many witnesses refused to answer their questions, citing their rights under the Fifth Amendment. Some people suggested repealing the amendment but Harvard law professor (and later solicitor general of the United States) Erwin Griswold reminded them of the necessity of the amendment in a 1955 booklet called "The 5th Amendment Today."

I would like to venture the suggestion that the privilege against self-incrimination is one of the great landmarks in man's struggle to make himself civilized. . . .The establishment of the privilege is closely linked historically with the abolition of torture. Now we look upon torture with abhorrence. But torture was once used by honest and conscientious public servants as a means of obtaining information about crimes which could not otherwise be disclosed. We want none of that today, I am sure. For a very similar reasons, we do not make even the most hardened criminal sign his own death warrant, or dig his own grave, or pull the lever that springs the trap on which he stands. We have through the course of history developed a considerable feeling of the dignity and intrinsic importance of the individual man. Even the evil man is a human being. If a man has done wrong, he should be punished. But the evidence against him should be produced, and evaluated by a proper court in a fair trial. Neither torture nor an oath nor the threat of punishment should be used to compel him to provide the evidence to accuse or to convict himself.

Witness Carole Tyler's lawyer provided her with a prepared response when she declined to answer the questions of a congressional committee investigating her boss, the Senate majority secretary Bobby Baker. The statement asserts her rights under the Fifth Amendment.

Hollywood screenwriter Ring Lardner Jr. is escorted to a hearing of the House Committee on Un-American Activities in 1947. His refusal to answer the committee's questions led to his serving a year in prison for contempt of Congress, and being blacklisted as a writer.

The Sixth Amendment upholds a defendant's right to a speedy and fair trial. The Seventh ensures that in civil cases (those not involving criminal charges) both the plaintiff (who makes the charges) and the defendant have the right to a trial by jury, so long as one side demands it. The Eighth Amendment requires that bail and fines should not be set excessively high, and that "cruel and unusual" punishment not be inflicted on those found guilty. This amendment has given rise to a debate as to whether the death penalty can be considered cruel and unusual punishment.

Following this list of specific prohibitions, the Ninth and Tenth Amendments added some broad generalizations. One reason why James Madison had initially opposed a Bill of Rights was his concern that not all rights could be anticipated and enumerated. The Ninth Amendment maintains that the people have other rights that cannot be suppressed simply because they are not mentioned in the Bill of Rights. For many years the Ninth Amendment went essentially unused. It was revived in the 1965 case of *Griswold* v. *Connecticut*, when the Supreme Court struck down a state law banning contraceptives. The justices cited the Bill of Rights collectively in asserting people's right to privacy in marital relations, and noted that the Ninth Amendment protected rights not specifically guaranteed in the Constitution. As Louis D. Brandeis wrote in an 1890 *Harvard Law Review* article (before he joined the Supreme Court), "the right to life has come to mean the right to enjoy life—the right to be let alone."

The Tenth Amendment stated that those powers not delegated to the U.S. government belonged to the states. Those who advocate a "strict construction" of the Constitution—that is, applying exactly what is written in it

A CONSUMER ADVOCATE DEFENDS THE RIGHT OF TRIAL BY JURY

Consumer advocate Ralph Nader described the value of jury trials in civil cases in his article "The Individual as Citizen," which was published in 1992 in The United States Constitution: Roots, Rights, and Responsibilities.

The Seventh Amendment to the federal Constitution preserves the right of trial by jury "in suits at common law." In recent years, that amendment has extended some remarkable benefits to the public. It was a worker sickened by asbestos who began the massive litigation that exposed the product's health risks as well as the lengthy and very extensive cover-up of those risks by certain of its manufacturers. In this case one man succeeded in humbling a large corporation into disclosing its illegal practices and compensating its victims. Also alerted into action and precaution were the long-indifferent regulatory agencies and society at large. But the litigant would not have had a chance had he been unable to secure his right to jury trial. Juries are instruments of law that reduce the disparity of power between the haves and the have-nots. At present, a mounting attack on juries and the jury system in civil liability cases is being waged by insurance companies, trade associations, and other corporations. Recently one of their lobbies offered legislation to Congress that would preempt or limit various decisions made by juries in state courts. This lobby is testing the waters, for it has a long history of favoring replacement of the jury system with compensation boards operated by political appointees. The core word they use is "predictability"; the real word is "controllability."

and no more—insist that the federal government may not perform any functions that are not specifically enumerated in the Constitution. Defenders of states rights complain that the growth of the federal government consumed many responsibilities that should have been left to the states. Yet, Chief Justice John Marshall reasoned in the case of *McCulloch* v. *Maryland* (1819) that the Constitution could not anticipate all the powers that the national government would need to meet future circumstances, and that therefore the provision that Congress could make all laws "necessary and proper" to carry out its responsibilities implies additional powers.

Young boys did dangerous work in the West Virginia coal mines in 1908, leading reformers to seek an amendment to the Constitution outlawing child labor. The amendment failed to be ratified but the Fair Labor Standards Act of 1938 finally accomplished the ban.

Tensions between these two positions reappear throughout American history. For instance, when the federal government tried to prohibit child labor, the Supreme Court in *Hammer* v. *Dagenhart* (1918), struck down these efforts as something that was more proper for the states to determine. A generation later, the Fair Labor Standards Act of 1938 again abolished child labor, and this time the courts accepted the law as constitutional.

Wartime fears have often strained the guarantees of the Bill of Rights. Responding to emergency situations, the government has argued for limiting individual rights to protect the national security. During the Civil War, President Abraham Lincoln suspended the right of habeas corpus to hold Confederate sympathizers without trial. By this method he prevented Maryland legislators from voting to secede, which would have isolated the capital of Washington, D.C., from the North. Lincoln explained that it was necessary for him to stretch the Constitution in order to save it. Not until after the war had been won did the Supreme Court uphold habeas corpus in the 1866 case of *Ex Parte Milligan*. During the First World War, the government prosecuted those who made public speeches against the war and the draft. During the Second World War, it sent thousands of Japanese Americans on the West Coast to inland internment centers. The Supreme Court ruled the internment camps unconstitutional in 1994. In 1990, the U.S. government formally apologized and paid reparations to the surviving internment camp prisoners. Following the terrorist attacks on September 11, 2001, Congress quickly passed the U.S.A. Patriot Act, which among other provisions vastly expanded the government's access to private records, from medical records to books that people check out of libraries.

The Bill of Rights protects people's civil liberties, which allow them to live their own lives according to their own consciences. Civil rights, by

The Japanese Americans seated on this train were being sent from their homes in Portland, Oregon, to internment camps during World War II. Although the Supreme Court ruled that the internment was constitutional, the U.S. government later apologized and paid reparations to those held in the camps.

contrast to liberties, generally refer to matters of equality. Just before the Civil War, in the 1857 case of *Dred Scott* v. *Sandford* the Supreme Court had ruled that slaves were not citizens and, therefore, had no constitutional rights. Following the war, the Thirteenth, Fourteenth, and Fifteenth Amendments outlawed slavery, forbade racial discrimination in voting, and guaranteed all citizens equal protection of the laws. Yet the civil rights embodied in these amendments went largely unenforced for the next century. When the southern states adopted racial segregation, the Supreme Court upheld the notion of "separate but equal" in the 1896 case of *Plessy* v. *Ferguson*. Later in *Brown* v. *Board of Education* (1954) the Court concluded that in education, separate was not equal. Congress further struck down racial segregation with the Civil Rights Act of 1964.

The argument then switched when affirmative action programs offered racial minorities an advantage in college enrollment, government contracts, and other areas. Critics complained that these programs amounted to "reverse discrimination." In *Regents of the University of California* v. *Bakke* (1978) the Supreme Court ruled in favor of a white student who had not been admitted into medical school despite having higher test scores than some of the minorities who had been accepted. The Court did not strike down all affirmative action plans, but said that universities could not set fixed enrollment quotas specifically for minority students. Otherwise, the Supreme Court has recognized that diversity

THE POLITICAL QUADRILLE
Music by Dred Scott

A cartoonist pictured Dred Scott playing the tune to which all of the Presidential candidates in 1860 danced—they each needed to react to the Supreme Court's decision in their campaigns. From the top left they are (clockwise) John C. Breckinridge, Abraham Lincoln, John Bell, and Stephen A. Douglas.

in education is constitutionally permissible, and that race can be considered as a factor in admissions.

An important right not guaranteed by the Bill of Rights was the right to vote. At the time that the first ten amendments were ratified, most of the states limited voting to white men who owned property. The states eventually dropped property requirements for voting, but it took several constitutional amendments to extend voting privileges to African Americans, women, and those between the ages of eighteen and twenty-one. In a democracy, the right to vote is as critical as any others guaranteed in the Constitution, and the responsibility of every citizen to exercise.

4

How Has the Constitution Expanded over Time?

"The powers of the legislature are defined and limited; and that those limits may not be mistaken, or forgotten, the constitution is written. To what purpose are powers limited, and to what purpose is that limitation committed to writing, if these limits may, at any time, be passed by those intended to be restrained? The distinction between a government with limited and unlimited powers, is abolished, if those limits do not confine the persons on whom they are imposed, and if acts prohibited and acts allowed, are of equal obligation."

—Chief Justice John Marshall,
majority opinion in
Marbury v. *Madison* (1803)

A constitutional amendment to permit students to pray in school; an amendment to guarantee women equal rights; an amendment to prohibit abortion; an amendment to define marriage; an amendment to make the District of Columbia a state: these are just a few of the more than eleven thousand proposed amendments formally introduced in Congress that have not become part of the Constitution. Since the Bill of Rights—the first ten amendments to the Constitution—was adopted in 1791, Congress has passed an additional twenty-three amendments, of which the states have ratified only seventeen. Such statistics indicate the magnitude of difficulty in amending the U.S. Constitution.

The few amendments that have been adopted have generally come about because of a widely recognized problem or a sustained campaign for reform. After the Nineteenth Amendment gave women the right to vote in 1920, Carrie Chapman Catt, one of the leaders of the woman suffrage movement, reflected that: "To get the word 'male' in effect out of the Constitution cost the women of the country fifty-two years of pauseless campaign." Given the difficulty of amending the Constitution, therefore, it is not surprising that change has more often occurred through judicial interpretation than through formal amendment.

The framers of the Constitution realized that change and reform would be necessary over time, and in Article V they spelled out several

In 1917 woman suffrage advocates marched down New York City's Fifth Avenue with this banner, encouraging men to support women's right to vote in state elections. Passage of the New York State suffrage amendment that November gave a boost to the national effort to amend the U.S. Constitution.

processes for amending this core document of the republic. Most commonly, amendments are approved by a two-thirds vote in both houses of Congress and then ratified by the legislatures of three-quarters of the states. Instead of the state legislatures, amendments can be ratified by conventions in three-quarters of the states. Voters in each state would elect members of these conventions. If Congress fails to respond to an issue important to the states, the states can also elect delegates to a constitutional convention that can propose amendments for the states to ratify. That procedure has not been used since the original Constitutional Convention in 1787.

The Articles of Confederation had required a unanimous vote of the states to approve any changes, which kept the Confederation Congress from fixing any of the weaknesses in the Articles. The Constitution's solution for cautious, well-considered revision was a vote in Congress and the states that was more than a majority but less than unanimity. The amendment process set high hurdles to clear, but still allowed the government to address new problems and adopt changes in the federal system peacefully, once a broad national consensus on the issue was achieved. The Constitution rests on the sovereign power of the people, who have the right to change aspects of their government when necessary. James Wilson, a delegate to the Constitutional Convention from Pennsylvania, explained in a lecture in 1791 that amendments were "not a principle of discord, rancor, or war," they were "a principle of melioration [reformation], contentment, and peace."

The first ten amendments satisfied complaints that the Constitution lacked specific guarantees of individual rights. After that, amendments were added individually to meet problems as they arose. The first added after the Bill of Rights was triggered by a lawsuit, filed by attorney Alexander Chisholm, who as executor of an estate for a South Carolina merchant, Robert Farquhar, sued the state of Georgia to secure payment for war supplies the state had purchased from Farquhar. The Supreme Court ruled in *Chisholm* v. *Georgia* (1793) that states could be sued. Georgia paid the claim, but called on its congressional delegation to support an amendment shielding the states from suits brought by citizens of another state or foreign country in federal court. Congress responded with what became the Eleventh Amendment, which the grateful states swiftly ratified. From then on, such claims could be filed only in state courts.

The unexpected outcome of the election of 1800 prompted the Twelfth Amendment. Thomas Jefferson and Aaron Burr ran as the Democratic-Republican candidates for President and Vice President. Although they defeated their Federalist rivals, Jefferson and Burr received an equal number of votes in the Electoral College. Because neither man had gotten a majority, the outcome of the election was left to the House of Representatives, which the opposition party controlled. Federalists who hated Jefferson voted for Burr for President. The House voted thirty-six times before it chose Jefferson for President, after the Federalist Party leader Alexander Hamilton threw his support to

Woman suffrage advocates used the image of a girl in Revolutionary War garb as a reminder of the Spirit of '76. Like the men who had fought against British taxation when they had no representation in the British parliament, the women declared "no taxation without representation."

Judges are like umpires.
Umpires don't make the rules;
they apply them. . . .
I will remember that it's my job
to call balls and strikes and
not to pitch or bat.

— Chief Justice John Roberts
at his confirmation hearing,
September 12, 2005

Jefferson, as the more able and honorable candidate. Jefferson became President and Burr became Vice President. (Burr later shot and killed Hamilton in a duel.) To prevent such a situation from happening again, the Twelfth Amendment, ratified in 1804, provided that the Electors vote separately for Presidential and Vice Presidential candidates. This meant that in the future, candidates for President would compete only against the other parties' Presidential candidates, not against their own Vice Presidential running mates.

More than sixty years passed before another amendment was added to the Constitution. Political pressure for new amendments lessened because of the Supreme Court's assertiveness in deciding constitutional issues. Starting with the 1803 case of *Marbury* v. *Madison*, the Supreme Court justices claimed the right to declare acts of Congress unconstitutional. As Chief Justice John Marshall wrote for the Court: "It is, emphatically, the province and duty of the judicial department, to say what the law is." The Court based its authority for this practice, known as judicial review, on Article III, section 2, which extended "judicial power" to all cases of law arising under the Constitution, along with the laws of the United States, and the treaties made with other nations. Also, state supreme courts had asserted the power of judicial review over state laws, establishing precedents for the national Supreme Court. Later, in *McCulloch* v. *Madison* (1819), the Supreme Court applied a broad interpretation of the federal government's right to take actions "necessary and proper" to meet the urgent needs of the nation. The Court's recognition of the flexibility and elasticity of the Constitution reduced the demand for new amendments.

Not everyone agreed with Chief Justice Marshall's reasoning regarding the power of the federal government. President James Madison personally favored spending federal money on "internal improvements" in the states—building roads and canals, for instance, to improve transportation and commerce—but he did not believe the Constitution permitted it. Madison vetoed an internal improvements bill based on this belief, but called for a constitutional amendment to allow for it. Though Congress could not override Madison's veto, neither did it pass the amendment he desired, and the issue of the federal government's authority to find internal improvements remained a lingering controversy between those who favored either stricter or looser interpretations of the Constitution.

No new amendments were adopted until after the Civil War. In 1860, the election of the first Republican President, Abraham Lincoln, triggered the secession of the Southern states. During the months between the election and Lincoln's inauguration, Congress nervously passed a constitutional amendment that would have protected slavery where it already existed. This last-ditch effort to preserve the Union stipulated that: "No amendment shall be made to the Constitution which will authorize or give to Congress the power to abolish or interfere, within any State, with the domestic institutions thereof, including that of persons held to labor or service by the laws of said State." The effort failed because the seceded states no longer felt bound by the Constitution and the remaining states—where antislavery sentiments ran high—chose not to appease them.

Five years later the Civil War led to an amendment that did the just opposite. The Thirteenth Amendment permanently abolished slavery throughout the United States. President Lincoln had signed the Emancipation Proclamation in 1863, but that order affected only the states in rebellion, and did not end slavery in the states that remained in the Union.

The abolition of slavery was the first of three amendments resulting from the Civil War that shifted more power from the states to the federal government. Congress drafted the Fourteenth Amendment to ensure that African Americans were recognized as citizens of the United States—contrary to the Supreme Court's ruling in *Dred Scott* v. *Sandford* (1857). The amendment tried to ensure that the freedmen would have rights

This nativist cartoon, published in California, warned against opening the ballot box to more than "the white race alone" by giving African Americans the right to vote. Uncle Sam (bottom left) admonishes Congress that the next step will be to give the vote to Asians and Native Americans, who are portrayed in grossly stereotypical images and dialogue.

"This great document is the
unique American contribution
to man's continuing search for a
society in which individual liberty
is secure against governmental
oppression."

—Justice Hugo L. Black,
A Constitutional Faith (1968)

equal to those of all other citizens. In order to be readmitted to the Union and end Reconstruction rule, the Southern states were required to adopt the Fourteenth Amendment, which was ratified in 1868. Over the next century, however, Court rulings narrowed the amendment's application, and shifted it from protecting individuals to protecting corporations from certain government regulation, on the grounds that corporations were "persons" entitled to equal rights and due process of the law.

The Fifteenth Amendment, ratified in 1870, prohibited denying someone the right to vote because of race. It was the first of several amendments that broadened the franchise—the right to vote. This post–Civil War amendment was intended to give the newly freed African Americans sufficient political power to protect their constitutional rights. It protected only men at the time, as no states then permitted women to vote. However, the Southern states soon undermined this amendment with a series of tactics, such as poll taxes and literacy requirements, that effectively disenfranchised their black citizens for another century.

After Reconstruction, there were no new amendments until the Progressive era early in the twentieth century, when reformers sought to

A collective image of the South Carolina state legislature in 1868 showed many African American members. The Reconstruction Amendments were designed to establish their political rights as equals in American society.

improve the workings of the federal government, and to reform American society. Two amendments were ratified in 1913. The first permitted the government to collect income taxes. Article I had prohibited Congress from imposing a "direct tax," but had not defined what this meant. During the Civil War, the federal government imposed an income tax to pay for the war's enormous expenses. The tax, which was not challenged at the time, expired in 1872. Later, in the 1890s, reformers proposed a tax on individual and corporate income as an alternative to raising tariffs to produce revenue. (The federal government received most of its operating expenses from duties imposed on imported goods, but high tariffs increased the cost of consumer goods.) In the 1895 case of *Pollock v. Farmer's Loan & Trust Co.*, the Supreme Court struck down the income tax as a direct tax. It took reformers another twenty years to gain the Sixteenth Amendment, which effectively reversed the court's ruling. At first, graduated income taxes were paid only by the people with the highest incomes. Not until World War II did average wage earners pay federal taxes that were withheld from payrolls.

A newspaper headline reports the controversy in Congress over an income tax on wealthy citizens. The Sixteenth Amendment allowed the federal government to levy an income tax.

Another Progressive-era reform, the Seventeenth Amendment, changed the way that senators were elected. The Constitution originally assigned the state legislatures to elect U.S. senators. Senators were seen as "ambassadors" from their states. The system produced some outstanding senators, including Henry Clay and Daniel Webster. Yet state legislatures sometimes deadlocked when choosing among candidates and were unable to fill Senate seats. Muckraking journalists—a term that Theodore Roosevelt applied to investigative journalists in 1906—raised the alarm that wealthy individuals were bribing legislatures to win Senate seats, where they protected special interests rather than the general public. In a series of magazine articles that ran under the title of "The Treason of the Senate," the muckraker David Graham Phillips denounced the senators as "perjurers," "bribers," and "thieves." Reformers proposed the amendment to allow citizens to elect their senators directly, and it was adopted in 1913. Unlike reformers in Britain at that time, who reduced the power of their House of Lords, the Seventeenth Amendment kept all the Senate's initial powers and responsibilities intact, leaving it one of the most powerful "upper houses" in any national legislature. (When parliamentary governments began, the aristocracy served in the "upper" chamber and the commoners in the "lower." The U.S. Congress makes no such class distinctions, but the Senate by virtue of being the smaller body with longer terms, and having the additional power of advice and consent over nominations and treaties, has often been called the "upper" body. Members of the House refer to it instead as the "other body.")

American participation in the First World War propelled two other reform amendments. The Eighteenth Amendment, ratified in 1919, was the culmination of a century-long crusade to ban the sale and consumption of alcohol. The amendment gained momentum during the war with successful efforts to ban the sale of intoxicating drinks in the vicinity of military bases. The Eighteenth Amendment was the first to set a time limit of seven years on its ratification. Some "wet" members of Congress, torn between their personal distaste for Prohibition and the large numbers of "dry" voters in their states, observed that fewer than three-quarters of the states had adopted some form of prohibition, suggesting that the amendment might not be ratified by a sufficient number of states. The time limit enabled them to vote for the amendment with some hope that the states would not ratify it. To their surprise enough states had responded in a little more than a year to ratify the amendment.

The Eighteenth Amendment banned "intoxicating beverages," but left it to Congress to define exactly which beverages were included. Responding to public opinion, in 1919, Congress passed the Volstead Act, which banned beer and wine along with hard liquor. The sweeping nature of Prohibition encouraged massive violations of the law during the Roaring Twenties. The mobster Al Capone bragged to newspaper reporters that by selling illegal liquor he was a simply supplying a public demand: "Some call it bootlegging. Some call it racketeering. I call it a business. They say I violate the prohibition law. Who doesn't?" To end the lawlessness that Prohibition stimulated, the Eighteenth Amendment was repealed by the Twenty-first Amendment in 1933, making it the only amendment to the Constitution to be voided.

During Prohibition, agents used many tactics to combat illegal alcohol, even liquor-sniffing dogs. Just as this dog finds a flask in the pocket of a man fishing, law enforcement authorities use dogs today to locate drugs and explosives.

The repeal of Prohibition has been the only amendment to be ratified by state conventions rather than by the legislatures. Advocates of repeal accepted ratification by convention because many state legislatures did not meet every year and waiting for them to convene would have delayed repeal. As the people would vote for state convention delegates, the convention system would also give repeal a popular mandate. Forty-three states established conventions and achieved the needed three-quarters ratification within four months. The states, however, retained the right to set their own laws regarding the transportation, sale, and consumption of alcohol.

The Eighteenth Amendment's widely perceived failure made some people cynical about amendments. In 1930 the caustic journalist H. L. Mencken asserted in a magazine article that there was one generalization that could be made about constitutional amendments: "They never work." Since then it has often been argued that social attitudes cannot be changed by laws or constitutional amendments. Yet the Nineteenth Amendment, ratified just after Prohibition, was highly successful. It ended a century of struggle by women seeking the right to vote. Some western states had already given women both the vote and the right to run for office. The first woman elected to the U.S. House of Representatives, Jeannette Rankin of Montana, was elected in 1916, before the Nineteenth Amendment extended woman suffrage to all the states. Women's active roles in many capacities during the First World War helped erode opposition to their right to vote.

Testifying in 1917, the woman suffrage lobbyist Maud Younger pointed out to a congressional committee the contradiction of fighting a war to "make the world safe for democracy," when so many American citizens were denied their democratic rights at home. "We thought, too, of the women of other nations, on the verge of enfranchisement [getting the vote] themselves," she said. "And we wondered how they would welcome the United States at the peace council to establish democracy for them—the United States which does not recognize its own women." In 1920, soon after the war ended, woman suffrage became part of the Constitution.

In 1933, the same year that Prohibition was repealed, the Twentieth Amendment revised the government's calendar. Known as the "lame duck" amendment, it pushed the beginning of Congress from December (thirteen months after the elections) back to January (two months after the election). This reduced the need for congressional sessions to be held after the elections, where many members who had retired or had been defeated continued to vote in Congress. These "lame ducks" no longer owned allegiance to the voters and were more susceptible to special interests. The Twentieth Amendment also shifted the President's inauguration from March 4 to January 20. The long delays that had made sense in earlier centuries, when transportation was slow, no longer made sense in the twentieth century, especially as the need for government action seemed more pressing.

Elected in November 1932, Franklin D. Roosevelt was the last President to have to wait until March for his inauguration. During the

"*Our country has deliberately undertaken a great social and economic experiment, noble in motive and far-reaching in purpose.*"

— President Herbert Hoover on Prohibition, in a letter to Senator W. H. Borah of February 23, 1928

On the cover of a speech by the woman suffrage leader Carrie Chapman Catt, a World War I soldier appeals to Uncle Sam to give his mother the right to vote.

Republicans who opposed Franklin D. Roosevelt's bid for an unprecedented third term as President put out this advertising flier in 1940. The ad suggests that Communists and Democratic Party bosses backed a third term, though respected American Presidents would have opposed it.

five-month interregnum before he took the oath of office, the national economy declined into the worst depression in American history. The government's inability to act vigorously during the transition made the need for constitutional change all the more obvious.

Once inaugurated, Roosevelt launched an ambitious New Deal program for economic relief and reform. The Democrats increased their majorities in Congress in 1934 and 1936, showing widespread popular support for Roosevelt's liberal program, but the Supreme Court remained dominated by Republican appointees. Conservative justices ruled unconstitutional such major New Deal initiatives as the National Industrial Recovery Act (aimed at improving business and labor conditions) and the Agricultural Adjustment Act (aimed at helping farmers). Having had no opportunity to appoint any justices to the Supreme Court during his first term, Roosevelt contemplated supporting a constitutional amendment that would require more than a simple majority vote on the Supreme Court to strike down an act of Congress. Instead, he decided to ask for legislation to enlarge the Court. His critics called this a "court packing" scheme and defeated it roundly. Within a few years, however, Roosevelt had appointed a majority of the Supreme Court justices. He appointed justices who generally favored a broad interpretation of the Constitution and were sympathetic to an active and innovative federal government.

Roosevelt's unprecedented election to four terms as President encouraged his opponents (after his death in 1945) to propose an amendment to limit Presidents to two terms. They worried that popular Presidents could use their incumbency to keep themselves in office for life, and potentially to evolve into dictators. Opponents of the amendment argued against limiting the people's right to choose their leader. After Republicans regained the majorities in the House and Senate, they proposed the Twenty-second Amendment, specifying a two-term limit. Strongly supported in state legislatures with Republican majorities, it was ratified in 1951. The Amendment exempted the incumbent President, Harry Truman, so that the first Presidents to feel this restriction, ironically, were popular Republicans, Dwight Eisenhower and Ronald Reagan. Not until Bill Clinton did a Democratic President serve two full terms and encounter the prohibition against running for a third term.

Ohio Republican senator John Bricker proposed another anti-Roosevelt amendment in 1953. Bricker's amendment would have required the Senate to vote on executive agreements as it did on treaties. Presidents negotiate executive agreements with other nations, as long as those agreements reflect the President's constitutional powers. For instance, as commander in chief the President can sign an executive agreement with another nation to station American troops in that country. The Bricker Amendment was in large part a reaction to President Franklin Roosevelt's secret agreements with the Soviet Union made at Yalta, in the Ukraine, near the end of World War II. Supporters of the amendment felt that the Senate should have been able to vote to approve or reject that agreement, the same as it would have handled a treaty. When Congress considered the Bricker Amendment, Republican President Dwight Eisenhower vigorously opposed it as an unnecessary restriction on the President's ability to conduct foreign policy. To Eisenhower's relief, the amendment narrowly failed to pass.

Judicial review continued to resolve conflict and uncertainty about the Constitution. Generally, the Supreme Court operated on precedent, honoring rulings made by previous judges. But the Court was not bound by precedent and could overturn earlier decisions when circumstances and opinion had shifted. The Court's decision in the 1954 case of *Brown* v. *Board of Education*, for instance, declared racial segregation in public schools unconstitutional. It reversed the earlier ruling in *Plessy* v. *Ferguson* (1896), which had upheld the notion that "separate but equal" facilities were acceptable Following the *Brown* decision, two constitutional amendments further chipped away at racial inequalities.

Ohio Senator John Bricker displays stacks of petitions from citizens supporting his effort to amend the Constitution to require Senate approval of executive agreements. Although Bricker failed in that effort, the photo demonstrates the First Amendment right to petition the government.

A child uses a drinking fountain marked "colored," in the era before the Civil Rights Act of 1964, when southern states required segregated fountains, restrooms, and other public facilities.

"Constitutions should consist only of general provisions: The reason is, that they must necessarily be permanent, and that they cannot calculate for the possible changes of things."

— Alexander Hamilton, speech to the New York ratification convention, June 28, 1788

The Twenty-third Amendment, ratified in 1961, gave the right to vote in Presidential elections to residents of the District of Columbia, where African Americans constituted a majority of the population. As the seat of the federal government, the district is not a state and has no senators, only a nonvoting delegate to the U.S. House of Representatives. The Twenty-fourth Amendment, ratified in 1964, abolished the poll taxes that some states had required citizens to pay in order to vote. Although poll taxes worked against poor people in general, they fell especially hard on African Americans in the South.

The shock of President John F. Kennedy's assassination in 1963 made Americans focus on the problem of Presidential succession. After Vice President Lyndon Johnson became President, the Vice Presidency remained vacant until the next election. Next in line of succession for the Presidency came the Speaker of the House and the president pro tempore of the Senate, both elderly men. People also wondered what might have occurred had President Kennedy been seriously wounded rather than killed. The Twenty-fifth Amendment, ratified in 1965, set up mechanisms to enable the Vice President to assume the Presidency if the President was incapable of functioning in office. When the Vice Presidency fell vacant, the President could nominate a replacement, with the consent of the Senate and House. Within a decade of the Twenty-fifth Amendment's ratification, it was activated to appoint two Vice Presidents: the first following the resignations of Vice President Spiro Agnew and then of President Richard Nixon.

The Vietnam War prompted ratification of the Twenty-sixth Amendment in 1971. Reformers pointed out that young men were subject

Infantrymen take a break in combat in Vietnam in January 1968. Until the Twenty-sixth Amendment in 1971, young men between eighteen and twenty-one could be drafted into the military, but could not cast votes for those who decided issues of war and peace.

When he appointed California governor Earl Warren to be chief justice of the United States in 1953, President Dwight D. Eisenhower had little idea of what a powerful champion of change Warren would become. The new chief justice took over leadership of a Court sharply divided between those who believed in judicial restraint and judicial activism. Warren proved adept at forging new majorities among the justices, and he unexpectedly became an advocate of individual rights and liberties. In his first major case, dealing with school desegregation, Warren argued strongly that segregation violated the Constitution's guarantee of equal protection of the laws. He convinced the other justices to join in a unanimous decision in *Brown* v. *Board of Education* (1954), which declared school segregation unconstitutional.

Warren was also proud of his leadership in striking down the old system of apportionment in state legislatures that gave more representation to sparsely populated rural districts than to large cities. "A citizen, a qualified voter," Warren asserted, "is no more or less so because he lives in the city or on a farm." In *Baker* v. *Carr* (1962), the Court ruled that all legislative districts must be equal in population.

The Warren Court never shied from controversy. In *Engel* v. *Vitale* (1962), it struck down school-sponsored prayer. In *Gideon* v. *Wainwright* (1963) it ruled that a poor defendant must be provided with a lawyer. In *Miranda* v. *Arizona* (1966) it declared that criminal suspects must be informed of their constitutional rights. Eisenhower shook his head and called appointing Warren the biggest mistake of his Presidency, but others applauded the Warren Court's vigorous defense of civil liberty and social reform.

to the military draft at the age of eighteen, and should therefore be able to vote for the leaders who were sending them into combat. A few states already allowed voters younger than twenty-one. The Twenty-sixth Amendment lowered the voting age to eighteen nationwide. However, younger Americans have often failed to take advantage of this right.

Under Chief Justice Earl Warren, who served from 1953 to 1969, the Supreme Court became more liberal and activist. It struck down school desegregation, school-sponsored prayer, and state legislatures that gave more seats to sparsely populated rural areas than to heavily populated cities. Noting that the Ninth Amendment did not limit people's rights to those enumerated in the Constitution, the Court ruled that citizens have a right to privacy, by which it overturned state laws banning contraceptives. Outraged opponents called for constitutional amendments to overturn the Court's rulings. In none of these efforts, however, could they muster sufficient support to attain the two-thirds votes needed in Congress for an amendment.

In 1972, Congress passed the Equal Rights Amendment, prohibiting discrimination on account of gender. While a majority of states ratified the proposed amendment, a vocal anti-feminist group called STOP ERA launched a counteroffensive that convinced enough states not to ratify it, killing the amendment. Congress then extended the deadline for ratifying the ERA, but the amendment again failed to win enough support from state legislatures. Opponents argued that the amendment was unnecessary because federal laws already protected equal rights for women.

Another failed amendment proposed in the 1970s would have made the District of Columbia a state, giving it two senators and at least one

When President Reagan nominated Sandra Day O'Connor in 1981, she became the first woman justice on the U.S. Supreme Court. Raised on an Arizona ranch, she had graduated third in her class at Stanford Law School in 1952, but, as she recalled in her commencement address at Stanford University on June 13, 2004, her academic brilliance did not lead directly to a post in private practice.

I was unable to obtain employment in a private law firm. I did receive one contingent offer of employment—as a legal secretary. But the gender walls that blocked me out of the private sector were more easily hurdled in the public sector, and I first found employment as a deputy county attorney of San Mateo County, California. While I was brought to the position by something short of choice, I came to realize almost immediately what a wonderful path I had taken. I was having a better time at my job than were those of my peers who had opted for private practice. Life as a public servant was more interesting. The work was more challenging. The encouragement and guidance from good mentors was more genuine. And the opportunities to take initiative and to see real results were more frequent. Ultimately, these forays into the exciting area of public service led me to the privilege of serving as an assistant attorney general in my state, a state senator, a state judge and a United States Supreme Court Justice.

Her prior career in public service made Justice O'Connor a pragmatist, and she adopted a middle-of-the-road, problem-solving approach to the law. With the Supreme Court's liberal and conservative wings closely balanced, she provided the critical swing vote on many five-to-four decisions, ranging widely from abortion rights to affirmative action. Although she was not chief justice, her critical swing votes shaped the outcome of so many decisions during her tenure that upon her retirement in 2005 many commentators called it the O'Connor Court.

representative. Although the district had a population comparable to that of several states, it was geographically tiny by comparison to the smallest state. Statehood raised questions about federal control of governmental areas within the district. Republicans also recognized that their party would have little chance of winning any of the congressional seats from the heavily Democratic District of Columbia. Only sixteen states had ratified the amendment when its time limit expired in 1985.

By contrast with the failure of these two amendments, after members of Congress raised their own salaries several times between 1987 and 1991, angry public opinion caused the states to belatedly ratify one of James Madison's original twelve amendments. What became the Twenty-seventh Amendment in 1992 stipulated that raises in congressional salaries would not go into effect until after the next election, giving the voters a chance to register their disapproval. Gregory Watson, a student at the University of Texas, had started the campaign to encourage the states to approve this long-forgotten amendment, for which Congress had set no time limit for ratification. Its cause was taken up by radio talk shows that appealed to a growing public disaffection with government. The states finally ratified the amendment more than two hundred years after Congress had passed it.

In 1994, for the first time in forty years, Republicans won the majority in the House of Representatives. They campaigned under the banner of a Contract with America, which advocated a Balanced Budget Amendment. With the United States running record high deficits, a mandatory balanced budget had gained many supporters in both parties. The House swiftly passed the amendment, but the Senate failed to achieve a two-thirds margin by a single vote. Oregon senator Mark Hatfield, the Republican chairman of the Senate Appropriations

Committee, refused to follow his party's lead on an amendment that he feared would hinder future government policy and cause more confusion than clarity. The drive for the amendment then lost steam when government balanced its budget without the constitutional mandate.

Conservatives also endorsed a host of other amendments concerning social issues. They sought to prohibit abortion, outlaw flag burning, and ban same-sex marriages. Some liberals also called for an amendment changing the Electoral College, after Al Gore, the Democratic Presidential candidate in 2000, won the popular vote but lost the electoral vote and the Presidency. Such amendments provided rallying cries during campaigns, motivating both supporters and opponents, but they lacked broad enough support for enactment in Congress. These failures led to calls from angry citizens for a new constitutional convention to propose amendments. Given the uncertain outcome of a convention, however, there was no groundswell for such a risky tactic.

Combined, all the amendments to the constitution do not equal the number of words in the original document, as concise as it was. Amending the Constitution has been difficult enough to discourage all but a tiny number of proposals from being adopted. Broad bipartisan national support is essential to alter the nation's fundamental charter. Yet the courts, together with the President and Congress, have steadily widened the scope of government and addressed new issues by reinterpreting the Constitution without always amending it.

> *"We do not consecrate the flag by punishing its desecration, for in doing so we dilute the freedom that this cherished emblem represents."*
>
> — Justice William J. Brennan Jr., *Texas* v. *Johnson* (1989)

President George H. W. Bush used the Marine Corps's Iwo Jima monument as a backdrop in 1989 when he endorsed a Constitutional amendment that would prohibit burning the American flag. The Supreme Court had ruled that flag burning was protected by the Constitution as symbolic speech.

5

How Is the Constitution Interpreted?

"Those who put their names in the Constitution understood the enormity of what they were attempting to do: to create a representative democracy, with a central government strong enough to unify a vast, diverse, then and now politically fractious nation; but a government limited enough to allow individual liberty and enterprise to flourish. Well, 213 years later, we can say with thanks, they succeeded. Not only in keeping liberty alive, but in providing a strong, yet flexible, framework within which America could keep moving forward, generation after generation, toward making real the pure ideals embodied in their words."

—President Bill Clinton, dedicating the National Constitution Center in Philadelphia on September 17, 2000

President Bill Clinton praised the foresight of the framers of the Constitution when he dedicated the National Constitution Center in Philadelphia in 2000. "We revere the Constitution," Clinton said, "because it is at the core of who we are."

It irked President Thomas Jefferson that the Supreme Court in *Marbury* v. *Madison* (1803) and other cases had taken upon itself the power to declare acts of Congress unconstitutional. "There is not a word in the Constitution that has given that power to them," Jefferson fumed in a letter to W. H. Torrance on March 11, 1815, about the Federalist justices who dominated the court in his day, "more than to the executive or the legislative branches." Since then, other Presidents and congressional leaders have expressed similar outrage over Court rulings that struck down their legislative accomplishments. Liberals and conservatives alike have decried "judicial activism," whenever rulings went against

them. Despite these complaints, the Supreme Court has reserved the final word on whether the actions of the executive and legislative branches comply with the Constitution.

Constitutional law consists of the applications and legal interpretations of the Constitution, as distinguished from statutory law (the acts of Congress) and common law (the precedents established by lower court rulings). Constitutional law deals with the government's legitimate functions and the limits that the Constitution places upon it. The executive and legislative branches constantly address new issues and establish new policies. Because Article III of the Constitution only gives federal courts the power to hear "cases or controversies," only those persons who have been harmed by a law will have "standing" to challenge it.

An example of the question of "standing" occurred in 1995, when Congress enacted a "line-item veto" that enabled Presidents to veto a single funding item within a larger appropriations bill without having to veto the whole bill. A few members of Congress who had voted against the line-item veto brought suit in the federal courts on the grounds that their legislative "power of the purse" had been diminished. However, a court found that they lacked standing—that is they had not been harmed by the line-item veto—and dismissed their suit. Then President Bill Clinton used the line-item veto to strike out funding that would have gone to New York City, and the courts heard the city's suit because it did clearly have standing. In *Clinton* v. *City of New York* (1998), the Supreme Court struck down the line-item veto as unconstitutional.

Although all federal officers take an oath to uphold the Constitution, they often read that document very differently. Presidents assert powers that they believe the Constitution gives them by implication. Congress enacts laws it deems "necessary and proper" to carry out its constitutional role. Their overlapping powers and responsibilities are an invitation to struggle. "The Constitution was designed to force conflict," said House Speaker Newt Gingrich in a December 6, 2004, interview on National Public Radio's *Morning Edition.* "You elect 100 senators, two per state. They're not part of the president's team. They work with the president, not for the president. You elect 435 House members by population; they work for the people who elect them. Then you have the president, who's elected every four years by the whole country." And, often the struggle between the executive branch and the legislature involves the President's nomination of and the Senate's right to approve or reject judicial appointments, who will interpret the Constitution.

Political parties also play a role in the varying interpretations of the Constitution, even though the Constitution made no mention of them. Those who favor a limited national government and more states' rights have gravitated toward one party, while those favoring a stronger, more active federal government tended toward another. Presidents George Washington and John Adams were identified with the Federalist Party, which tended toward a dominant federal government, but their party lost the Presidency and majorities in both houses of Congress to the

A piece of pottery promoted John Adams's candidacy for President, describing him as a man "full of love for thee and thine." When Adams lost his race for reelection in 1800, the nation experienced the first transfer of power from one political party to another under the constitutional system.

Democratic-Republicans, who favored states' rights, in the election of 1800. This first transfer of power between the parties left only the judiciary under the control of the Federalists, since only Federalist-appointed judges were then serving. President Thomas Jefferson, a Democratic-Republican, then set out to purge the Supreme Court by encouraging his supporters in the House to impeach Supreme Court justice Samuel Chase. A bitter partisan who never hesitated to speak his mind, Justice Chase struck many of Jefferson's supporters as lacking a judicial temperament; however, this was hardly an impeachable offense. Jeffersonians in the House accused Chase of some minor infractions on the bench, but essentially accused him of having rendering legal interpretations of the law in "an arbitrary, oppressive, and unjust way." Had these trumped-up charges succeeded in convicting Chase, the Jeffersonians might have also tried to remove Chief Justice John Marshall. However, Justice Chase was acquitted at his Senate trial, discrediting the notion of using impeachment as a political tool.

Within a few years, the Federalist Party crumbled and the United States entered into a period of one-party rule, called the Era of Good Feelings. Although unified on the surface, political leaders had sharply different opinions over what the Constitution meant and how the government should operate. The Era of Good Feelings ended with the hotly contested election of 1824, in which Andrew Jackson won the greatest share of the popular vote but lost the election in the House of Representatives to John Quincy Adams. Jackson's followers created their own party, the Democrats, while his opponents called themselves the Whigs, borrowing that name from the British political party that opposed the king, and supported social reforms in Parliament. In 1828 Jackson won the Presidency and began to spar with the Whigs in Congress—where the majorities fluctuated between Democrats and Whigs.

One of the clashes during this period between the executive and judicial branches dealt with efforts to remove Native Americans from their lands in the East and relocate them west of the Mississippi River. After the discovery of gold on Cherokee lands, the state of Georgia refused to recognize the Cherokees as a sovereign nation and opened tribal lands to white settlers. The Cherokees appealed to the courts, and in the case of *Cherokee Nation* v. *Georgia* (1832), Chief Justice John Marshall upheld their rights. President Jackson, who disagreed with the Court's order, refused to carry it out. "John Marshall has rendered his decision," Jackson supposedly said, "now let him enforce it." Jackson instead supported the Indian Removal Act, which paid the tribes for their land in the East and relocated them to new territory in the West. In 1838 the U.S. Army carried out that act and forcibly evicted the Cherokees who had resisted,

The Whig Party used this banner in the 1840s as a symbol of its program of internal improvements, to bolster both urban and agricultural development. Their opponents argued that such national initiatives were unconstitutional and should be left to the states.

sending them on the Trail of Tears to Oklahoma, so named because so many Cherokees died on the rugged journey.

Slavery also became a political and constitutional question. The question of whether slavery should be allowed to spread into the newly acquired western territories split apart the existing parties and encouraged the creation of the new Republican Party. When Abraham Lincoln became the first Republican to be elected President, eleven Southern states seceded from the Union out of concern that Lincoln would prevent the extension of slavery into the West, and perhaps move to abolish

The government prepared this map to designate western lands reserved for "emigrant Indians," those who were displaced from their traditional lands in the East and forced to move West. The move took place despite the Supreme Court's support for Indian land claims in Cherokee Nation v. Georgia *(1832).*

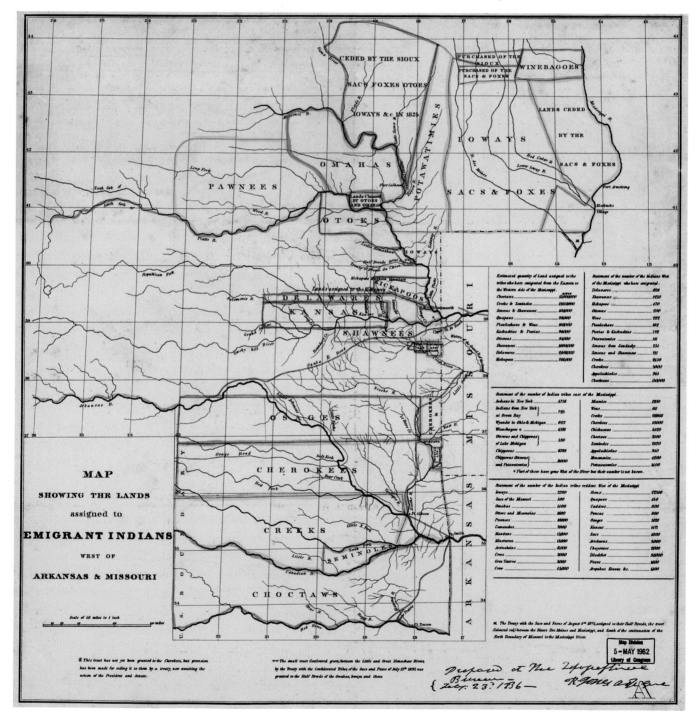

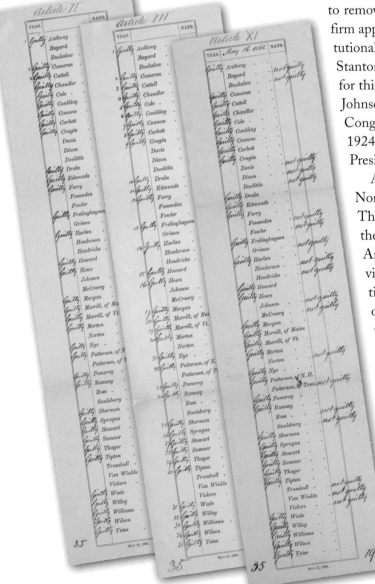

President Andrew Johnson came within a single vote of being removed from office at his Senate trial in 1868. These were the official tallies kept by Senate clerks to determine how senators voted on three articles of impeachment.

it completely. Lincoln denied being an abolitionist. Although he opposed the spread of slavery, he believed that the Constitution protected slave-holding where it already existed. During the Civil War, Lincoln signed an executive order known as the Emancipation Proclamation that freed people enslaved in territories under insurrection against the federal government. This act did not free anyone in the border states that had remained within the Union. Not until after the South was defeated did the Thirteenth Amendment abolish slavery entirely.

After Lincoln's assassination, in the period of Reconstruction that followed the war, Congress fought fiercely with President Andrew Johnson over how to treat the defeated southern states. Johnson believed in carrying out Lincoln's lenient policies, while congressional Republicans preferred a much tougher stance designed to protect the newly freed African Americans in the South. To prevent the President from dismissing cabinet officers sympathetic to the congressional Republicans, the Tenure of Office Act in 1867 required Senate approval to remove a cabinet officer, just as the Senate needed to confirm appointments. President Johnson called the act unconstitutional and defiantly fired his secretary of war, Edwin Stanton. The House of Representatives impeached Johnson for this action and related issues in 1868. At his Senate trial, Johnson came within one vote of being removed from office. Congress later repealed the Tenure of Office Act, and in 1924 the Supreme Court belatedly confirmed the President's right to remove executive branch appointees.

As a condition for being readmitted to the Union, the North required the southern states to ratify the Thirteenth, Fourteenth, and Fifteenth Amendments to the Constitution, known as the Reconstruction Amendments. On the surface, the amendments provided African Americans with citizenship, equal protection of the laws, and the right to vote. But, the language of the amendments, especially the sweeping nature of the Fourteenth Amendment, opened wide new areas for Congress to legislate and for the Court to interpret.

As the United States became a more industrial nation, the Supreme Court recognized the rights of corporations as "persons" under the Fourteenth Amendment and struck down efforts by the state and federal governments to regulate business as a violation of the amendment's guarantee that no state shall "deprive any person of life, liberty, or property, without due process of law." It would take another half century before the Supreme Court revised its interpretation of the amendment to permit laws that prohibited child labor, protected women workers, and set minimum wages for workers in general. Increasingly, the courts also used the Fourteenth Amendment to apply the restrictions and guarantees of the Bill of Rights to the states as well as to the federal government, using it to interpret laws related to voting and the rights of aliens and of criminal defendants. As the American industrial society developed, the federal courts changed their positions, becoming more tolerant of Presidential and legislative efforts to experiment with new means of protecting and improving the public welfare.

For the most part, the judicial branch has resisted intervening in the internal operations of the Congress. In the 1920s, when the Senate held highly publicized investigations into executive branch corruption, the Supreme Court confirmed the right of Congress to call any witnesses, even those who were not government officials, and to investigate anything remotely related to its legislative functions. Drawing on this authority, in the 1930s, congressional committees aggressively investigated the economic conditions that contributed to the Great Depression, the use of business lobbyists to shape legislation, and other issues.

After the Second World War, committees in both the House and Senate held sensationalized hearings into alleged Communist infiltration and subversion of government agencies. They subpoenaed numerous witnesses who had little connection with the government and interrogated them about their past political beliefs and activities, particularly any involvement with the Communist Party. The Supreme Court eventually concluded that these practices had overstepped constitutional bounds. In *Watkins* v. *United States* (1957) the court insisted that an investigative committee had to demonstrate a legislative purpose to jus-

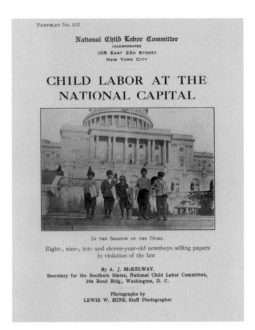

Newsboys in front of the U.S. Capitol were photographed by opponents of child labor as a way of demonstrating the pervasiveness of the issue. Not until the 1930s did the Supreme Court interpret the Fourteenth Amendment broadly enough to uphold anti–child labor laws.

JUSTICE JOHN MARSHALL HARLAN DISSENTS

The highest courts in some countries issue rulings without indicating what the votes of the justices were, or publishing dissenting opinions. The U.S. Supreme Court by contrast identifies how the justices voted and allows the majority to explain its rationale and the dissenters to explain their objections. As social thinking and public opinion change over time, however, these dissenting opinions may eventually prevail.

In the late nineteenth century, many southern states passed laws, called Jim Crow laws, requiring racial segregation in schools, transportation, and other public accommodations. African Americans sued on the grounds that these Jim Crow laws violated their civil rights under the Fourteenth Amendment's guarantee of equal protection of the laws. When the African American Homer A. Plessy refused to leave the first-class compart-

ment of a train in Louisiana, for which he had purchased a ticket, he was arrested and convicted of violating state law. The case went to the Supreme Court, which, in *Plessy* v. *Ferguson* (1896), decided that racial separation was constitutional so long as both races were treated equally, this became known as the doctrine of separate but equal. Justice John Marshall Harlan vigorously dissented from that opinion, arguing that "the thin disguise of 'equal' accommodations . . . will not mislead anyone, nor atone for the wrong this day done."

Born in Kentucky, Justice Harlan had fought in the Union Army during the Civil War. President Rutherford B. Hayes, who had served as a Union general nominated him to the Supreme Court in 1877. A strong advocate of civil rights and civil liberties, Justice Harlan consistently argued in favor of a

color-blind Constitution that would equally protect all citizens, black and white, and argued that Congress had the authority under the Fourteenth Amendment to protect the rights of African Americans.

Although Justice Harlan was far out of step with his times, his arguments won favor with later generations. After the Supreme Court allowed segregation in general to continue for another half century, it voted unanimously in the case of *Brown* v. *Board of Education of Topeka, Kansas* (1954) to strike down segregation in public schools. Regardless of whether equal facilities were provided, the court now decided, segregation was inherently unequal because it created feelings of inferiority in those who were being segregated. Although he had died forty years earlier, Justice Harlan's reasoning had finally prevailed.

tify its probing. The Supreme Court further ruled that the Bill of Rights applied fully to all witnesses before Congress.

The civil rights movement for racial equality also pressed the various branches of the federal government to readjust their thinking. Since its 1896 ruling in *Plessy* v. *Ferguson*, the Supreme Court had tolerated racial segregation as long as all races were treated equally. In the 1954 case of *Brown* v. *Board of Education*, the Supreme Court reversed itself and found that segregated schools violated the constitutional ideal of equal treatment. Concluding that "separate but equal" facilities had been, in reality, grievously unequal, the Court ordered school integration "with all deliberate speed."

Some southern states resisted this order, and when the governor of Arkansas refused to protect African American students trying to attend a previously all-white high school, President Dwight D. Eisenhower sent in the National Guard to ensure the students' safety. When the state of Arkansas asserted that it had not been a party to the *Brown* v. *Board of Education* case and therefore was not bound by the Court's decision, the Supreme Court responded unanimously. In the 1958 case of *Cooper* v. *Aaron* the Court ruled that it would tolerate no resistance to its judicial authority.

While the courts struck down segregation in schools, Congress enacted legislation to require racial integration in all forms of public transportation and accommodation. The legislation passed the House of Representatives but encountered a filibuster in the Senate. Opponents of the legislation conducted the longest filibuster in the Senate's history, from March until June 1964, until a coalition of Democrats and Republicans gained enough votes to invoke cloture and shut off the

Alabama governor George Wallace stood in the doorway to block the admission of the first African American students at the University of Alabama in 1962, but moved after Assistant Attorney General Nicholas Katzenbach (at the right) asked him to step aside. Desegregation of public education in America moved slowly despite the Supreme Court's ruling for it.

debate. The Civil Rights Act of 1964 then won speedy passage.

The Supreme Court's reversal of its stand on segregation marked the beginning of a dramatic shift in the Court's outlook. Chief Justice Earl Warren's dramatic rulings struck down traditionally sanctioned behavior as unconstitutional. Warren believed that the Supreme Court itself had contributed to national problems by not taking bolder action in the past. He pointed out that for most of the twentieth century, the population of the United States had been shifting from rural to urban areas, but state legislatures had not been redistricted to reflect these changes, and the courts had not objected. "Because of its timidity, it made change hopeless," Warren wrote in his memoirs about the Supreme Court before his tenure. "It refused to enter, or to permit lower federal courts to consider, any litigation [or lawsuits] seeking to remedy unequal apportionment." The justices had not intervened because they saw reapportionment as a political question best handled by the politicians. But the Warren Court, in the 1962 case of Baker v. Carr insisted that all legislatures must be reapportioned to guarantee one person, one vote.

Justice William J. Brennan Jr., who served on the Supreme Court from 1956 to 1990, promoted the idea of a "living Constitution," in which legislators and federal judges adapted the Constitution "to cope with current problems and current needs." For example, Justice Brennan believed that even though the death penalty had existed when the Constitution was adopted, it had become "cruel and unusual punishment" by modern values and could therefore be declared unconstitutional. Justice Brennan's arguments had a profound impact on the way the Court dealt with such issues as voting rights, free speech, and the separation of church and state. A liberal in outlook, Brennan believed that the Court should promote broader notions of opportunity, liberty, equality, and human dignity.

Conservatives countered this notion of a "living Constitution" with an insistence that the courts should limit their rulings to the original intent of the framers of the Constitution. Justice Antonin Scalia, who joined the Supreme Court in 1986, called himself an "originalist." At a conference in 2005 he declared that "the Constitution is not a living organism, for Pete's sake; it's a legal document and like all legal documents, it says some things and it doesn't say others." He explained that he did not mean that the Constitution has to be interpreted strictly, but it needs to be interpreted reasonably. "I do believe you give the text the meaning it had when it was adopted." Justice Scalia dissented in the case

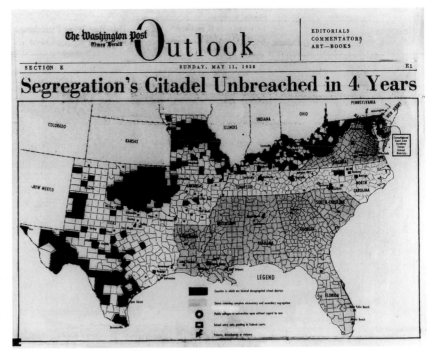

The Washington Post *ran this map of the southern states in 1958, showing the patterns of school desegregation throughout the southern states. Integration occurred more quickly outside the Deep South, where the largest numbers of African Americans lived.*

"*The powers of the legislature are defined and limited; and that those limits may not be mistaken, or forgotten, the constitution is written. . . . The distinction between a government with limited and unlimited powers, is abolished, if those limits do not confine the persons on whom they are imposed, and if acts prohibited and acts allowed, are of equal obligation.*"

— Chief Justice John Marshall,
Marbury v. *Madison* (1803)

"It is obvious, that there can be no security to the people in any constitution of government, if they are not to judge of it by the fair meaning of the words of the text."

— Justice Joseph Story,
Commentaries on the Constitution of the United States,
(1833)

of *Roper* v. *Simmons* (2005), which banned the execution of convicted criminals less than eighteen years old. He reasoned that because minors could be executed in 1787, it was still constitutional. He used the same reason for disagreeing with *Roe* v. *Wade* (1972), which permitted abortions, arguing that abortion was largely illegal when the Fourteenth Amendment was first adopted.

Those who argue for "original intent," say that the courts should leave social change to elected officials who can pass laws or introduce constitutional amendments to bring about such changes. President George W. Bush pledged to appoint judges who would not try to "legislate from the bench," that is, who would apply the law as written and leave policy decisions to the politicians. By this, Bush meant that he intended to appoint neutral, apolitical, but ideologically conservative judges. Yet, those who spoke for a "living Constitution" pointed out that conservative justices have been just as likely to overturn legislation as liberals, although for different reasons.

The debate between "original intent" and a "living Constitution" has taken place essentially between those who view the Constitution as a limit on the powers of government and those who believe that the Constitution is flexible enough to cover modern contingencies without frequent amendment. Senator Barry Goldwater insisted in his 1960 book *The Conscience of a Conservative* that "the Constitution is what its authors intended it to be and said it was—not what the Supreme Court says it is." Justice Brennan responded that the Constitution should not be judged in terms of "a world dead and gone," but that judges should apply the Constitution's basic principles to modern problems.

Justice Thurgood Marshall, the first African American to serve on the Supreme Court, from 1967 to 1991, commented that he did not accept the notion that the Philadelphia convention had forever "fixed" the Constitution. Instead he believed that the compromise with slavery had made a government that was "defective from the start" and it took a civil war, a civil rights movement, and several constitutional amendments to develop a federal system that respected the individual rights and freedoms of all its citizens. Yet, Marshall appreciated the progress that the United States had made over the past two centuries, and at the time of the Constitutional bicentennial in 1987 he said that he would "celebrate the bicentennial of the Constitution as a living document, including the Bill of Rights, and other amendments protecting individual freedoms and human rights."

This debate has taken place against the backdrop of major clashes between the branches of the federal government. The Vietnam War and the Watergate scandal helped further refine interpretations of the Constitution. In 1971, the Supreme Court upheld the right of the *New York Times* and other newspapers to publish classified government documents on how the United States had gone to war in Vietnam, despite the government's protests that the "Pentagon Papers" jeopardized national security.

After five men were arrested while breaking into the Democratic National Committee offices in the Watergate building to plant eavesdropping devices in 1972, evidence mounted that implicated members of President Richard Nixon's administration. The Senate appointed a special committee to investigate these allegations, and during its hearings the committee learned that President Nixon had been secretly tape-recording his conversations in the White House. The committee subpoenaed the tapes, but Nixon resisted, citing executive privilege. The case went to the Supreme Court, where eight of the nine justices, including those he had appointed, ruled that executive privilege did not cover evidence in a criminal case. (The decision was still unanimous as Justice William H. Rehnquist recused himself as a former official in the Nixon Justice Department.) The forced release of the tapes provided evidence that President Nixon had participated in a cover-up of the crime, forcing his resignation. The outcome of the Watergate scandal demonstrated that no one, not even the President of the United States, is above the law.

Following Watergate, Congress reasserted much of the authority it had lost to the Presidency over past decades. Sparring between the President and Congress grew more intense, particularly over the appointment of judges. In 1987, the Senate rejected President Ronald Reagan's nomination of Robert Bork to the Supreme Court. Although the former law professor and judge had extensive experience, liberal Democrats, who held the majority in the Senate, complained that his

THE FIGHT OVER THE WATERGATE TAPES

A mighty struggle took place between all three branches of the government over the release of President Richard M. Nixon's secret tape-recordings. This struggle tested the separation of powers, with the Congress, a special prosecutor, and the President disagreeing over the release of the tapes and the Supreme Court deciding among them.

In 1973, a special committee of the Senate was investigating irregularities in the previous year's Presidential campaign. Men associated with the Committee to Reelect the President had been arrested while breaking into Democratic National Committee headquarters at the Watergate building in Washington, D.C., in order to plant listening devices. The Senate Watergate Committee called various White House officials to testify, and one of them admitted that the President had secretly tape-recorded his own conversations in the Oval Office. The Committee immediately sought access to the tapes,

but President Nixon refused to provide them on the grounds that the information they contained was covered by "executive privilege." The President argued that in order for the officers of the executive branch to make internal decisions and weigh policy choices they are entitled to keep internal discussions private and should not have to provide them to Congress or the courts. Although President Nixon later agreed to provide edited transcripts of selective tapes, he effectively stonewalled the committee's request.

At the same time, Archibald Cox, a special prosecutor looking into the Watergate break-in sought access to the tapes. President Nixon not only refused to comply but also fired Cox. Public opinion was so outraged over his action that Nixon eventually bowed to public

pressure and appointed another special prosecutor, Leon Jaworski. Jaworski also demanded the tapes, taking his case to the U.S. Supreme Court. In *Nixon* v. *United States* (1974), the Court ruled 8-to-0 that executive privilege did not cover evidence needed for criminal prosecution. (Justice William Rehnquist did not participate because he had been previously involved in the case while he served in the Justice Department.) The Court ordered the President to turn the requested tape recordings over to the special prosecutor, which he did. One of these recordings, known as the "smoking gun," gave evidence that the President had been personally involved in a cover-up of the Watergate burglary. With that revelation, Congress moved to impeach the President, who chose to resign from office instead.

"Our Constitution was
not written in the sands to be
washed away by each wave
of new judges blown in by
each successive political wind."

—Justice Hugo L. Black,
dissenting opinion,
Turner v. *United States* (1970)

conservative ideology was beyond the mainstream. Bork's defeat was followed by accusations on both sides that political "litmus tests" were being applied to nominees, whose nominations and confirmations often depended on how they stood on the most controversial issues of the day, rather than their legal qualifications.

Changes in the political parties created further tensions. For most of the twentieth century, both the Democratic and Republican Parties had been internally divided between liberals, moderates, and conservatives. As a result, there were few straight party-line votes in Congress, as bipartisan coalitions of conservatives voted against similarly bipartisan coalitions of liberals. By the 1990s, the two parties had grown far more internally cohesive. In Congress, the party members stuck together until almost every vote became a party-line vote, with the balance occasionally tipped one way or the other by a small number of moderates who forged compromises.

In 1994, Republicans won control of both houses of Congress and positioned themselves against the Democratic President Bill Clinton. A dispute between the President and Congress over federal funding in 1995 led to a brief shut-down of government agencies. The Senate also opposed many of Clinton's more liberal judicial nominees and appointments to key governmental positions. When a special prosecutor brought charges that Clinton had lied to a grand jury about his inappropriate relationship with a White House intern almost all the Republicans in the House of Representatives voted to impeach the President, while almost all the Democrats voted against impeachment. The Senate held a trial, where the vote fell far short of the two-thirds needed to convict the President and remove him from office.

During the Presidency of George W. Bush, a conservative Republican, liberal Democrats filibustered to block the confirmation of a number of his judicial nominees. Republicans in the Senate protested that the Constitution required only a majority vote for nominations and that all nominees deserved an "up or down" vote, that is, a vote in favor or against without obstruction. The intensity of the struggle testified to how seriously the executive and legislative branches take lifetime appointments to the independent judiciary, which has the final word in interpreting our Constitution.

Robert Bork (seated alone, at left) faced the Senate Judiciary Committee when President Ronald Reagan nominated him for the Supreme Court in 1987. Exercising its power to offer advice and consent, the Senate rejected Bork's nomination.

THE U.S. CONSTITUTION

Preamble

The Constitution's opening words, "We the People," make clear that the new government derived its powers from the whole people rather than from the individual states.

WHAT IT SAYS

We the People of the United States, in Order to form a more perfect Union, establish Justice, insure domestic Tranquility, provide for the common defence, promote the general Welfare, and secure the Blessings of Liberty to ourselves and our Posterity, do ordain and establish this Constitution for the United States of America.

BY COMPARISON: THE PREAMBLE TO THE DECLARATION OF INDEPENDENCE

On July 4, 1776, the Continental Congress declared America's independence from Great Britain and converted the thirteen colonies into the United States of America. The Declaration of Independence's justification for that break later influenced the language of the preamble to the Constitution.

We hold these truths to be self-evident, that all men are created equal, that they are endowed by their Creator with certain unalienable Rights, that among these are Life, Liberty, and the pursuit of Happiness—

That to secure these rights, Governments are instituted among Men, deriving their just powers from the consent of the governed,—

That whenever any Form of Government becomes destructive of these ends, it is the Right of the People to alter or to abolish it, and to institute new Government, laying its foundation on such principles and organizing its powers in such form, as to them shall seem most likely to effect their Safety and Happiness.

Dedicated to the American people on July 4, 1950, by the artist Arthur Szyk, this painting of the Declaration of Independence features the flags and seals of the original thirteen states, portraits of George Washington and Paul Revere, the American eagle, and scenes of American soldiers.

of the United States, in Order to form a more perfect Union, establish Justice,
...efence, promote the general Welfare, and secure the Blessings of Liberty to ourselves
...tion for the United States of America.

WHAT IT MEANS

The preamble expresses the purpose of the U.S. Constitution. The federal government gains its power from the people rather than from the states. The government exists to maintain peace at home, provide national defense, promote the well-being of the people, and protect their liberties. Importantly, the Supreme Court has held, in *Jacobson* v. *Massachusetts* (1905), that the preamble itself is not a source of federal power or individual rights. Rather, all rights and powers are set out in the articles and amendments that follow.

FIRST DRAFT OF THE PREAMBLE TO THE CONSTITUTION

At the Constitutional Convention on August 6, 1787, the Committee of Detail submitted this first draft of the preamble, which began with a list of the states, as did the Articles of Confederation.

We, the people of the states of New Hampshire, Massachusetts, Rhode-Island and Providence Plantations, Connecticut, New York, New-Jersey, Pennsylvania, Delaware, Maryland, Virginia, North-Carolina, South-Carolina and Georgia, do ordain, declare, and establish, the following Constitution for the Government of Ourselves and our Posterity.

However, ratification of the Constitution did not require the unanimous consent of all thirteen states, and future states were expected to join the Union, so the convention dropped the names of the first states. This revision strengthened the idea that "the people" rather than "the states" created the government. Gouverneur Morris, a delegate from Pennsylvania, rewrote the preamble, crafting the more eloquent explanation that the convention finally adopted.

"*Earlier today, we heard the beginning of the Preamble to the Constitution of the United States, 'We, the people.' It's a very eloquent beginning. But when that document was completed, on the seventeenth of September in 1787, I was not included in that 'We, the people.' I felt somehow for many years that George Washington and Alexander Hamilton just left me out by mistake. But through the process of amendment, interpretation, and court decision, I have finally been included in 'We, the people.'*"

— Representative Barbara Jordan, an African American, speaking in the House Judiciary Committee on July 25, 1974

Article I
Section 1

> "I believe all of us—
> regardless of party—
> can respect one another, even
> as we fiercely disagree on
> particular issues."
>
> —Representative
> J. Dennis Hastert,
> on becoming Speaker
> of the House in 1999

John Plumbe Jr. took the first known photograph of the U.S. Capitol in 1846. The admission of new states into the Union would soon require a major expansion of the building to house the many new senators and representatives.

WHAT IT SAYS

All legislative Powers herein granted shall be vested in a Congress of the United States, which shall consist of a Senate and House of Representatives.

WHAT IT MEANS

The framers of the Constitution separated the powers of government into three branches, granting legislative power (the power to pass laws) to Congress, executive power (the power to administer the laws) to the President, and judicial power (the power to interpret laws and decide legal disputes) to the courts. The unique and limited powers of the Congress are specified in Article I.

This separation of powers ensures that no one person or group could create, administer, and interpret the laws at the same time, and that each branch would serve as a check on the power of the other two branches. In some instances, the spheres of the three branches overlap, such as when Senate approval is required to confirm the President's nominees to the Supreme Court, or when the President can veto acts of Congress or pardon convicted criminals.

Section 1 also specifies that the Congress of the United States shall be bicameral, that is, it will be divided into two houses, the Senate and the House of Representatives. The previous government under the Articles of Confederation had only a single lawmaking body, as did some of the states. The creation of two legislative bodies reflected a compromise between the power of the states and the power of the people. The number of seats in the House of Representatives is based on population.

HOW A BICAMERAL LEGISLATURE WORKS

For any bill to become ready to send to the President for approval, both the Senate and the House of Representatives must pass it in exactly the same form. Members of the House or Senate will introduce the bill, which will then be referred to the committee that holds jurisdiction over its subject matter. A bill proposing to improve the quality of drinking water, for instance, would be referred to the Environmental Committee. A subcommittee investigates the matter, holds hearings, takes testimony, collects evidence, and perhaps amends the proposal before voting on it and submitting it to the full committee. The committee might further amend the bill before reporting it to the full House. The House Rules Committee would determine whether it could be amended any further on the House floor. Once the House passes the bill it will be submitted to the Senate (or, if it began in the Senate, it will be submitted to the House).

Then, the process begins all over again, with introduction by a senator or representative, submission to the appropriate committee, and perhaps another round of hearings. Those groups who oppose provisions of the original bill will seek to have it improved through additional amendments. The Senate Rules Committee, however, plays no role in the process and the bill will be more open to amendment than in the House. By the time the bill is passed, it may differ significantly from the original version.

In order to resolve the differences between the versions of the bill passed by the House and the Senate, the legislative leaders will appoint a conference committee of senators and representatives. The conferees will negotiate and vote on a single version of the bill. They then send the conference report, as this final version is called, back to the House and Senate for an "up or down vote" in which members may vote to approve or disapprove but not to make any more changes. Once both houses approve the final version, it goes to the White House, where the President may approve or veto the bill. It takes a two-thirds vote of both houses to override a Presidential veto. This complex system makes it difficult to pass legislation hastily. Except in time of national emergency, the process usually permits much input from those most affected by the proposed legislation and stimulates debate that helps build public awareness and support for its objectives.

The Whig Party formed in opposition to "King" Andrew Jackson, as this editorial cartoon portrayed him. Whig legislators objected to Jackson's assertion of Presidential power, particularly in his opposition to rechartering the Bank of the United States.

The larger and more urban states have more representatives than the more rural, sparsely populated states. Regardless of their size, the states are equal in the Senate, with two senators from each state. In order to create a law, both the House of Representatives and the Senate must pass the proposed legislation in exactly the same form, and it then must be approved, or at least not vetoed, by the President.

Article I
Section 2

Clauses 1–2

WHAT IT SAYS

[1] The House of Representatives shall be composed of Members chosen every second Year by the People of the several States, and the Electors in each State shall have the Qualifications requisite for Electors of the most numerous Branch of the State Legislature.

[2] No Person shall be a Representative who shall not have attained to the Age of twenty five Years, and been seven Years a Citizen of the United States, and who shall not, when elected, be an Inhabitant of the State in which he shall be chosen.

This painting by Samuel F. B. Morse depicts a night session of the House of Representatives in 1822. At the time, the House was the only part of the federal government directly elected by the people.

WHAT IT MEANS

The House of Representatives is composed of members chosen every two years by the voters of each state. There are only three qualifications: representatives must be at least twenty-five years old, must have been citizens of the United States for at least seven years, and must live in the state from which they are chosen. The states may not add any further controls on members of Congress, such as term limits or recall—special elections in which voters can remove public officials midterm—because these provisions are not specified by the Constitution. The Constitution allows the states to determine who is eligible to vote (the Constitution calls voters "electors"). Whatever requirements are necessary to cast a vote for members of the larger house of the state legislatures will be sufficient to vote for the U.S. House of Representatives.

In recent years, the Supreme Court has used the notion "by the people of the several states" in Article I along with the Fourteenth Amendment's "equal protection" clause to require that each congressional district contain roughly the same number of people. This ensures that each person has an equal vote in a congressional election.

The U.S. House of Representatives uses this mace as the symbol of its authority. The silver mace consists of thirteen rods (one for each of the original states) bound together by bands and topped by a globe and eagle.

APPOINTMENTS TO THE PEOPLE'S HOUSE

On September 11, 2001, after hijacked passenger planes crashed into the World Trade Center in New York City and the Pentagon in Washington, D.C., the U.S. Capitol and the Senate and House office buildings were evacuated for fear that the Capitol might be the next target. Both the Senate and House returned to session the next day, but the incident raised questions about the continuity of operations of the legislative branch. If a large number of senators died at the same time, the Constitution and most state laws provided for the governors of their states to appoint replacements immediately. There is no constitutional provision for the appointment of House members. Instead their states usually hold special elections to fill the empty seats. Some observers asked whether the Congress could function properly in the months that it would take for such elections to be held. Two Washington-based think tanks, the Brookings Institution and the American Enterprise Institute, created a Continuity of Government Commission that studied the problem and called for a constitutional amendment to allow for the temporary replacement of House members in the case of catastrophic attack. However, the amendment confronted a proud tradition that no representative had ever entered the "people's house" except by popular election. It also raised the question of whether governors could appoint anyone they pleased or if they were obligated to appoint someone from the same political party as the representative being replaced, as large scale replacements could change the political control of the House. Such complications stalled the progress of the amendment, despite the enormity of the problem it sought to address.

Article I
Section 2

Clauses 3–5

Congressional leaders visit the White House in 1949 to get a preview of President Harry Truman's message seeking approval of a new arms program. From left to right, Senate Foreign Relations Committee chairman Tom Connally, House Speaker Sam Rayburn, and House majority leader John McCormack all supported the President's proposal.

WHAT IT SAYS

[3] [Representatives and direct Taxes shall be apportioned among the several States which may be included within this Union, according to their respective Numbers, which shall be determined by adding to the whole Number of free Persons, including those bound to Service for a Term of Years, and excluding Indians not taxed, three fifths of all other Persons.]* The actual Enumeration shall be made within three Years after the first Meeting of the Congress of the United States, and within every subsequent Term of ten Years, in such Manner as they shall by Law direct. The Number of Representatives shall not exceed one for every thirty Thousand, but each State shall have at Least one Representative; and until such enumeration shall be made, the State of New Hampshire shall be entitled to chuse three, Massachusetts eight, Rhode-Island and Providence Plantations** one, Connecticut five, New-York six, New Jersey four, Pennsylvania eight, Delaware one, Maryland six, Virginia ten, North Carolina five, South Carolina five, and Georgia three.

[4] When vacancies happen in the Representation from any State, the Executive Authority thereof shall issue Writs of Election to fill such Vacancies.

[5] The House of Representatives shall chuse their Speaker and other Officers; and shall have the sole Power of Impeachment.

*Changed by the Fourteenth Amendment, Section 2.
**The colonial name Rhode-Island and Providence Plantations remains the official name of the state commonly called Rhode Island.

WHAT IT MEANS

The Constitution set the number of members of the first House of Representatives from each of the original thirteen states and declared that the amount of direct taxes would depend on the number of citizens in each state. At that time, when slavery was still legal, it specified that slaves did not count as full citizens. The "three-fifths compromise" at the Constitutional Convention counted slaves as three-fifths of a citizen for purposes of state representation and taxation. This provision was changed following the Civil War with the passage of the Thirteenth, Fourteenth,

A POWERFUL SPEAKER OF THE HOUSE: HENRY CLAY

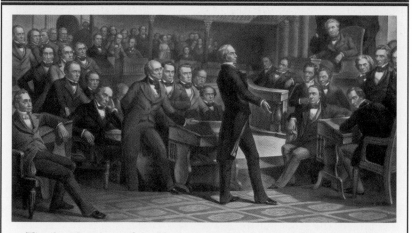

The first Speakers of the House limited their role to that of neutral presiding officer. It was not until the thirty-four-year-old Henry Clay of Kentucky took the office in 1811 that the Speaker became the political leader of the House. Elected Speaker on his first day in the House, the magnetic Clay was one of the congressional "war hawks" who drew the United States into the War of 1812. At the war's end, President James Madison sent Clay to Ghent in Belgium to negotiate a peace treaty with Great Britain. Clay also promoted an ambitious program of protective tariffs along with roads, harbors, and canals and other internal improvements, which he called the American System. Trying to end the heated debate over the spread of slavery into the western territories, Speaker Clay also promoted the Missouri Compromise of 1820. His efforts won him renown as the Great Compromiser. Clay dominated the House through his interpretation of its rules, his decrees as presiding officer, and his skills as an orator. Most notably, he expanded the number of standing committees, which improved the efficiency of the House and enabled it to handle a dramatic increase in the number of bills and resolution during his long tenure.

Clay went on to serve as Secretary of State and U.S. Senator from Kentucky. To the end he continued to forge legislative compromises, and he is pictured above delivering his most famous address to the Senate on February 5, 1850. Arguing in favor of the Compromise of 1850, he implored Senators "to repress the ardor of their passions" and determine what was best for the country with regard to allowing or prohibiting slavery in the new western territories.

"The hardest part of leadership is compromise. People often think when you compromise, you are compromising your morals or your principles. That's not what political compromise is. Political compromise is deferring your ideas so a majority can be reached. That's what Congress does."

—House Speaker Tip O'Neill, *All Politics Is Local, and Other Rules of the Game* (1994)

The efforts by Massachusetts Republicans to apportion legislative districts to favor their party in 1812 created an odd shape that an editorial cartoonist portrayed as a "Gerrymander." The name combines the name of the governor of Massachusetts at the time, Elbridge Gerry, with the slithery amphibian the salamander.

and Fifteenth Amendments that abolished slavery, guaranteed equal protection, and extended voting rights to African Americans. Since then, all citizens, regardless of race, are fully counted in each census.

Clause 3 also establishes that the census (an enumeration or headcount) will be conducted every ten years. Every adult in the country must answer a survey, which Congress then uses to determine how many representatives are to come from each state and how to distribute federal funds among the states. Every state must have at least one representative, but Congress sets the maximum number of members.

The Constitution specified the original number of representatives each state should have, but did not draw the district lines, a function it left to the states. As a result, the political party in power in each state legislature is able to define districts in such a way that benefits its own candidates. Extreme cases, which result in oddly shaped districts, are called gerrymandering, after a plan devised when Elbridge Gerry was governor of Massachusetts in 1812. An editorial cartoonist, looking at such a district, compared it to the mythical lizard-like creature the salamander, added the governor's name, and coined the term gerrymander.

If a member of the House dies or resigns in midterm, the governor of the representative's state can call for a special election, with a "writ of election," to fill the vacancy. Unlike the Senate, where a governor can appoint someone to serve until the next election, no one has ever been appointed to the House of Representatives.

The Constitution authorizes the House to elect its own Speaker. The Speaker of the House presides over its meetings or authorizes another member to preside in his place. By act of Congress, the Speaker is next in line to become President, if both the President and Vice President are unable to serve. The House may also choose other officers, such as its chaplain, clerk of the House, and sergeant at arms.

The House also holds the power of impeachment. Akin to an indictment, impeachment of a federal officer—whether a judge, a cabinet secretary, or the President—requires only a simple majority in the House. A two-thirds vote of the Senate is then required to convict and remove from office the impeached official. Members of the House act as prosecutors during the trial in the Senate chamber. If a President is impeached, the chief justice of the United States presides over the Senate trial, rather than the Vice President, who stands to benefit from the President's removal.

Frederick Augustus Muhlenberg
(Federalist, Pennsylvania)   1789–1791, 1793–1795

Jonathan Trumbull
(Federalist, Connecticut)   1791–1793

Jonathan Dayton
(Democratic-Republican, New Jersey)   1795–1799

Theodore Sedgwick
(Federalist, Massachusetts)   1799–1801

Nathaniel Macon
(Democratic-Republican, North Carolina)   1801–1807

Joseph B. Varnum
(Democratic-Republican, Massachusetts)   1807–1811

Henry Clay
(Democratic-Republican, Kentucky)
          1811–1814, 1815–1820, 1823–1825

Langdon Chives
(Democratic-Republican, South Carolina)   1814–1815

John W. Taylor
(Democratic-Republican, New York)   1820–1821, 1825–1827

Philip B. Barbour
(Democratic-Republican, Virginia)   1821–1823

Andrew Stevenson
(Democrat, Virginia)   1827–1834

John Bell
(Whig, Tennessee)   1834–1835

James K. Polk
(Democrat, Tennessee)   1835–1839

Robert M. T. Hunter
(Whig, Virginia)   1839–1841

John White
(Whig, Kentucky)   1841–1843

John W. Jones
(Democrat, Virginia)   1843–1845

John Wesley Davis
(Democrat, Indiana)   1845–1847

Robert C. Winthrop
(Whig, Massachusetts)   1847–1849

Howell G. Cobb
(Democrat, Georgia)   1849–1851

Linn Boyd
(Democrat, Kentucky)   1851–1855

Nathaniel P. Banks
(Republican, Massachusetts)   1856–1857

James L. Orr
(Democrat, South Carolina)   1857–1859

William Pennington
(Republican, New Jersey)   1860–1861

Galusha A. Grow
(Republican, Pennsylvania)   1861–1863

Schuyler Colfax
(Republican, Indiana)   1863–1869

Theodore M. Pomeroy
(Republican, New York)   1869

James G. Blaine
(Republican, Maine)   1869–1875

Michael C. Kerr
(Democrat, Indiana)   1875–1876

Samuel J. Randall
(Democrat, Pennsylvania)   1876–1881

J. Warren Keifer
(Republican, Ohio)   1881–1883

John G. Carlisle
(Democrat, Kentucky)   1883–1889

Thomas B. Reed
(Republican, Maine)   1889–1891, 1895–1899

Charles F. Crisp
(Democrat, Georgia)   1891–1895

David B. Henderson
(Republican, Iowa)   1899–1903

Joseph G. Cannon
(Republican, Illinois)   1903–1911

James Beauchamp "Champ" Clark
(Democrat, Missouri)   1911–1919

Frederick H. Gillett
(Republican, Massachusetts)   1919–1925

Nicholas Longworth
(Republican, Ohio)   1925–1931

John Nance Garner
(Democrat, Texas)   1931–1933

Henry T. Rainey
(Democrat, Illinois)   1933–1934

Joseph W. Byrnes
(Democrat, Tennessee)   1935–1936

William Bankhead
(Democrat, Alabama)   1936–1940

Sam Rayburn
(Democrat, Texas)   1940–1947, 1949–1952, 1955–1961

Joseph W. Martin
(Republican, Massachusetts)   1947–1948, 1953–1954

John W. McCormack
(Democrat, Massachusetts)   1962–1971

Carl Albert
(Democrat, Oklahoma)   1971–1977

Thomas P. "Tip" O'Neill Jr.
(Democrat, Massachusetts)   1977–1987

Jim Wright
(Democrat, Texas)   1987–1989

Thomas S. Foley
(Democrat, Washington)   1989–1995

Newt Gingrich
(Republican, Georgia)   1995–1999

J. Dennis Hastert
(Republican, Illinois)   1999–present

WHAT IT SAYS

[1] The Senate of the United States shall be composed of two Senators from each state, [chosen by the Legislature] thereof,* for six Years; and each Senator shall have one Vote.

[2] Immediately after they shall be assembled in Consequence of the first Election, they shall be divided as equally as may be into three Classes. The Seats of the Senators of the first Class shall be vacated at the Expiration of the second Year, of the second Class at the Expiration of the fourth Year, and of the third Class at the Expiration of the sixth Year; so that one-third may be chosen every second Year; [and if Vacancies happen by Resignation, or otherwise, during the Recess of the Legislature of any State, the Executive thereof may make temporary Appointments until the next Meeting of the Legislature, which shall then fill such Vacancies].**

[3] No Person shall be a Senator who shall not have attained to the Age of thirty Years, and been nine Years a Citizen of the United States, and who shall not, when elected, be an Inhabitant of that State for which he shall be chosen.

JOHN EATON, AN UNDERAGE SENATOR

In seeking to establish an older, more experienced, and more deliberative legislative body, the framers of the Constitution required that senators be at least thirty years of age—five years older than the minimum age for representatives. John Eaton, however, was only twenty-eight when he took his seat as senator from Tennessee in 1818. At the time, no one questioned his qualifications. He had practiced law in Tennessee and served in the state legislature before he was appointed to fill a vacancy in the Senate. This violation of the Constitution did not hinder his political career. He was elected to a full term in 1821 and later served as secretary of war in Andrew Jackson's cabinet.

Although Eaton was the youngest, two other U.S. senators in the nineteenth century were also underage. In 1806, Henry Clay became a senator from Kentucky at age twenty-nine, and in 1816 Armistead Mason became a senator from Virginia at age twenty-eight, because no one questioned them publicly. By the twentieth century, the Senate was paying more careful attention to the age of its incoming members. In 1934 West Virginia elected Rush Holt to the Senate, although he was only twenty-nine. Holt had to wait six months after his election, until he turned thirty, before he could take the oath of office as a senator.

* Changed by the Seventeenth Amendment.
** Changed by the Seventeenth Amendment.

WHAT IT MEANS

The Senate, which now has one hundred members, has two senators from each state. Originally elected by state legislatures, senators have been directly elected by the people since ratification of the Seventeenth Amendment in 1913. Senators must be more than thirty years old, must have been an American citizen for at least nine years, and must live in the state they represent. Senators can serve for an unlimited number of six-year terms.

The Senate is divided into three "classes," and elections are held on a staggered basis so that one class, or one-third of the senators, stands for election every two years. When a state entered the Union, its first senators flipped a coin to determine which class they would enter, with the result that one received a longer term than the other. If senators leave office before the end of their terms, the state legislature may authorize the governor of their state to appoint someone to fill the vacant seat until the next election.

"The only other qualification is, that the senator shall, when elected, be an inhabitant of the state, for which he is chosen. This scarcely requires any comment; for it is manifestly proper, that a state should be represented by one, who, besides an intimate knowledge of all its wants and wishes, and local pursuits, should have a personal and immediate interest in all measures touching its sovereignty, its rights, or its influence."

— Supreme Court Justice Joseph Story, *Commentaries on the Constitution of the United States* (1833)

Welcomed by Wisconsin Senator Alexander Wiley (left), Alaska's first senators, Ernest Gruening (center) and E. L. Bartlett (right), displayed a forty-nine-star flag when Alaska became a state in 1959. New states enter the Union on an equal basis with the other states.

Article I
Section 3

Clauses 4–7

"Has the president committed offenses and planned and directed and acquiesced in a course of conduct which the Constitution will not tolerate? That is the question."

—Representative Barbara Jordan, during the House Judiciary Committee's deliberation over the impeachment of President Richard Nixon, 1974

WHAT IT SAYS

[4] The Vice President of the United States shall be President of the Senate, but shall have no Vote, unless they be equally divided.

[5] The Senate shall choose their other Officers, and also a President pro tempore, in the absence of the Vice President, or when he shall exercise the Office of President of the United States.

[6] The Senate shall have the sole Power to try all Impeachments. When sitting for that Purpose, they shall be on Oath or Affirmation. When the President of the United States is tried, the Chief Justice shall preside: And no Person shall be convicted without the Concurrence of two-thirds of the Members present.

[7] Judgment in Cases of Impeachment shall not extend further than to removal from Office, and disqualification to hold and enjoy any Office of honor, Trust or Profit under the United States: but the Party convicted shall nevertheless be liable and subject to Indictment, Trial, Judgment and Punishment, according to Law.

Chief Justice William Rehnquist presides over the impeachment trial of President Bill Clinton. Although the House could impeach the President on a near party-line vote, the Senate needed a bipartisan two-thirds majority to convict. Two votes of 55 not guilty to 45 guilty, and 50-50, acquitted the President.

WHAT IT MEANS

The Vice President of the United States is also the president of the Senate. The Vice President may preside over the Senate but can vote only to break a tie. To preside in the absence of the Vice President, the Senate elects a president pro tempore (literally, for the time being). Like the Speaker of the House, the president pro tempore is in the line of Presidential succession. By modern custom the president pro tempore is the senior member of the Senate's majority party. The Senate may also create and fill its other offices, such as the chaplain, secretary of the Senate, and sergeant at arms.

If the House of Representatives votes to impeach a federal official, the Senate holds a trial to convict or acquit that officer. The Vice President presides, except when a President has been impeached. The chief justice of the United States presides over Presidential trials. A vote of two-thirds of the senators present (sixty-seven if all one hundred are present) is necessary to remove someone from office. This means that while a simple majority in the House may impeach an official, a larger consensus in the Senate is needed for conviction. In the cases of impeached Presidents Andrew Johnson and Bill Clinton, fewer than two-thirds of the senators voted to convict them, and they were acquitted. Those convicted by the Senate are removed from office, but Congress can inflict no further punishment on them, other than barring them from holding future office. Officials who have been removed may still be prosecuted criminally or sued, just like any other citizen.

The House of Representatives impeached Tennessee senator William Blount on charges of treason. Blount resigned and the Senate voted to expel him formally rather than hold an impeachment trial.

IMPEACHMENT TRIALS HELD IN THE SENATE

1. William Blount, senator from Tennessee, for disloyalty to the United States; in 1799 the Senate expelled Blount and dismissed the impeachment charges against him.

2. John Pickering, federal judge; in 1804 the Senate found him guilty of charges of drunkenness and unlawful rulings and removed him from office.

3. Samuel Chase, Supreme Court justice; in 1805 the Senate found him not guilty of his alleged mishandling of a trial.

4. James H. Peck, federal judge; in 1831 the Senate found him not guilty of his alleged misuse of the contempt power against a lawyer.

5. West H. Humphreys, federal judge; in 1862 the Senate found him guilty of supporting the Confederate rebellion.

6. Andrew Johnson, President; in 1868 the Senate found him not guilty of violating federal laws.

7. Mark H. Delahay, federal judge; resigned in 1873 over charges of drunkenness; the Senate took no action against him.

8. William Belknap, secretary of war; in 1876 the Senate found him not guilty of bribery and corruption.

9. Charles Swayne, federal judge; in 1905 the Senate found him not guilty of improperly convicting lawyers for contempt.

10. Robert Archbald, federal judge; in 1913 the Senate found him guilty of soliciting bribes and removed him from office.

11. George W. English, federal judge; in 1926 he resigned and the Senate dismissed the charges of abusive treatment of lawyers and litigants against him.

12. Harold Louderback, federal judge; in 1933 the Senate found him not guilty of partiality and favoritism.

13. Halsted Ritter, federal judge; in 1936, the Senate found him guilty of tax evasion and removed him from office.

14. Harry E. Claiborne, federal judge; in 1986 the Senate found him guilty of falsifying his tax returns and removed him from office.

15. Alcee Hastings, federal judge; in 1989 the Senate found him guilty of bribery and perjury and removed him from office. (In 1992, Hastings was elected to the U.S. House of Representatives from Florida.)

16. Walter Nixon, federal judge; in 1989 the Senate found him guilty of perjury and removed him from office.

17. William J. Clinton, President; in 1999 the Senate found him not guilty of charges of perjury.

Article I
Section 4

Clauses 1–2

"No right is more precious in a free country than that of having a voice in the election of those who make the laws under which, as good citizens, we must live."

— Justice Hugo L. Black,
Westberry v. Saunders (1964)

Abraham Lincoln and Stephen Douglas participated in a celebrated series of public debates during their senatorial campaign in Illinois in 1858. The state legislature eventually reelected Douglas.

WHAT IT SAYS

[1]   The Times, Places and Manner of holding Elections for Senators and Representatives, shall be prescribed in each State by the Legislature thereof; but the Congress may at any time by Law make or alter such Regulations, except as to the Places of choosing Senators.

[2]   The Congress shall assemble at least once in every Year, and such Meeting shall [be on the first Monday in December,]* unless they shall by Law appoint a different Day.

SETTING A NATIONAL ELECTION DAY

After the ratification of the Constitution, the states held elections for the President and members of Congress. The Constitution left it to the states to set a date for these elections, which ranged between November 24, 1788, and June 22, 1789. The states continued to vote on different days until 1848, when Congress fixed a standard day for congressional elections. Some members of Congress had worried that this would be an encroachment on states' rights, but the majority felt that a uniform date would reduce the chance of corruption, keeping some voters from crossing state lines to cast ballots in different states. Congress set the first Tuesday after the first Monday in November as the Election Day for federal elections. The exception was the state of Maine, which because of its severe weather conditions continued to hold its elections in September. The vote in Maine was seen to foretell the national election results, as expressed in the oft-repeated slogan, "As Maine goes, so goes the nation." Finally, in 1958, Maine shifted its elections to November to vote with the rest of the nation.

*Changed by the Twentieth Amendment

The Constitution gives the state legislatures the task of determining how congressional elections are held. For example, the state legislatures determine when elections are scheduled, how voters can register, and where they can cast their ballots. But, Congress has the right to change these state rules to set a uniform date for federal elections and to provide national protection for the right to vote. The first federal election law prohibited false registrations, bribery of election officials, and reporting false election returns. Congress passed this law after the Civil War as a means of enforcing the prohibitions against racial discrimination in voting contained in the Fifteenth Amendment. With the passage of the Civil Rights Acts of 1957 and 1964 and the Voting Rights Act of 1965, Congress enacted greater protections for the right to vote in federal, state, and local elections.

As a general rule, Congress sets its own schedule for how frequently it meets. The Constitution provides only that it must meet once a year. Originally, Congress convened on the first Monday in December, a year and a month after the congressional elections. In 1933 the Twentieth Amendment moved this date forward to January 3, unless the members specify a different schedule.

In the years before the Civil War, the U.S. House of Representatives met under this statue of Clio, the classical image of history. She is recording events while riding in a chariot whose wheel is a clock symbolizing the passage of time.

In 1969, Shirley Chisholm of New York became the first African American woman to serve in Congress. House Speaker John McCormack administered the oath of office.

Article I
Section 5

Clauses 1–4

"I have begun a sketch, which those who come after me will successively fill up, till a code of rules shall be formed for the use of the Senate, the effects of which may be accuracy in business, economy of time, order, uniformity, and impartiality."

— Thomas Jefferson, preface to *Manual of Parliamentary Practice* (1801), which he compiled while presiding over the Senate as Vice President

WHAT IT SAYS

[1] Each House shall be the Judge of the Elections, Returns and Qualifications of its own Members, and a Majority of each shall constitute a Quorum to do Business; but a smaller Number may adjourn from day to day, and may be authorized to compel the Attendance of absent Members, in such Manner, and under such Penalties as each House may provide.

[2] Each House may determine the Rules of its Proceedings, punish its Members for disorderly Behavior, and, with the Concurrence of two thirds, expel a Member.

[3] Each House shall keep a Journal of its Proceedings, and from time to time publish the same, excepting such Parts as may in their Judgment require Secrecy; and the Yeas and Nays of the Members of either House on any question shall, at the Desire of one fifth of those Present, be entered on the Journal.

[4] Neither House, during the Session of Congress, shall, without the Consent of the other, adjourn for more than three days, nor to any other Place than that in which the two Houses shall be sitting.

THE CONGRESSIONAL RECORD

Any day that the House and Senate are in session, official reporters of debate take down every word spoken, collect copies of all bills introduced, and record every vote taken. The next day this information is published in the *Congressional Record*. As the Constitution requires, each house publishes a journal of its proceedings, but these are minute books without the verbatim text of speeches. Since 1789, clerks of the House and Senate have prepared these journals.

In contrast, the *Congressional Record* evolved from the notes of stenographers hired by private newspapers, first in New York City, then in Philadelphia, and finally in Washington, D.C. During the early nineteenth century, such Washington-based papers as the *National Intelligencer* and the *Globe* published the congressional debates. These reporters' notes occasionally contained mistakes, which suspicious members of Congress suspected were politically motivated to embarrass them. In the 1840s, the reporters of debate were hired as congressional employees. At the same time, advances in stenography ensured more accurate transcripts. Not until 1873 did the Government Printing Office take over this responsibility and began to publish the *Congressional Record*. Today, in addition to past and current copies of the these volumes held by libraries, the *Congressional Record* can be accessed online at http://www.gpoaccess.gov/crecord/.

WHAT IT MEANS

Both the House of Representatives and the Senate are in charge of determining whether an election of one of its own members is legitimate. The losing candidate in an election may bring charges before the appropriate House or Senate committee, which will sift through the evidence and render a judgment. Similarly, the House and Senate can establish their own rules, punish members for disorderly behavior, and, if two-thirds of its members agree, expel a member.

Both the House and Senate need a quorum to do business—meaning that a majority of members must be present. A full majority need not always be present in the chamber but must be close enough to respond to quorum calls. Business in the chamber stops if a member calls attention to the absence of a quorum. Bells then ring through the Capitol and office buildings summoning enough members to establish a quorum. Each house may authorize its sergeant at arms to arrest absent members and compel their attendance to establish a quorum to do business.

Tempers ran high during the debate over the Compromise of 1850. Mississippi Senator Henry Foote (left) felt threatened by and pulled a pistol on Missouri Senator Thomas Hart Benton (center, hands on his chest). Although the Senate's rules require decorum, senators took no formal action to discipline Foote or Benton.

Both bodies must keep and publish a journal of their proceedings, including how members voted. Congress can decide that some discussions and votes are to be kept secret, but if one-fifth of the members demand that a vote be recorded, it must be. To keep the two chambers operating on similar schedules, the Constitution requires that neither the House nor the Senate can close down or move proceedings from their usual location for a period longer than three days without the consent of the other chamber. To avoid having to ask each other's permission, either the House or the Senate will often hold pro forma (for form) sessions, where only a few members are present and no business is conducted, at times when the other body is meeting. So, for instance, if the House is meeting to handle some unfinished business, but the Senate has nothing on its agenda, and most senators are out of town that week, one senator will agree to stay behind and call the Senate to order each day, and then immediately adjourn. The presiding senator sometimes tries to see how fast he or she can strike the gavel calling the Senate to order and then immediately adjourning it, as a sort of game. This meets the constitutional requirement that both houses be in session at the same time.

Perhaps bored by the debates, congressional reporter Thomas Lloyd drew sketches on his notes on the proceedings of the First Congress. The first congressional reporters of debate were hired by private newspapers rather than by Congress.

Article I
Section 6

Clauses 1–2

[1] The Senators and Representatives shall receive a Compensation for their Services, to be ascertained by Law, and paid out of the Treasury of the United States. They shall in all Cases, except Treason, Felony and Breach of the Peace, be privileged from Arrest during their Attendance at the Session of their respective Houses, and in going to and returning from the same; and for any Speech or Debate in either House, they shall not be questioned in any other Place.

[2] No Senator or Representative shall, during the Time for which he was elected, be appointed to any civil Office under the Authority of the United States, which shall have been created, or the Emoluments whereof shall have been increased during such time; and no Person holding any Office under the United States, shall be a Member of either House during his Continuance in Office.

SUING A SENATOR FOR LIBEL

Senator William Proxmire, a Wisconsin Democrat, regularly bestowed "golden fleece" awards on people and organizations he felt were wasting federal funds. In 1975 one of these awards went to the National Science Foundation for funding Ronald R. Hutchinson, a scientist who studied physical signs of aggression in monkeys. When the senator claimed that "the good doctor has made a fortune from his monkeys and in the process made a monkey out of the American taxpayer," the scientist sued for libel. The lower federal courts ruled that Proxmire held immunity under the Constitution's "speech and debate" clause, but in *Hutchinson* v. *Proxmire* (1979) the Supreme Court ruled that while his speeches in the Senate were protected, his press releases and newsletters were not. Chief Justice Warren Burger wrote the majority opinion, asserting that the constitutional protection was limited to actions essential to the legislative process. Only Justice William Brennan dissented, arguing that "in my view, public expenditure, whatever its form, is a legislative act shielded by the Speech and Debate Clause."

WHAT IT MEANS

Members of Congress are entitled to be paid for their service from the U.S. Treasury. Because members must vote to raise their own salaries, the Twenty-seventh Amendment, ratified in 1992, provides that salary increases can take effect only after the next election, giving voters a chance to register their approval or disapproval at the polls.

The Constitution protects legislators from arrests in civil lawsuits while they are in session, but they may be arrested in criminal matters. Members of Congress are granted immunity from criminal prosecution and civil lawsuits for the things they say and the work they do as legislators. This protection prevents prosecutors and others from using the courts to intimidate legislators because they do not like their views.

To ensure the separation of powers between the legislative, executive, and judicial branches of government, senators and representatives are prohibited from holding any other federal office during their service in Congress.

"The doctrine of separation of powers was adopted by the Convention of 1787, not to promote efficiency but to preclude the exercise of arbitrary power. The purpose was not to avoid friction, but, by means of the inevitable friction incident to the distribution of the government powers among three departments, to save the people from autocracy."

—Justice Louis D. Brandeis, dissenting opinion, *Myers* v. *United States* (1926)

Article I
Section 7

Clauses 1–3

"The fact that a given law or procedure is efficient, convenient, and useful in facilitating functions of government, standing alone, will not save it if it is contrary to the Constitution."

— Chief Justice Warren E. Burger, *INS* v. *Chadha* (1983)

WHAT IT SAYS

[1] All Bills for raising Revenue shall originate in the House of Representatives; but the Senate may propose or concur with Amendments as on other Bills.

[2] Every Bill which shall have passed the House of Representatives and the Senate, shall, before it becomes a Law, be presented to the President of the United States; if he approve he shall sign it, but if not he shall return it, with his Objections to that House in which it shall have originated, who shall enter the Objections at large on their Journal, and proceed to reconsider it. If after such Reconsideration two thirds of that House shall agree to pass the Bill, it shall be sent, together with the Objections, to the other House, by which it shall likewise be reconsidered, and if approved by two thirds of that House, it shall become a Law. But in all such Cases the Votes of both Houses shall be determined by yeas and Nays, and the Names of the Persons voting for and against the Bill shall be entered on the Journal of each House respectively. If any Bill shall not be returned by the President within ten Days (Sundays excepted) after it shall have been presented to him, the Same shall be a Law, in like Manner as if he had signed it, unless the Congress by their Adjournment prevent its Return, in which Case it shall not be a Law.

[3] Every Order, Resolution, or Vote to which the Concurrence of the Senate and House of Representatives may be necessary (except on a question of Adjournment) shall be presented to the President of the United States; and before the Same shall take Effect, shall be approved by him, or being disapproved by him, shall be repassed by two thirds of the Senate and House of Representatives, according to the Rules and Limitations prescribed in the Case of a Bill.

THE LINE-ITEM VETO

Presidents have been reluctant to veto a tax or spending bill because they objected to just a part of it. This has forced Presidents to agree to spending items they opposed in order to get other items they supported. In 1995, advocates of balancing the federal budget proposed a line-item veto, by which the President can approve a bill but veto some of its specific provisions, and in 1996 Congress granted the President this power. In the eighteen months after the line-item veto was approved, President Bill Clinton used it eighty-two times. The city of New York objected to one of his line-item vetoes, which affected some tax breaks tied to the city's Medicare program. New York filed suit in federal court, and eventually the Supreme Court, in *City of New York* v. *William J. Clinton* (1998). The Court struck down the line-item veto as unconstitutional because it violated the Constitution's requirement that bills be presented in their entirety for the President's signature or veto.

President Bill Clinton signs the Family Leave Act (making it easier for workers to take leave during family medical crises), which had been vetoed by his predecessor George H.W. Bush. Looking on are the bill's sponsor, Senator George Mitchell (standing, center), and Vice President Al Gore (right).

WHAT IT MEANS

When it comes to raising and spending money, the House of Representatives must begin the process. The Senate can offer changes and must ultimately approve the bills before they can go to the President. If the President signs the bill, it becomes a law. If the President does nothing for ten days, not including Sundays, the bill also automatically becomes law, except during the last few days of a congressional session. In that period of time, the President can use a "pocket veto." By doing nothing, the President automatically vetoes the bill. If the President sends a vetoed bill back to Congress with objections, it takes a two-thirds vote in both the House and Senate to override the veto in order for the bill to become law. Congress can also change the bill to make it more acceptable to the President. For political reasons, Presidents may be cautious about vetoing legislation, but just the threat of a veto may press members of Congress to work out a compromise. Similarly, if Congress has the necessary votes to override a veto, it is likely that the President will make every effort to compromise on the issue.

In 1792, George Washington signed the first Presidential veto in American history, rejecting an apportionment bill because it would not ensure congressional districts of equal size. A Presidential veto can be overridden only by a two-thirds vote of both houses of Congress.

PRESIDENT	R	P	O
R=regular; P=pocket; O=overridden			
Washington	2	0	0
J. Adams	0	0	0
Jefferson	0	0	0
Madison	5	2	0
Monroe	1	0	0
J. Q. Adams	0	0	0
Jackson	5	7	0
Van Buren	0	1	0
W. Harrison	0	0	0
Tyler	6	4	1
Polk	2	1	0
Taylor	0	0	0
Fillmore	0	0	0
Pierce	9	0	5
Buchanan	4	3	0
Lincoln	2	5	0
A. Johnson	21	8	15
Grant	45	49	4
Hayes	12	1	1
Garfield	0	0	0
Arthur	4	8	1
Cleveland	346	238	7
B. Harrison	19	25	1
McKinley	6	36	0
T. Roosevelt	42	40	1
Taft	30	9	1
Wilson	33	11	6
Harding	5	1	0
Coolidge	20	30	4
Hoover	21	16	3
F. Roosevelt	372	263	9
Truman	180	70	12
Eisenhower	73	108	2
Kennedy	12	9	0
L. Johnson	16	14	0
Nixon	26	17	7
Ford	48	18	12
Carter	13	18	2
Reagan	39	39	9
G. H. W. Bush	29	17	1
Clinton	36	1	2
G. W. Bush	0	0	0
Total	**1,484**	**1,069**	**106**

Article I
Section 8

~

Clauses 1–4

~

"The power to tax involves the power to destroy."

— Chief Justice John Marshall, *McCulloch* v. *Maryland* (1819)

~

WHAT IT SAYS

[1]   The Congress shall have Power To lay and collect Taxes, Duties, Imposts and Excises, to pay the Debts and provide for the common Defense and general Welfare of the United States; but all Duties, Imposts and Excises shall be uniform throughout the United States;

[2]   To borrow Money on the credit of the United States;

[3]   To regulate Commerce with foreign Nations, and among the several States, and with the Indian Tribes;

[4]   To establish an uniform Rule of Naturalization, and uniform Laws on the subject of Bankruptcies throughout the United States;

THE FIRST FEDERAL TAX TRIGGERS A REBELLION

During the "Whiskey Rebellion" of 1797, a cartoon mocked the tax collectors who would be lured by demon rum, or "grog," and then tarred and feathered. Congress sets all taxes and the executive branch collects them.

Whiskey was the first commodity that Congress taxed. In 1791, Secretary of the Treasury Alexander Hamilton proposed this tax as a way of helping pay for the states' Revolutionary War debts. But because distilling grain into whiskey was an inexpensive and profitable way for farmers to transport their product to market—due to the nation's poor roads—this tax fell hardest on the farmers of the western frontier. In western Pennsylvania angry farmers tarred and feathered the federal agents who tried to collect the unpopular tax and set fire to one tax collector's home. President George Washington and Treasury Secretary Hamilton responded to this Whiskey Rebellion by personally calling up and leading some 13,000 militiamen from Virginia, Maryland, Pennsylvania, and New Jersey against the rebels, who were speedily rounded up and arrested. This action left no doubt about the federal government's power to levy taxes.

WHAT IT MEANS

The eighteen clauses of Article I, section 8 specify the powers of Congress in great detail. These powers are limited to those listed and those that are "necessary and proper" to carry them out. All other lawmaking powers are left to the states. The First Congress, concerned that the limited nature of the federal government was not clear enough in the original Constitution, adopted the Tenth Amendment, which reserved to the states all the powers not specifically granted to the federal government.

Over time, federal legislation has dealt with many matters that the states had previously managed. In passing these laws, Congress has often relied on the power granted it by the commerce clause (clause 3), which allows Congress to regulate business activities "among the states," because so much business today, either in manufacturing or distribution, crosses state lines. But the commerce clause powers are not unlimited. In recent years, the Supreme Court has expressed greater concern for states' rights. It has issued a series of rulings that limit the power of Congress to pass legislation under the commerce clause or other powers contained in Article I, section 8. For example, these rulings have found unconstitutional federal laws aimed at protecting battered women or protecting schools from gun violence on the ground that these types of police matters are usually managed by the states.

The most important of the specific powers that the Constitution enumerates is the power to set taxes, tariffs (which the Constitution refers to as imposts), and other means of raising federal revenue, and to authorize the expenditure of all federal funds. In addition to the tax powers in Article I, the Sixteenth Amendment (1913) authorized Congress to establish a national income tax. The power to appropriate federal funds is known as the "power of the purse." It gives Congress its greatest authority over the executive branch, which must appeal to Congress for all its funding.

The federal government borrows money by issuing bonds. This creates a national debt, which the United States is obligated to repay. Congress also determines how individuals and corporations can declare bankruptcy. It also has the responsibility of determining naturalization—how immigrants become citizens. Such laws must apply uniformly to all states and cannot be modified by the states. Although bankruptcy and immigration are unrelated, they are linked in this clause by the Constitution's intention to set uniform laws on such national issues.

A World War I poster exhorts American women to help their sons win the war by buying Liberty Bonds. The government can fund wartime expenses through taxes and the sale of bonds.

A poster issued just after World War I encourages immigrants to the United States to become citizens. Congress is authorized to establish uniform laws of naturalization.

Article I
Section 8

⁓

Clauses 5–8

[5]   To coin Money, regulate the Value thereof, and of foreign Coin, and fix the Standard of Weights and Measures;

[6]   To provide for the Punishment of counterfeiting the Securities and current Coin of the United States;

[7]   To establish Post Offices and post Roads;

[8]   To promote the Progress of Science and useful Arts, by securing for limited Times to Authors and Inventors the exclusive Right to their respective Writings and Discoveries;

A frontier post office connected Dorrance, Kansas, with the rest of the nation and the world. The Constitution authorizes Congress to build post offices and post roads—roads built for the purpose of delivering the mail.

WHAT IT MEANS

Congress determines what type of money the federal government will issue, both coins and bills, and sets punishments for anyone who tries to counterfeit that currency. In order to deliver the mail across the country, the Constitution authorized Congress to create the necessary infrastructure—post offices and roads. For the general improvement of society, Congress has the right to establish copyright laws and provide patent protection for authors and inventors, so their creative work cannot be pirated.

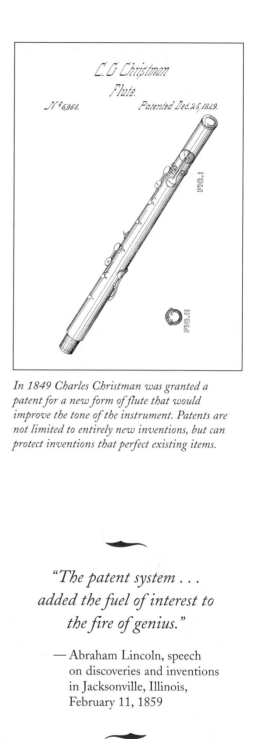

In 1849 Charles Christman was granted a patent for a new form of flute that would improve the tone of the instrument. Patents are not limited to entirely new inventions, but can protect inventions that perfect existing items.

"The patent system . . . added the fuel of interest to the fire of genius."

— Abraham Lincoln, speech on discoveries and inventions in Jacksonville, Illinois, February 11, 1859

L. Frank Baum filed for copyright for a musical composition based on his children's book The Wonderful Wizard of Oz. *The Constitution provides for copyright and patents to protect original work.*

Article I
Section 8

Clauses 9–11

[9] To constitute Tribunals inferior to the supreme Court;

[10] To define and punish Piracies and Felonies committed on the high Seas, and Offences against the Law of Nations;

[11] To declare War, grant Letters of Marque and Reprisal and make Rules concerning Captures on Land and Water;

FORMAL DECLARATIONS OF WAR		
WAR	**SENATE VOTE**	**HOUSE VOTE**
War of 1812 against Great Britain	June 17, 1812, 19–13	June 4, 1812, 79–49
War with Mexico	May 12, 1846, 40–2	May 11, 1846, 174–14
War with Spain	April 25, 1898, voice vote	April 25, 1898, voice vote
World War I, against Germany	April 4, 1917, 82–6	April 6, 1917, 373–50
World War I, against Austria-Hungary	December 7, 1917, 74–0	December 7, 1917, 365–1
World War II, against Japan	December 8, 1941, 82–0	December 8, 1941, 388–1
World War II, against Germany	December 11, 1941, 88–0	December 11, 1941, 393–0
World War II, against Italy	December 11, 1941, 90–0	December 11, 1941, 399–0
World War II, against Bulgaria	June 4, 1942, 73–0	June 3, 1942, 357–0
World War II, against Hungary	June 4, 1942, 73–0	June 3, 1942, 360–0
World War II, against Romania	June 4, 1942, 73–0	June 3, 1942, 361–0

General Andrew Jackson commanded the American forces that won the Battle of New Orleans against the British in January 1814. Unknown to both sides, a peace treaty had already been signed in Europe, but that did not stop Jackson from being hailed as a hero, as demonstrated by this idealized painting of a century later.

WHAT IT MEANS

In Article III the Constitution established the Supreme Court, but it was left to Congress to create the lower federal court system, such as federal district courts and courts of appeal. Congress may also enact laws to protect American shipping on the seas beyond the national boundaries.

Although the President is the commander in chief, Congress has the constitutional responsibility to declare war. However, Congress has not formally declared war since World War II. Since then it has generally passed resolutions authorizing Presidents to use military forces where necessary. Congress has also relied more on the power of the purse to shape military policy, most notably when it cut off funds for further military action in Southeast Asia in 1975.

Letters of marque and reprisal were eighteenth-century documents that authorized "privateers," or private merchants to seize other nations' ships and cargoes in reprisal for having been pirated themselves. This section of the Constitution has become obsolete over time.

"It is inconsistent to decry war and maintain law, for if there were no need of war there would be no need of law."

— Henry David Thoreau
in his journal (1842)

A POLICE ACTION IN KOREA

When North Korea invaded South Korea on June 1, 1950, the United States sent troops to aid South Korea but never formally declared war. Instead, on June 25, the United Nations Security Council declared North Korea's action "a breach of the peace" and called on its members to repel the aggressors. Because most Americans believed that the United States should support its ally South Korea, congressional leaders urged the President to call for a declaration of war that would authorize America's military intervention in the conflict. Instead, President Harry Truman agreed with his secretary of state Dean Acheson, who advised that the president could endorse the United Nations resolution on his authority as commander in chief rather than request congressional approval. Rather than seek a declaration of war, therefore, President Truman cited the UN resolution as his reason for engaging America militarily. The President referred to the Korean situation as a "police action" rather than a war.

"Not only has the President the authority to use the Armed Forces in carrying out the broad foreign policy of the United States and implementing treaties," said Secretary of State Acheson, "but it is equally clear that this authority may not be interfered with by the Congress in the exercise of powers which it has under the Constitution." The war in Korea lasted much longer and was much more difficult to fight than either Truman or Acheson had anticipated. As casualties mounted, members of Congress grew more critical of a war they had never endorsed. "This Korean War is a Truman War," claimed his opposition, a charge to which Truman had left himself vulnerable with his decision not to seek congressional approval.

American soldiers heading for the front pass a line of refugees during the Korean War. The United States never formally declared war against North Korea but instead supported a United Nations resolution to protect South Korea.

War Powers

The United States takes military action without a declaration of war

1801

When the United States refuses to pay tribute to the North African Barbary pirates, who have been raiding its ships in the Mediterranean, the pasha of Tripoli declares war on the United States. President Thomas Jefferson exerts his powers as commander in chief to set a naval blockade of Tripoli that results in a peace treaty in 1805.

Congress enacts the first declaration of war

1812

Britain's interference with American shipping and a blockade of U.S. ports leads President James Madison to ask Congress for a declaration of war against Great Britain. The House votes 79 to 49 for war on June 4. The Senate votes more narrowly for war, 19 to 13, on June 18. In August 1814, British troops invade Washington, D.C., and burn the White House and Capitol, but are eventually turned back at Baltimore. The inconclusive war is ended by the Treaty of Ghent, but, before word of the treaty reached the United States, Americans score a morale-building victory at the Battle of New Orleans in January 1815.

War with Mexico adds vast territories

1846

A border clash between the United States and Mexico over disputed territory between the Rio Grande and Nueces Rivers, leaves eleven Americans dead. President James K. Polk asks Congress for a declaration of war. The House votes 174 to 14 for war on May 11, and the Senate adopts a war resolution the next day by a vote of 40 to 2. American troops capture the Mexican capital of Mexico City. By the Treaty of Guadalupe Hidalgo, Mexico, cedes its northernmost territory to the United States, lands that today include the states of California, Arizona, Utah, Nevada, New Mexico, Colorado, and Wyoming.

Congress enacts the last official declarations of war

1941

On December 7, 1941, a Japanese surprise attack destroys the U.S. fleet at Pearl Harbor, Hawaii, which is a U.S. territory. President Franklin Roosevelt calls for a declaration of war against Japan, which Congress adopts with only one dissenting vote in the House. Japan's allies, Germany and Italy, also declare war on the United States, and Congress unanimously declares war against them. In June 1942, Congress again unanimously declares war on three of Germany's allies, Bulgaria, Hungary, and Romania. Italy is defeated in 1943, and Germany surrenders in May 1945. Following the use of atomic weapons against Hiroshima and Nagasaki, Japan surrenders in August 1945. World War II marks the last time that the U.S. Congress officially declares war against another nation.

The United States engages in a police action in Korea, bypassing Congress

1950

North Korean troops invade South Korea in 1950. President Harry S. Truman does not ask Congress for a declaration of war in support of South Korea but instead dispatches U.S. troops to support the United Nations' effort in Korea, which he calls a police action. An armistice reached in 1953 leaves Korea divided.

The Gulf of Tonkin Resolution substitutes for a declaration of war

1964

After President Lyndon Johnson reports that North Vietnamese patrol boats have fired on American naval vessels in the Gulf of Tonkin, Congress passes the Gulf of Tonkin Resolution. It authorizes the President to take all necessary measures to repel another armed attack and to prevent further aggression. President Johnson later uses the Gulf of Tonkin Resolution as a declaration of war enabling him to commit several hundred thousand American troops to South Vietnam. The United States withdraws its troops from South Vietnam in 1973, after signing a peace treaty. Hostilities between the North and South continue until Congress finally cuts off all military aid to the South in 1975. North Vietnam prevails and unites Vietnam under its rule.

TIMELINE

The North views secession as an insurrection

1861

Soon after the election of President Abraham Lincoln, eleven southern states secede from the Union and form the Confederacy. When Lincoln declines to surrender Fort Sumter in the harbor of Charleston, South Carolina, Confederate forces fire upon and capture the fort. Lincoln then declares that an insurrection exists and calls on Northerners to volunteer for military service. Lincoln calls

Congress into emergency session on July 4 but does not seek a formal declaration of war. After four brutal years of fighting, the South surrenders in April 1865.

The Spanish-American War ends swiftly

1898

The American public is outraged over reports of Spanish atrocities in Cuba, and the explosion and sinking of the USS *Maine* in Havana Harbor. President William McKinley responds to sentiments in Congress with a war message on April 11. On April 25, the House and Senate declare war by voice votes. The brief conflict sees American victories against the Spanish in Cuba and the Philippines.

The United States is drawn into a European war

1917

In 1914 the Triple Entente of Great Britain, France, and Russia goes to war against the Triple Alliance of Germany, Austria-Hungary, and Italy. The United States stays neutral until German attacks on American shipping convince President Woodrow Wilson to ask Congress, in 1917, for a declaration of war. The Senate passes the war resolution by a vote of 82 to 6 on April 4, and the House by a vote of 373 to 50 on April 6. Entry of U.S. forces into the conflict tips the balance against Germany, which accepts an armistice in November 1918. The Senate twice defeats the Treaty of Versailles. But, the Senate finally approves a treaty with Germany that formally ends the war in 1921.

Congress reasserts its authority with the War Powers Resolution

1973

Congressional frustration with the prolonged war in Vietnam leads to passage of the War Powers Resolution in 1973, over President Nixon's veto. The War Powers Resolution requires Presidents to notify Congress within forty-eight hours after committing U.S. combat troops abroad, and establishes a sixty-day limit on the deployment of American troops in combat overseas without congressional approval.

The United States goes to war in the Persian Gulf by UN resolution

1991

After Iraq invades Kuwait and threatens Saudi Arabia, President George H. W. Bush organizes a multinational coalition and persuades the United Nations to impose sanctions on Iraq and set a deadline for Iraq's withdrawal. Congress passes a resolution authorizing the use of force in support of the United Nations. On January 16, 1991, American-led coalition forces attack Iraqi positions. The war ends in one hundred hours, with Kuwait freed from Iraqi occupation.

The United States responds to terrorism

2001

The United States responds to terrorist attacks in New York City and Washington, D.C., on September 11, 2001, by attacking Afghanistan, which had hosted the terrorist organization responsible for the attacks. President George W. Bush then asserts the nation's right to fight preemptive wars. He identifies Iraq as having links to terrorists and warns that it possesses weapons of mass destruction. When the United Nations fails to authorize the use of force against Iraq, Congress grants President Bush authority to commit U.S. forces, which invade and defeat Iraq, capturing its leader, Saddam Hussein.

Article I
Section 8

Clauses 12–16

[12] To raise and support Armies, but no Appropriation of Money to that Use shall be for a longer Term than two Years;

[13] To provide and maintain a Navy;

[14] To make Rules for the Government and Regulation of the land and naval Forces;

[15] To provide for calling forth the Militia to execute the Laws of the Union, suppress Insurrections and repel Invasions;

[16] To provide for organizing, arming, and disciplining the Militia, and for governing such Part of them as may be employed in the Service of the United States, reserving to the States respectively, the Appointment of the Officers, and the Authority of training the Militia according to the discipline prescribed by Congress;

EISENHOWER CALLS UP THE ARKANSAS NATIONAL GUARD

Shocked by the Supreme Court's ruling in *Brown* v. *Board of Education* (1954), southern states resisted racial desegregation of their public schools. In 1957, a federal court approved a plan for the gradual integration of the all-white Central High School in Little Rock, Arkansas. Rejecting a more comprehensive proposal by civil rights advocates, the court ordered that just nine African American students be admitted at first. Arkansas governor Orval Faubus then posted troops from the state's National Guard outside the school—to prevent violence, he said. When the African American students attempted to enter the school, the troops barred their way.

President Dwight D. Eisenhower strongly encouraged Governor Faubus to honor the court's ruling. But the governor simply withdrew the National Guard and left the students to the mercy of an angry mob that forced them away from the school. President Eisenhower declared that he would not

allow such defiance of a federal court's ruling. He took charge of the Arkansas National Guard and sent a thousand U.S. Army paratroopers to Little Rock to ring the school and allow the students to enter safely. The troops protected the students for the rest of the

school year. Governor Faubus ordered all of Little Rock's public high schools to close for the next year, until a federal court then struck down Arkansas's school closing law as unconstitutional. In 1959, Arkansas's integrated schools reopened.

WHAT IT MEANS

Congress grants the military authority and appropriations to maintain forts, arsenals, and naval yards. The executive branch can spend only what Congress appropriates, and Congress may not pass any appropriation of funds for longer than two years. Traditionally, Congress makes only annual appropriations, requiring all military and civilian agencies to request funds every year. This "power of the purse" gives Congress the opportunity to review and to influence military policy.

The states operate militias, such as the National Guard, under the laws passed by Congress. The federal government may call up these forces in times of national emergency. For instance, in 1795, Congress authorized President George Washington to use the militia to suppress the antitax Whiskey Rebellion in western Pennsylvania. In 1957, President Dwight D. Eisenhower used the Arkansas National Guard to protect students integrating a Little Rock high school. In 2003, President George W. Bush sent National Guard troops into combat in Iraq.

THE APPROPRIATIONS COMMITTEES

Among the most powerful committees of the Senate and House of Representatives are the Appropriations Committees. Each of their subcommittees deals with specific areas of the government, such as the armed services, the courts, the cabinet departments, and the legislative branch itself. The chairmen of these subcommittees are known as the "cardinals" in recognition of their prestige and influence. Senators and representatives seek membership on the Appropriations Committees as a way of channeling federal funds back to their home states and districts. For instance, a representative's membership on the Appropriations Committee may help secure funds to build a highway through his or her congressional district, or locate a veterans hospital there.

At different times in the nineteenth century, Congress experimented with having all its standing committees appropriate funds in their areas of jurisdiction. Having authorized legislation, these committees naturally wanted to fully fund all their projects. This created a lack of control over spending and persuaded Congress to concentrate the power of the purse in its Appropriations Committees.

"Judges are not given the task of running the Army. The responsibility for setting up the channels through which such grievances can be considered and fairly settled rests upon the Congress and upon the President of the United States and his subordinates. The military constitutes a separate discipline from that of the civilian."

—Justice Robert H. Jackson, *Orloff* v. *Willoughby* (1953)

Article I
Section 8

Clauses 17–18

Pierre L'Enfant designed the street plan for the federal capital in the District of Columbia, creating a north-south, east-west grid crisscrossed by broad avenues named for the states. The Constitution authorized Congress to establish this new seat of government.

WHAT IT SAYS

[17] To exercise exclusive Legislation in all Cases whatsoever, over such District (not exceeding ten Miles square) as may, by Cession of particular States, and the acceptance of Congress, become the Seat of the Government of the United States, and to exercise like Authority over all Places purchased by the Consent of the Legislature of the State in which the Same shall be, for the Erection of Forts, Magazines, Arsenals, dock-Yards, and other needful Buildings;—And

[18] To make all Laws which shall be necessary and proper for carrying into Execution the foregoing Powers, and all other Powers vested by this Constitution in the Government of the United States, or in any Department or Officer thereof.

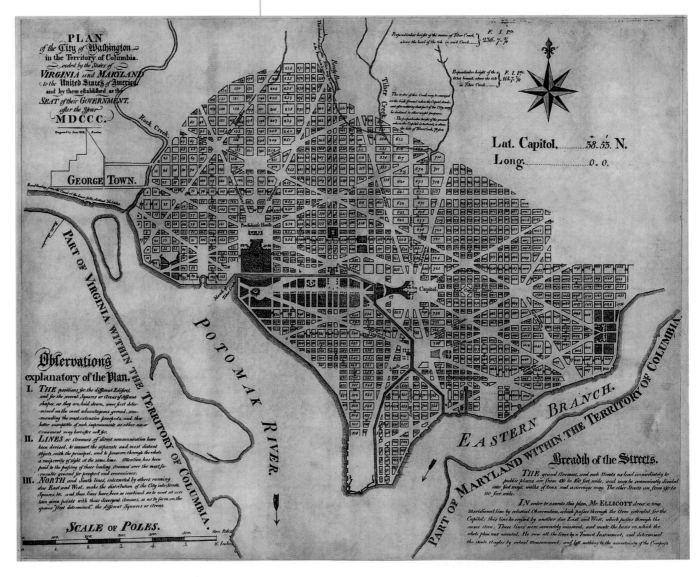

Since 1800, the federal government has operated within the District of Columbia, an area consisting of land ceded by the states of Maryland and Virginia. For many years, Congress directly governed the District, but in 1967 it established a locally elected government. Even with such "home rule," Congress retained oversight over the District's laws and budget.

Because the framers of the Constitution could not anticipate the range of issues that Congress would face in the future, they gave Congress great latitude in making all laws "necessary and proper" to carry out its general powers. This is known as the "elastic clause," and it enables Congress to address new problems as they arise so long as these laws are consistent with the powers stated above.

> *"The Constitution was not made to fit us like a strait jacket. In its elasticity lies its chief greatness."*
>
> —Woodrow Wilson,
> public address at Cooper Union in New York City on November 19, 1904

HOME RULE FOR THE NATION'S CAPITAL

The half million residents of the District of Columbia, the nation's capital, have no senators and only a single nonvoting delegate in the House of Representatives. Until the ratification of the Twenty-first Amendment in 1961, people living in the District could not vote for President. The Constitution gives Congress control over the District, and for many years the District of Columbia Committees of the Senate and House essentially operated as the local government.

In 1968, at the urging of President Lyndon B. Johnson, Congress approved a "home rule" bill that enabled the District to elect a mayor and city council. While this government has much autonomy in day-to-day operations, Congress retains the power to reject the District's tax and spending programs. In 1978, Congress passed a constitutional amendment that would have made the District of Columbia a state with full representation in Congress. Yet only sixteen states ratified the amendment within the allotted seven years, and it failed to become part of the Constitution.

Article I
Section 9

Clauses 1–4

[1] [The Migration or Importation of Such Persons as any of the States now existing shall think proper to admit, shall not be prohibited by the Congress prior to the Year one thousand eight hundred and eight, but a tax or duty may be imposed on such Importation, not exceeding ten dollars for each Person.]*

[2] The Privilege of the Writ of Habeas Corpus shall not be suspended, unless when in Cases of Rebellion or Invasion the public Safety may require it.

[3] No Bill of Attainder or ex post facto Law shall be passed.

[4] [No capitation, or other direct, Tax shall be laid, unless in Proportion to the Census or Enumeration herein before directed to be taken.]**

HOLDING PRISONERS INDEFINITELY AT THE GUANTANAMO NAVAL BASE

After the radical Islamic group al Qaeda committed vicious acts of terrorism against the World Trade Center in New York City and the Pentagon in Washington, D.C., on September 11, 2001, Congress authorized President George W. Bush to use military force against the "nations, organizations, or persons" who planned the attacks. The United States quickly sent armed forces to Afghanistan, where the country's rulers, the Taliban, had allowed al Qaeda terrorists to set up bases. U.S. forces captured many prisoners who were suspected of having aided the Taliban and the terrorists.

President Bush signed a military order that permitted U.S. Defense Department officials to hold such prisoners indefinitely without trial, because they posed a threat to national security. The President's order allowed those arrested to be held without charges and without the right to counsel. The President further directed the Pentagon to create military tribunals, but set no deadline for them, so the detainees were held for years without trial at the U.S. naval base in Guantanamo Bay, Cuba.

On behalf of the 595 detainees, the Center for Constitutional Rights, a civil liberties organization, filed a habeas corpus suit against the government. The Supreme Court ruled in *Rasul* v. *Bush* (2004) that the due process clause requires that even in time of war the foreign prisoners who claimed they were being unlawfully imprisoned could take their cases to U.S. civilian courts. Because the base was outside the United States, the Bush administration argued that anyone held there was outside the jurisdiction of the U.S. civilian courts.

A suspected foreign terrorist held at the U.S. naval base at Guantanamo Bay, Cuba. With Presidential authority the Defense Department can hold these prisoners indefinitely without trial.

* This provision became obsolete after 1808, when the Constitution prohibited further importation of slaves.

** Revised by the Sixteenth Amendment.

WHAT IT MEANS

Article I, section 9, details areas in which Congress cannot legislate. In the first clause, the Constitution banned Congress from ending the slave trade before the year 1808.

In the second and third clauses, the Constitution specifically guarantees rights to those accused of crimes. It provides that a writ of habeas corpus (a Latin phrase meaning "produce the body"), which allows prisoners the right to challenge their detention, cannot be suspended except under extreme circumstances, such as rebellion or invasion, when there is a public danger. Habeas corpus has been suspended only on rare occasions in American history. For example, President Abraham Lincoln suspended the writ during the Civil War. In 1871, the federal government also suspended habeas corpus in South Carolina to combat the Ku Klux Klan.

The Constitution similarly prohibits bills of attainder, which are laws directed against specific individuals or groups, declaring them guilty of a serious crime—such as treason—by legislation rather than by a jury trial. This ban was intended to ensure that the legislative branch did not bypass the courts and deny people the protections designed for criminal defendants and guaranteed elsewhere in the Constitution. In addition, there can be no "ex post facto" (Latin for "after the fact") laws—or laws passed to make an action illegal after it has already happened. This protection guarantees that individuals are warned ahead of time that their actions are illegal.

The fourth clause, which prevented the imposition of direct taxes, caused the Supreme Court to strike down a national income tax in 1895. To expand federal revenues, Congress proposed and the states ratified the Sixteenth Amendment (1913), permitting the federal government to levy an income tax.

"If I be wrong on this question of Constitutional power [suspension of habeas corpus], my error lies in believing that certain proceedings are constitutional, when, in cases of rebellion or invasion, the public safety requires them."

— Abraham Lincoln,
letter to Erastus Corning,
June 12, 1863

Wooden sailing ships like these in Charleston harbor in 1767 imported slave labor. The Constitution banned any further importation of slaves after 1808.

Article I
Section 9

Clauses 5–8

"It was my understanding of both English and Roman history that inspired me in opposing the Reagan and Bush Administration's efforts to grasp more and more power at the expense of the legislative branch— particularly with regard to . . . the Congressional power over the public purse."

— Senator Robert C. Byrd, address to the American Historical Society, January 8, 2004

WHAT IT SAYS

[5] No Tax or Duty shall be laid on Articles exported from any State.

[6] No Preference shall be given by any Regulation of Commerce or Revenue to the Ports of one State over those of another; nor shall Vessels bound to, or from, one State, be obliged to enter, clear, or pay Duties in another.

[7] No Money shall be drawn from the Treasury, but in Consequence of Appropriations made by Law; and a regular Statement and Account of the Receipts and Expenditures of all public Money shall be published from time to time.

[8] No Title of Nobility shall be granted by the United States: And no Person holding any Office of Profit or Trust under them, shall, without the Consent of the Congress, accept of any present, Emolument, Office, or Title, of any kind whatever, from any King, Prince, or foreign State.

A 1904 campaign advertisement showed President Theodore Roosevelt sowing seeds of prosperity among agriculture, industry, and other aspects of society. By banning taxes on goods shipped from one state to the next and forbidding preferences in regulation of ports in various states, the Constitution aimed to create a national economy.

General Dwight D. Eisenhower (center, with striped tie) testified before the Senate Appropriations Committee about the U.S. military budget early in the Cold War. The Constitution gave Congress the power to appropriate all federal funds.

WHAT IT MEANS

In order to ensure equality between the states, the Constitution prohibits states from imposing taxes upon goods coming into their states from another state and prevents Congress from favoring the ports of one state over the ports of others. This provision made the entire United States a free trade zone, where no fees would be charged to import or export goods from state to state. Further, Congress could enact tariffs on goods imported from abroad, but it could not tax goods exported from any of the states.

The government cannot spend any public money unless Congress has appropriated it. Furthermore, Congress is required to produce a regular accounting of all the money the government spends.

Having fought a revolution to end aristocratic rule, and rejecting government by monarchy, the framers of the Constitution forbid Congress from establishing any American titles of nobility. It prohibited federal officials from accepting a title of nobility, office, or gifts from any foreign nation without congressional authorization.

STATE TARIFFS

Under the Articles of Confederation, the states could set tariffs on goods imported from other nations and from other states. In attempts to raise revenue and to protect their own industries, various states imposed tariffs on woolen and cotton cloth, silks, hats, jewelry, silverware, and other goods. These tariffs disturbed European nations that exported the goods, including France, a strong ally during the American Revolution. Anti-British feelings still ran strong, and some states imposed specific taxes on British shipments to the United States. Only the northern states imposed such tariffs. The agrarian southern states depended on imported goods and wanted to avoid retaliatory tariffs imposed on their own agricultural products.

Both shippers and consumers sought a uniform national trade policy, but the Articles of Confederation did not extend this power to Congress. Congress could only request that the states take action, and each acted to its own perceived benefit. Amending the articles required the unanimous approval of all the states, which proved impossible to attain. It was a question of trade between the states that led Virginia to call for the Annapolis Convention of 1786, and eventually resulted in the Constitutional Convention of 1787. Setting restrictions on the states and granting the federal government authority over interstate and international trade were therefore prime reasons for writing a new constitution.

Article I
Section 10

Clauses 1–3

A cartoonist portrayed Senator Henry Clay sewing President Andrew Jackson's lips together as a means of stopping his protests over the Bank of the United States. The President and his congressional opponents disagreed about the bank's constitutionality.

WHAT IT SAYS

[1] No State shall enter into any Treaty, Alliance, or Confederation; grant Letters of Marque and Reprisal; coin Money; emit Bills of Credit; make any Thing but gold and silver Coin a Tender in Payment of Debts; pass any Bill of Attainder, ex post facto Law, or Law impairing the Obligation of Contracts, or grant any Title of Nobility.

[2] No State shall, without the Consent of the Congress, lay any Imposts or Duties on Imports or Exports, except what may be absolutely necessary for executing its inspection Laws; and the net Produce of all Duties and Imposts, laid by any State on Imports or Exports, shall be for the Use of the Treasury of the United States; and all such Laws shall be subject to the Revision and Control of the Congress.

[3] No State shall, without the Consent of Congress, lay any duty of Tonnage, keep Troops, or Ships of War in time of Peace, enter into any Agreement or Compact with another State, or with a foreign Power, or engage in War, unless actually invaded, or in such imminent Danger as will not admit of delay.

WHAT IT MEANS

Article I, section 10 limits the power of the states. No state may enter into a treaty with a foreign nation as that power belongs to the President, with the advice and consent of two-thirds of the Senate. States cannot make their own money nor can they grant any titles of nobility. Like Congress, the states are prohibited from passing laws that assign guilt to someone without court proceedings (bills of attainder), that make some act illegal retroactively (ex post facto laws), or that interfere with legal contracts.

Under the federal system, the states retain sovereignty but the Constitution prohibits them from exercising powers granted to Congress, such as collecting taxes on exports and imports, building an army or keeping warships in time of peace, or otherwise engaging in war unless invaded or in imminent danger. States are also prohibited from charging "duties of tonnage," which refers to fees on the cargo-carrying capabilities of any ship.

STATE BANK NOTES VERSUS FEDERAL DOLLARS

During the colonial era, the colonies relied on Europe to mint silver and gold coins and printed their own money. To finance the American Revolution, the Continental Congress authorized the printing of paper money, known as Continentals, which soon became devalued. This practice gave rise to the then-popular expression that something that was worthless was "not worth a Continental."

Although the Constitution prohibited the states from coining money and left matters of currency to the federal government, Congress authorized the private Bank of the United States to issue paper currency. This system continued until 1832, when President Andrew Jackson vetoed the renewal of the bank's charter. Without a national bank, state banks began issuing paper currency. This situation produced a wide variety of bills in different sizes, shapes, colors, and designs, many of them drawn on dubious banks and not worth their face value. To bring some order to American currency, Congress passed the National Bank Act of 1863, which enabled the federal government to print and issue federal bank notes. The system remained unstable, however, and in 1913 Congress set up the Federal Reserve Board to regulate the money supply by setting interest rates and to regulate the nation's banks. Today's dollar bills, therefore, are Federal Reserve notes, issued by the Federal Reserve Banks.

"For most men and women now living, national loyalty [as opposed to state loyalty] dates from the earliest memory or from adolescence, and because that is true, state sovereignty is a lifeless legalism."

— Irving Brandt,
Storm over the Constitution (1936)

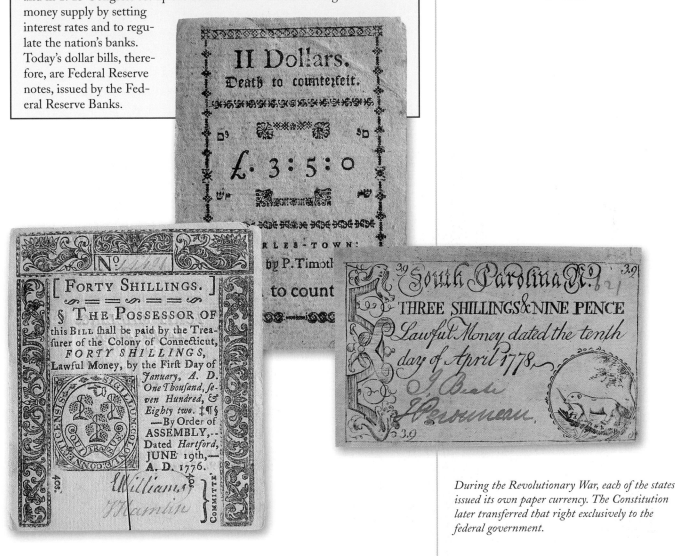

During the Revolutionary War, each of the states issued its own paper currency. The Constitution later transferred that right exclusively to the federal government.

Article II
Section 1

Clauses 1–3

"The President is at liberty, both in law and conscience, to be as big a man as he can. His capacity will set the limit; and if Congress be overborne by him, it will be no fault of the makers of the Constitution."

— Woodrow Wilson,
Congressional Government in the United States (1908)

Congress counted the electoral ballots after the election of 1789 and declared that George Washington had won election as President and John Adams as Vice President. Washington was the only President ever elected with the unanimous vote of the electoral college.

WHAT IT SAYS

[1]   The executive Power shall be vested in a President of the United States of America. He shall hold his Office during the Term of four years, and, together with the Vice-President, chosen for the same Term, be elected, as follows:

[2]   Each State shall appoint, in such Manner as the Legislature thereof may direct, a Number of Electors, equal to the whole Number of Senators and Representatives to which the State may be entitled in the Congress: but no Senator or Representative, or Person holding an Office of Trust or Profit under the United States, shall be appointed an Elector.

[The Electors shall meet in their respective States, and vote by Ballot for two Persons, of whom one at least shall not be an Inhabitant of the same State with themselves. And they shall make a List of all the Persons voted for, and of the Number of Votes for each; which List they shall sign and certify, and transmit sealed to the Seat of the Government of the United States, directed to the President of the Senate. The President of the Senate shall, in the Presence of the Senate and House of Representatives, open all the Certificates, and the Votes shall then be counted. The Person having the greatest Number of Votes shall be the President, if such Number be a Majority of the whole Number of Electors appointed; and if there be more than one who have such Majority, and have an equal Number of Votes, then the House of Representatives shall immediately chuse by Ballot one of them for President; and if no Person have a Majority, then from the five highest on the List the said House shall in like Manner chuse the President. But in chusing the President, the Votes shall be taken by States, the Representation from each State having one Vote; A quorum for this Purpose shall consist of a Member or Members from two-thirds of the States, and a Majority of all the States shall be necessary to a Choice. In every Case, after the Choice of the President, the Person having the greatest Number of Votes of the Electors shall be the Vice-President. But if there should remain two or more who have equal Votes, the Senate shall chuse from them by Ballot the Vice-President.]*

[3] The Congress may determine the Time of chusing the Electors, and the Day on which they shall give their Votes; which Day shall be the same throughout the United States.

* Replaced by the Twelfth Amendment.

The Constitution establishes that the President of the United States has the power to run the executive branch of the government. This section, later modified by the Twelfth Amendment, establishes the Electoral College (the process by which the President and Vice President are elected).

This section says that the President and Vice President are elected at the same time and serve the same four-year term. Originally, there was no limit to the number of

At a joint session of Congress in January 1945, clerks counted the electoral ballots that gave Franklin D. Roosevelt an unprecedented fourth term as President.

times a President could run for reelection. George Washington set the tradition of serving for no more than two terms. After Franklin Roosevelt was elected for four terms, the ratification of the Twenty-second Amendment limited Presidents to no more than two four-year terms. A Vice President who assumes the Presidency and serves more than two years of the remaining term is limited to one additional term.

Rather than being elected directly by the people, the President is elected by members of the Electoral College. It is not really a college but a group of people who are elected in each of the states. To keep elections national, rather than to favor any single state, the electors have to choose one candidate for President or Vice President who is not from their own states. The electors then vote for the Presidential candidate who won the majority of the popular vote in their states. (In a few states, laws specify that electors will cast their ballots according to the percentage of votes that each candidate received.) The number of electors from a state is equal to the number of senators and representatives from that state. Neither members of Congress nor other federal officials can serve as electors. The Electoral College gives more weight to the smaller states, rather than allowing the more populous states to control who becomes President, since all states have two senators, regardless of the size of their population. Should no one receive a majority in the Electoral College, then the House of Representatives chooses the President and the Senate chooses the Vice President.

Presidential elections are held on the Tuesday that follows the first Monday in November. After the people cast their votes, the electors meet in their respective states to ballot on the Monday following the second Wednesday in December. The electoral ballots are then counted at a joint session of Congress, held on January 6.

The election of 2000 reminded Americans that the Electoral College, not a direct popular vote, elects their Presidents. Vice President Al Gore, the Democratic candidate, polled a half-million more votes than did Texas governor George W. Bush, the Republican candidate. Final returns showed Governor Bush winning a narrow lead in the crucial state of Florida, and therefore gaining an electoral majority. Florida's margin was so thin, however, that it triggered an automatic vote recount. Although the recount confirmed Bush's lead, reported problems with the state's antiquated voting machinery became so numerous that Gore called for recounting the ballots by hand in certain districts. The Florida Supreme Court ruled in Gore's favor, but by a 5-to-4 vote the U.S. Supreme Court overturned the state court's decision. Citing the equal protection clause of the Fourteenth Amendment, the Supreme Court justices reasoned that insufficient time remained to conduct a thorough and fair recount, and that Florida lacked any established means of conducting a uniform statewide recount of all eligible ballots. Florida's electoral votes went to Bush, giving him a majority in the Electoral College. This marked the first time since 1888 that a candidate had won the Presidency with fewer popular votes than his opponent.

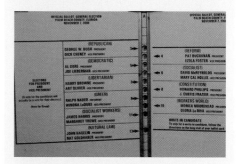

A "butterfly"–or fold-out–ballot used in Florida during the election of 2000 caused controversy because voters had difficulty in determining how to mark their choices correctly. The Supreme Court eventually settled the election results in the case of Bush v. Gore.

Article II
Section 1

Clauses 4–7

VICE PRESIDENTS WHO ASSUMED THE PRESIDENCY ON THE DEATH OR RESIGNATION OF THE PRESIDENT

John Tyler (1841)
succeeded William Henry Harrison

Millard Fillmore (1850)
succeeded Zachary Taylor

Andrew Johnson (1865)
succeeded Abraham Lincoln

Chester Allan Arthur (1881)
succeeded James A. Garfield

Theodore Roosevelt (1901)
succeeded William McKinley

Calvin Coolidge (1923)
succeeded Warren G. Harding

Harry S. Truman (1945)
succeeded Franklin D. Roosevelt

Lyndon B. Johnson (1963)
succeeded John F. Kennedy

Gerald R. Ford (1974)
succeeded Richard M. Nixon

WHAT IT SAYS

[4] No Person except a natural born Citizen, or a Citizen of the United States, at the time of the Adoption of this Constitution, shall be eligible to the Office of President; neither shall any person be eligible to that Office who shall not have attained to the Age of thirty-five Years, and been fourteen Years a Resident within the United States.

[5] In Case of the Removal of the President from Office, or of his Death, resignation, or Inability to discharge the Powers and Duties of the said Office, the same shall devolve on the Vice President, and the Congress may by Law provide for the Case of Removal, Death, Resignation or Inability, both of the President and Vice President, declaring what Officer shall then act as President, and such Officer shall act accordingly, until the Disability be removed, or a President shall be elected.

[6] The President shall, at stated Times, receive for his Services, a Compensation, which shall neither be increased nor diminished during the Period for which he shall have been elected, and he shall not receive within that Period any other Emolument from the United States, or any of them.

[7] Before he enter on the Execution of his Office, he shall take the following Oath or Affirmation:—"I do solemnly swear (or affirm) that I will faithfully execute the Office of President of the United States, and will to the best of my Ability, preserve, protect and defend the Constitution of the United States."

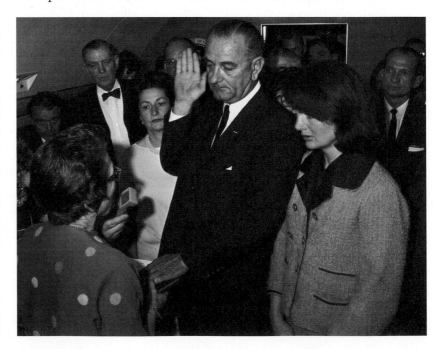

Vice President Lyndon B. Johnson took the oath of office as President on board Air Force One *in Dallas, Texas, following John F. Kennedy's assassination. In the event of the death, incapacitation, or resignation of the President, the Constitution provides that the Vice President will succeed to the Presidency.*

Just a month after William Henry Harrison was inaugurated as President in 1841, he died of pneumonia. On April 5, 1841, messengers from Washington arrived at the home of Vice President John Tyler in Williamsburg, Virginia, to inform him that the President had died. Tyler then hurried back to Washington, where he took the oath of office as President. Some people argued that Tyler was still Vice President and only the acting President. There were even calls for a special election. The House of Representatives, meeting in special session, prepared to send a resolution to Tyler as President, one member sought to amend the wording of the resolution by replacing "President" with "Vice President now exercising the office of President." Tyler rejected the notion that he was in any way "acting President" and asserted the full powers of the Presidency. The majority of the House agreed and struck down the amendment to the resolution. They therefore established the precedent that has applied to all other Vice Presidents when the office of the Presidency suddenly fell upon them.

WHAT IT MEANS

There are three minimum requirements to be President: one must be a natural-born citizen of the United States, have lived in the United States for at least fourteen years, and must be at least thirty-five years old. A natural-born citizen is a person either born in this country or born to American parents living abroad.

If the President dies or resigns, the Vice President becomes President. Congress has designated other officials to be in the line of succession, including the Speaker of the House, the president pro tempore of the Senate, and members of the cabinet. The Twenty-fifth Amendment, added in 1967, allowed for the appointment of a new Vice President in case that office becomes vacant.

Congress sets the President's salary. To prevent Congress from punishing or rewarding the President financially, the Constitution prohibits any change in salary during a President's current term, but it could be increased in a second term. The President is prohibited from receiving any other type of compensation while in office. However, Congress also provides funds to pay for Presidential expenses in operating the White House, hosting social functions, and traveling. Ethics laws also determine what gifts a President can accept and what belongs to the government.

On taking office, Presidents take an oath to do their best to uphold the United States Constitution as the law of the land. The wording of this oath is written into the Constitution. All other federal officers take an oath enacted by Congress.

"The second office of this government is honorable and easy. The first is but a splendid misery."

— Thomas Jefferson, comparing the Vice Presidency to the Presidency, letter to Elbridge Gerry (1797)

In 1923 Vice President Calvin Coolidge was sworn in as President at his father's Vermont farmhouse by his father, a justice of the peace. Coolidge succeeded President Warren G. Harding, who died unexpectedly of an apparent brain hemorrhage.

Article II
Section 2

Clauses 1–3

"It will be the office of the President to nominate, and with the advice and consent of the Senate to appoint. There will, of course, be no exertion of choice on the part of the Senators. They may defeat one choice of the Executive and oblige him to make another; but they cannot themselves choose—they can only ratify or reject the choice of the President."

— Alexander Hamilton,
The Federalist, No. 66,
March 8, 1788

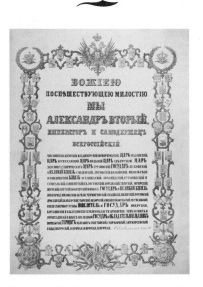

By this treaty, the Russian government sold Alaska to the United States in 1867.

WHAT IT SAYS

[1]   The President shall be Commander in Chief of the Army and Navy of the United States, and of the Militia of the several States, when called into the actual Service of the United States; he may require the Opinion, in writing, of the principal Officer in each of the executive Departments, upon any Subject relating to the Duties of their respective Offices, and he shall have Power to Grant Reprieves and Pardons for Offences against the United States, except in Cases of Impeachment.

[2]   He shall have Power, by and with the Advice and Consent of the Senate, to make Treaties, provided two-thirds of the Senators present concur; and he shall nominate, and by and with the Advice and Consent of the Senate, shall appoint Ambassadors, other public Ministers and Consuls, Judges of the supreme Court, and all other Officers of the United States, whose Appointments are not herein otherwise provided for, and which shall be established by law: but the Congress may by Law vest the Appointment of such inferior Officers, as they think proper, in the President alone, in the Courts of Law, or in the Heads of Departments.

[3]   The President shall have Power to fill up all Vacancies that may happen during the Recess of the Senate, by granting Commissions which shall expire at the End of their next Session.

THE CABINET THEN AND NOW

The Constitution refers to the executive departments, and in 1789 Congress created four such departments. President George Washington appointed the first cabinet officers to head them: the secretary of state, secretary of the treasury, secretary of war, and postmaster general. Washington also appointed an attorney general, although there was not yet a Department of Justice.

Two centuries later, the cabinet has grown to include the secretary of state, secretary of the treasury, secretary of defense, attorney general, secretary of agriculture, secretary of the interior, secretary of commerce, secretary of labor, secretary of health and human services, secretary of housing and urban development, secretary of energy, secretary of education, secretary of veterans affairs, and secretary of homeland security. Several other agency heads also have cabinet status: the director of the Office of Management and Budget, the administrator of the Environmental Protection Agency, the United States trade representative, and the director of the Office of National Drug Control Policy, together with the Vice President and the White House chief of staff.

WHAT IT MEANS

The President serves not only as head of the executive branch of government but also as the commander in chief of the armed forces (including the National Guard of each state when they are called upon to serve with the federal armed forces). All U.S. military forces are therefore subordinate to the civilian government. The President appoints a secretary of defense and other civilian officials to supervise the armed forces. Being commander in chief has given Presidents immense power in wartime, and over time has allowed them to assert greater control over foreign and military policy.

As chief executive, the President is responsible for the different executive offices. These include the high-level cabinet departments, such as the Department of the Treasury, and also many smaller, specialized agencies, such as the National Aeronautics and Space Administration (NASA).

With the permission of two-thirds of the Senate, the President can make treaties with other nations, and with the approval of a majority of senators, the President appoints U.S. ambassadors to other countries, federal judges including Supreme Court justices, cabinet officers, agency heads, and other officers of the government. Congress may choose to allow the President to appoint lower-level positions without Senate approval. When the Senate is not in session, the president can appoint people without Senate approval. Known as "recess appointments," these appointees' terms end when the next Senate session ends—unless the Senate votes to confirm their nominations.

During the Civil War, President Abraham Lincoln met with Union generals at their field camp near Sharpsburg, Maryland, on October 3, 1862. As commander in chief, Lincoln took an active part in battlefield decisions and soon afterward dismissed General George McClellan for not pursuing the Confederates more aggressively.

Section 2, clause 2 grants the President the power to make treaties and appointments with "the Advice and Consent of the Senate." The Constitution explains how the Senate offers its consent: requiring a two-thirds vote to approve treaties, and a majority to confirm nominations, but it does not define how it should offer its advice. Senators in the First Congress called on President George Washington to present all nominations and treaties in the Senate chamber. Washington declined to deliver nominations personally, as there were far too many nominations to make. Instead, he agreed to bring treaties to the Senate chamber to seek the body's advice. In August 1789, President Washington and Secretary of War Henry Knox went before the Senate with a list of questions about treaties with Indian tribes in the South. The senators felt uncomfortable debating these questions in front of Washington and referred them to a committee to study. "This defeats my very purpose of being here!" Washington angrily protested. The President returned a few days later when the committee issued its report. After that, he and most other Presidents have chosen to submit treaties to the Senate in writing rather than in person. As agreed Washington sent his judicial nominations to the Senate, rather than delivering them in person. From the start, the Senate resisted simply ratifying the President's choices. For instance, in 1795, senators rejected Washington's nomination of John Rutledge for chief justice of the United States, after he gave a speech attacking a treaty that the Senate had just ratified.

Treaty-Making Authority

Washington seeks the Senate's advice on Indian treaties

1798

The Senate requests that President Washington personally deliver treaties to the Senate to seek its advice. On August 22, 1789, he appears in the Senate chamber with a series of questions about treaties with Indian tribes. When senators refer his questions to a committee, Washington exclaims "This defeats every purpose of my coming here!" He returns a few days later to receive the Senate's responses but thereafter discontinues the practice of presenting treaties in person.

GEORGE WASHINGTON
PRESIDENT.
1792.

The Senate and House consider Jay's Treaty

1795

As a special envoy, Chief Justice John Jay negotiates a treaty in which Great Britain withdraws from its forts in the American Northwest and opens ports in the West Indies to American shipping, in return for payment of America's pre–Revolutionary War debts. Jay's Treaty is highly unpopular, especially in the southern states. The Senate ratifies it, but opponents in the House try to block the treaty by refusing to pass appropriations for its enforcement. President Washington responds that the Constitution requires only Senate approval for treaties. The House then narrowly approves the appropriation.

Louisiana Territory is purchased by treaty

1803

In the Louisiana Purchase, France sells its vast North American territory to the United States, which doubles the size of the nation. As the Constitution makes no mention of purchasing land from foreign nations, President Jefferson considers asking for an amendment to allow him to proceed. Realizing that ratifying an amendment would take too long, Jefferson instead interprets the existing constitutional power to govern territories as implying the ability to purchase them. The Senate approves the treaty by a vote of 24 to 7.

The Treaty of Guadalupe Hidalgo ends the Mexican War

1848

The annexation of Texas leads to war with Mexico, which is concluded by the Treaty of Guadalupe Hidalgo. In it, Mexico agrees to sell to the United States a vast territory covering the future states of California, Arizona, New Mexico, Nevada, Utah, Wyoming, and Colorado. Although President James K. Polk had not authorized the negotiations that led to the treaty, he submits it to the Senate, where it passes by a vote of 38 to 14. An effort by antislavery senators to attach to the treaty the Wilmot Proviso, banning slavery from the new territories, fails 38 to 15.

The Supreme Court upholds the Senate's right to amend treaties

1869

In *Haver* v. *Yaker* (1869) the Supreme Court declares that because treaties are the law of the land, the Senate has the right to amend a treaty like any other law, rather than simply adopting or rejecting it as a whole. Amendments that change the wording of a treaty require only a simple majority vote. The Senate can also pass reservations that indicate a change in interpretation of the treaty. Such adjustments help senators to build the coalitions needed to gain a two-thirds vote for ratification.

The Senate rejects the Treaty of Versailles

1919–1920

President Woodrow Wilson personally negotiates the Treaty of Versailles, ending the First World War and creating a League of Nations to foster international cooperation. Wilson, a Democrat, did not take Republican senators to the peace talks. Republicans win control of the Senate in 1918 and oppose the League of Nations, arguing it gives away too much American sovereignty. When Senator Henry Cabot Lodge offers a series of reservations to make the treaty more acceptable, Wilson rejects them. Wilson takes his case to the American people, but suffers a stroke that leaves him incapacitated. Without his leadership, the Senate twice rejects the treaty, by a vote of 38 to 53 in 1919, and 49 to 35 in 1920. The United States never joins the League of Nations.

TIMELINE

The Treaty of Ghent is approved

1815

House Speaker Henry Clay resigns his position to go to Ghent in Belgium to negotiate an end to the War of 1812 with Great Britain. The treaty restores peace, but settles none of the issues that caused the war. The negotiators sign the treaty on December 24, 1814, but before the news reaches America, General Andrew Jackson scores a dramatic victory over the British at the Battle of New Orleans in January 1815. With the nation's morale boosted, the Senate unanimously approves the Treaty of Ghent.

The Senate rejects its first treaty

1825

By a vote of 40 to 0, the Senate rejects a treaty with Colombia on the suppression of the African slave trade. Senators from slave states had loaded a similar treaty with Great Britain with amendments to make it unacceptable to the British. The Colombia treaty, dealing with the same issues, is caught in the backlash.

The Senate rejects a treaty to annex Texas

1844

After Texas wins its independence from Mexico in 1836, it applies for statehood. President Andrew Jackson hesitates out of concern over northern opposition to adding more slaveholding states and over the possibility of starting a war with Mexico. Jackson instead signs a resolution recognizing Texas as an independent republic. In 1844, Secretary of State John C. Calhoun sends a treaty of annexation to the Senate, but it is defeated by a vote of 35 to 16. The next year, Congress annexes Texas by a resolution, which requires a majority vote in both houses, rather than two-thirds of the Senate.

The Vandenberg Resolution and the North Atlantic Treaty

1948–1949

Before World War II, Michigan senator Arthur Vandenberg argues that the United States should avoid all foreign entanglements. The Japanese attack on Pearl Harbor converts him from isolationism to internationalism. The Republican Vandenberg then works closely with the Democratic President Harry Truman to forge a bipartisan foreign policy. In 1948, he writes the Vandenberg Resolution that endorses regional defense alliances. This leads to the Senate's approval in 1949 of the North Atlantic Treaty, which founds NATO, a defensive alliance between the United States and the Western European nations against the Soviet Union and its Eastern European satellites.

The Senate defeats the Comprehensive Nuclear Test Ban Treaty

1999

In 1994, Republicans win control of both houses of Congress for the first time in forty years. In the majority, they engage in a series of confrontations with Democratic President Bill Clinton. The Comprehensive Nuclear Test Ban Treaty is negotiated in 1996 as a means of stopping the global arms race. Although 154 nations join the treaty, opponents in the Senate point out that many of the nations that possess nuclear weapons have not signed it. The Senate then defeats the treaty by a vote of 48 yeas to 51 nays.

President Bush withdraws from the Kyoto Treaty

2001

In 1997 Vice President Al Gore flies to Kyoto, Japan, to break a diplomatic logjam over a multinational treaty aimed at reducing the carbon dioxide emissions blamed for global warming. The agreement places larger restrictions on industrially developed nations such as the United States than on developing nations such as India and China. Sensing there is no chance of passage, President Bill Clinton does not submit the treaty to the Senate. When Gore runs for President in 2000, he wins the popular vote but loses in the Electoral College. The victor, President George W. Bush, promptly announces that the United States will never sign the Kyoto Treaty.

Article II
Sections 3–4

He shall from time to time give to the Congress Information on the State of the Union, and recommend to their Consideration such Measures as he shall judge necessary and expedient; he may, on extraordinary Occasions, convene both Houses, or either of them, and in Case of Disagreement between them, with Respect to the Time of Adjournment, he may adjourn them to such Time as he shall think proper; he shall receive Ambassadors and other public Ministers; he shall take Care that the Laws be faithfully executed, and shall Commission all the Officers of the United States.

The President, Vice President and all civil Officers of the United States, shall be removed from Office on Impeachment for, and Conviction of, Treason, Bribery, or other high Crimes and Misdemeanors.

President Franklin D. Roosevelt called Congress into special session when war broke out in Europe in 1939. The Constitution authorizes the President to call Congress back during emergencies.

WHAT IT MEANS

Most years the President reports to Congress about how things are going in the country. Although the Constitution only requires a State of the Union speech "from time to time," Presidents use the opportunity annually to present their agenda for legislative action. This section also grants the President the power to call the House of Representatives and the Senate back into special session after they have adjourned, to deal with a crisis or some other business that cannot wait. Although the President is also granted the power to adjourn Congress, that has never been done. The President meets with representatives of other nations on behalf of the United States and otherwise runs the country by enforcing the laws and directing its officers and staff.

The President, Vice President, and other federal officers can be removed from office through impeachment and conviction of treason, bribery, or other high crimes. The process begins in the House, where a simple majority is needed to impeach. The accused official then stands trial in the Senate, where a two-thirds vote must be achieved for conviction. President Richard Nixon resigned from office as the House prepared to vote to impeach him. Presidents Andrew Johnson and Bill Clinton were impeached in the House but acquitted in the Senate. If convicted, the official is removed from office.

Women filled the "Ladies' Gallery" of the U.S. Senate during the impeachment trial of President Andrew Johnson in 1868. Although the Constitution does not require Congress to meet in public session, both the House and Senate provide public galleries.

CHANGING TRADITIONS OF THE STATE OF THE UNION ADDRESS

President George Washington and John Adams both appeared before Congress to deliver their State of the Union messages in person. In 1801, President Thomas Jefferson discontinued this practice, which to him seemed too aristocratic. Jefferson believed it resembled the British monarch's appearances before the Houses of Parliament. He began the practice of sending his annual messages to Congress, where they were read aloud by clerks of the House and Senate. Throughout the nineteenth century, all Presidents followed Jefferson's precedent. In 1913, Woodrow Wilson broke with tradition and appeared in person to deliver his State of the Union message before a joint session of Congress. Wilson believed this dramatic gesture would help build support for his legislative agenda. Since then most Presidents—although not all—have appeared in person. In 1923, Calvin Coolidge's State of the Union message was broadcast over the radio, and in 1947 Harry Truman's message was covered on television, giving Presidents a vastly expanded national audience for this important address.

President Ronald Reagan delivered his State of the Union message to a joint session of Congress in January 1983, during a severe recession. "As we gather here tonight, the state of our Union is strong, but our economy is troubled," he said. "We must all do everything in our power . . . to begin the hard but necessary task of building a better future for ourselves and our children."

Article III
Section 1

"The complete independence of the courts of justice is peculiarly essential in a limited constitution."

— Alexander Hamilton,
The Federalist, No. 78,
May 28, 1788

The judicial Power of the United States, shall be vested in one supreme Court, and in such inferior Courts as the Congress may from time to time ordain and establish. The Judges, both of the supreme and inferior Courts, shall hold their Offices during good Behaviour, and shall, at stated Times, receive for their Services a Compensation which shall not be diminished during their Continuance in Office.

THE FEDERAL JUDICIARY ACT

Among its many significant achievements, the First Congress passed the Federal Judiciary Act of 1789, which established a judiciary. However, the Constitution left the details largely undefined. The act set the number of justices on the Supreme Court (originally only six, now nine) and created thirteen district courts, along with a number of circuit courts to which Supreme Court justices and district court judges would travel. Today, there are ninety-one district courts in the fifty states, the District of Columbia, and the Commonwealth of Puerto Rico, and twelve circuit courts of appeal. Connecticut senator Oliver Ellsworth, who had been a delegate to the Constitutional Convention and who would later become chief justice of the United States, was the act's principal author.

Section 1. Be it enacted by the Senate and the House of Representatives of the United States of America in Congress assembled, That the supreme court of the United States shall consist of a chief justice and five associate justices, any four of whom shall be a quorum, and shall hold annually at the seat of government two sessions, the one commencing the first Monday of February, and the other the first Monday of August. That the associate justices shall have precedence according to the date of their commissions, or when the commissions of two or more of them bear date on the same day, according to their respective ages.

A German news photographer surreptitiously photographed the Supreme Court in session in 1935. This is one of very few such pictures—the Court has traditionally opposed photography during its proceedings.

WHAT IT MEANS

Article III establishes the federal court system. The first section creates the U.S. Supreme Court as the federal system's highest court. The Supreme Court has the final say on matters of federal law that come before it. The Constitution specifies that judges will serve "during good Behaviour," meaning for life—so long as they do not violate their oath of office by taking an impeachable action—and that their salaries cannot be cut as a means of controlling or punishing them. This assures an independent judiciary. The Supreme Court today has nine members, who are appointed by the President with the consent of a majority of the Senate. Congress has the power to create and organize the lower federal courts, which operate in every state. A case is filed and tried in the federal district courts or in some specialty courts, such as admiralty or bankruptcy courts. The trial courts look at the facts of the case and decide guilt or innocence, or which side is right in a dispute. If the losing side appeals the outcome, the appellate courts determine whether the trial was fair and followed the rules, and whether the law was correctly applied. A case may be appealed as far as the Supreme Court, although the Supreme Court hears only a small number of cases.

The Constitution made the U.S. Supreme Court the highest court in the land. Its nine members hold lifetime appointments.

Judges and lawyers gather on the steps of the federal courthouse in Brooklyn, New York, in 1873. These brownstones served as the first U.S. District Court in Brooklyn, from 1867 to 1873.

Article III
Section 2

Clauses 1–3

> "Life is breathed into a judicial decision by the persistent exercise of legal rights until they become usual and ordinary in human experience."
>
> — Martin Luther King Jr., "The Case against Tokenism" (1962)

WHAT IT SAYS

[1] The judicial Power shall extend to all Cases, in Law and Equity, arising under this Constitution, the Laws of the United States, and Treaties made, or which shall be made, under their Authority;—to all Cases affecting Ambassadors, other public ministers and Consuls;—to all Cases of admiralty and maritime Jurisdiction;—to Controversies to which the United States shall be a Party;—to Controversies between two or more States—between a State and Citizens of another State;—between Citizens of different States;—between Citizens of the same State claiming Lands under Grants of different States, and between a State, or the Citizens thereof, and foreign States, Citizens or Subjects.

[2] In all Cases affecting Ambassadors, other public Ministers and Consuls, and those in which a State shall be Party, the supreme Court shall have original Jurisdiction. In all the other Cases before mentioned, the supreme Court shall have appellate Jurisdiction, both as to Law and Fact, with such Exceptions, and under such Regulations as the Congress shall make.

[3] The trial of all Crimes, except in Cases of Impeachment, shall be by Jury; and such Trial shall be held in the State where the said Crimes shall have been committed; but when not committed within any State, the Trial shall be at such Place or Places as the Congress may by Law have directed.

THE SUPREME COURT REJECTS PRESIDENT TRUMAN'S SEIZURE OF THE STEEL MILLS

Judicial power was dramatically demonstrated in 1952 when the U.S. Supreme Court stopped the President of the United States from seizing a vital defense industry to prevent a strike that could damage the national interest. U.S. combat troops were fighting in Korea when federal labor mediation broke down between the unions and the steel industry, and the unions called a nationwide steel strike. President Harry S. Truman ordered his secretary of commerce to seize and operate the nation's steel mills. No law existed that authorized the President to take such an action, but President Truman asserted that responding to a wartime emergency was an "inherent power" of the Presidency necessary to promote the general welfare, as well as his responsibility as commander in chief of the armed forces. The steel companies sued the government on the ground that the President lacked the authority to take over their industry.

The Supreme Court surprised the President with its ruling in *Youngstown Sheet & Tool Company* v. *Sawyer* (1952), when it concluded that the President could not seize the steel mills. By acting without

congressional authority, Truman had violated the separation of powers, regardless of the emergency. Moreover, the Court ruled that a President's war powers could not be applied to domestic policies. Although he disagreed with the ruling—and always insisted that a President must act in a national emergency—President Truman complied with the Court's ruling. The steel seizure case confirmed that judicial power extended even to war powers, and even during a war.

WHAT IT MEANS

The federal courts decide arguments over how to interpret the Constitution, all laws passed by Congress, and the nation's rights and responsibilities in agreements with other nations. Federal courts can hear disputes that may arise between states, between citizens of different states, and between states and the federal government.

In the case of *Marbury* v. *Madison* (1803), the Supreme Court interpreted Articles III and IV as giving the federal courts the final say over the meaning of the Constitution and all federal laws, as well as the power to order state and federal officials to comply with its rulings. The federal courts can make decisions only on cases that are brought to them through the appeals process. Federal courts cannot create cases on their own—even if they believe that a law is unconstitutional. A person adversely affected by the law must bring suit against the government in order for the courts to rule on the matter.

Almost all federal cases start in the federal district court, where motions are decided and trials are held. Then, if the outcome of the trial is questioned by one of the parties, the cases are heard on appeal by the federal court of appeals and possibly by the Supreme Court. The Supreme Court accepts only a small number of cases for review, typically about eighty cases each year.

The federal courts also have final say over guilt or innocence in federal criminal cases, such as kidnapping, wiretapping, or narcotics smuggling. U.S. attorneys in the various states bring charges against those accused of breaking federal law. The Justice Department also brings suits and prosecutes alleged offenders. Defendants in criminal cases, except impeachment, have a right to have their cases heard by a jury in the state where the crime occurred.

William Marbury (above) was appointed a justice of the peace by the outgoing President John Adams, but the incoming Secretary of State James Madison refused to deliver Marbury's commission (below). The document was later damaged in a fire. In deciding the case of Marbury v. Madison *the Supreme Court for the first time declared an act of Congress unconstitutional.*

Article III
Section 3

Clauses 1–2

[1]   Treason against the United States, shall consist only in levying War against them, or in adhering to their Enemies, giving them Aid and Comfort. No Person shall be convicted of Treason unless on the Testimony of two Witnesses to the same overt Act, or on Confession in open Court.

[2]   The Congress shall have Power to declare the Punishment of Treason, but no Attainder of Treason shall work Corruption of Blood, or Forfeiture except during the Life of the Person attainted.

These pistols were used by former Treasury Secretary Alexander Hamilton and Vice President Aaron Burr when they fought an illegal duel (right) in Weehawken, New Jersey, in 1804. The two men had long been political rivals. The duel resulted in Hamilton's death and Burr's political disgrace.

A VICE PRESIDENT CHARGED WITH TREASON

The nation's most controversial Vice President, Aaron Burr, always played by his own rules. He began his term in 1800 by receiving a tie vote in the Electoral College with his running mate, Thomas Jefferson, and ended his term by shooting former secretary of the treasury Alexander Hamilton in a duel. Dropped by his party from their national ticket in 1804, Burr headed west. Soon the federal government began receiving reports that Burr was involved in a scheme by which the western states and territories would secede to form a new nation, which he would lead. Burr was arrested in 1807 and brought to Richmond, Virginia, to stand trial for treason. The chief justice of the United States, John Marshall, presided reminding federal prosecutors that the Constitution required either a confession or the testimony of at least two witnesses who had seen Burr commit an act of treason. Lacking either a confession or credible witnesses, the federal case collapsed and the jury found him innocent. The disgraced former Vice President then left the country to live in exile in Europe.

A Japanese American, Iva Ikuko Toguri, was convicted of treason in 1949 for having performed as "Tokyo Rose," broadcasting propaganda to American troops over Radio Tokyo during World War II. Although she argued that she had been coerced by the Japanese military police and was only one of several English-speaking women on Radio Tokyo, she was sentenced to ten years in prison. In 1977 President Gerald Ford granted her a full pardon.

"When our forefathers took up the task of forming an independent political organization for New World society . . . they were far more awake to powerful enemies with designs on this continent than some of the intervening generations have been."

—Justice Robert H. Jackson, *Cramer v. United States* (1945)

WHAT IT MEANS

Treason is the only crime specifically defined in the Constitution. Individuals may be found guilty of treason if they go to war against the United States or give "aid or comfort" to its enemies. They do not have to physically pick up a weapon and fight in combat against U.S. troops. Actively helping the enemy by passing along classified information or supplying weapons can lead to the charge of treason. Vocal opposition to a U.S. war effort through protest and demonstration, however, is protected by the free speech clause in the First Amendment.

A conviction of treason must be based either on an admission of guilt or on the testimony of two witnesses. Congress may set a punishment, but it must be directed only at the guilty persons and not against their friends or family, if they were not involved in the crime. The Constitution's strange reference to corrupt blood or forfeiture was intended to negate the English common law that prevented blood relatives of person convicted of treason from inheriting that person's property. This became an issue when the government was dealing with the property of Confederates after the Civil War.

The Federal Judiciary

Congress passes the Judiciary Act
1798

Congress responds to its constitutional authority to establish the lower federal courts by passing the Judiciary Act. Senator Oliver Ellsworth, who was a delegate to the Constitutional Convention, takes the lead in drafting the legislation that provides for six justices on the Supreme Court, thirteen district courts in the major cities, and three circuit courts to cover other areas. Initially, the Supreme Court serves as the only court of appeals.

The Senate rejects John Rutledge as Chief Justice
1795

President George Washington nominates John Rutledge to be chief justice of the United States. Rutledge, who previously served as an associate justice on the Supreme Court, has resigned to become chief justice of the South Carolina Supreme Court. Rutledge, however, has just given a speech denouncing the Jay Treaty, which the Senate has just approved. The outraged senators then vote 14 to 10 against his nomination, making him the first chief justice to be rejected.

The Supreme Court asserts the right of judicial review
1803

Outgoing President John Adams signs the commission for William Marbury to become a justice of the peace in Washington, D.C., but the incoming Secretary of State James Madison refuses to deliver the commission. Marbury files a writ directly with the Supreme Court, as the law permits, demanding his commission. Chief Justice John Marshall in his opinion in *Marbury* v. *Madison* declares the law that permitted Marbury to appeal to the Supreme Court to be unconstitutional. This marks the first instance in which the Supreme Court claims the right of judicial review over acts of Congress.

Congress creates the U.S. Courts of Appeals
1891

Since the Judiciary Act of 1789, Supreme Court justices had "ridden circuit," serving as trial judges for the circuit courts. In 1891, Congress creates the U.S. Courts of Appeals, but allows the circuit courts to continue for twenty additional years. In 1911, the circuit courts are abolished and their jurisdictions are transferred to the district courts. In the early twenty-first century, there are ninety-four U.S. judicial districts organized into twelve regional circuits, each one having a U.S. Court of Appeals.

Uniformity of Federal Court procedures is sought
1922

The growth of the federal courts in the twentieth century forces Congress to develop a means to improve their administration and operations. In 1922, Congress establishes the Conference of Senior Circuit Judges, which in 1948 is renamed the Judicial Conference of the United States to "serve as the principal policy making body concerned with the administration of the United States Courts." The Judicial Conference keeps track of the business of the federal courts, and makes suggestions for promoting uniformity of procedures and conduct of court business.

FDR tries to "pack" the Supreme Court
1937

After the Supreme Court strikes down the National Industrial Recovery Act, Agricultural Adjustment Act, and other New Deal legislation as unconstitutional, President Franklin D. Roosevelt complains that the Court is still operating in the "horse and buggy" era, out of step with the times. Unable to appoint any justices during his first term, he follows his landslide reelection with a proposal to expand the Court by adding one new justice for every sitting justice over the age of seventy. This "Court packing" plan bitterly divides congressional Democrats and is never adopted. Yet, in his next three terms as President, Roosevelt is able to appoint all the members of Supreme Court, and the new justices are more sympathetic to expanded federal regulation of the economy.

TIMELINE

The House impeaches a Supreme Court Justice

→ 1804

In 1804, the Jeffersonian Republicans in the House of Representatives vote to impeach Justice Samuel Chase, a Federalist who has served on the Supreme Court since 1796. He is accused of behaving in an "arbitrary, oppressive, and unjust" manner on the bench. The Senate conducts a trial in 1805, in which Justice Chase defends himself by declaring that he is being prosecuted for his political convictions rather than having committed any "high crimes or misdemeanors," as the Constitution specifies. Six Republicans join with nine Federalist senators to acquit Chase on all counts. He remains on the Supreme Court until he dies in 1811.

Congress creates a Court of Claims

→ 1855

To relieve itself of petitions for financial claims, Congress in 1855 establishes the Court of Claims, giving it jurisdiction to decide the validity of all monetary claims based upon the laws, regulations, or contracts with the U.S. government. The three judges on the Court of Claims are nominated by the President and confirmed by the Senate for lifetime appointments. In 1982, Congress abolishes the Court of Claims and divides its jurisdiction between the new U.S. Court of Appeals for the Federal Circuit and the U.S. Court of Federal Claims.

The size of the Supreme Court fluctuates

→ 1863–1867

In 1863 the new Republican majorities in Congress expand the Supreme Court to ten, allowing President Abraham Lincoln to make an appointment to the Court. After Lincoln dies, however, Congress strongly disagrees with his successor, Andrew Johnson, over Reconstruction policies. To prevent Johnson from appointing any justices, Congress reduces the number of justices to eight in 1867. After Johnson's term ends in 1869, Congress returns the Supreme Court to nine justices.

The District of Columbia gets a Court of Appeals

→ 1970

The District of Columbia is not a state but instead is operated by Congress as the seat of government. In 1970, Congress establishes a court of appeals as the highest court for the District of Columbia, the equivalent of a state supreme court.

Congress creates the U.S. Court of International Trade

→ 1980

To reduce some of the workload of the U.S. district courts, Congress establishes a Board of General Appraisers in 1890 to decide disputes involving imports, exports, and tariffs. The board operates within the Treasury Department. In 1909, Congress creates a Court of Customs Appeals to hear all challenges to the board's decisions. By 1980, in recognition that the work has become more judicial than administrative, Congress reorganizes these bodies into the U.S. Court of International Trade.

Three Federal judges are impeached and removed from the bench

→ 1986–1989

Although rarely used, impeachment remains the only way that Congress can consider removing a federal judge with a lifetime appointment. Between 1986 and 1989, the House of Representatives impeaches three federal judges on charges ranging from income tax evasion to accepting a bribe. The Senate designates a committee to hear the evidence and then votes to remove judges Harry Claiborne, Alcee Hastings, and Walter Nixon.

Article IV
Section 1

Full Faith and Credit shall be given in each State to the public Acts, Records, and judicial Proceedings of every other State. And the Congress may by general Laws prescribe the Manner in which such Acts, Records and Proceedings shall be proved, and the Effect thereof.

At a time when divorce was difficult to obtain in most states, people traveled to Reno, Nevada, and stayed in "divorce ranches" like the Biltmore motel to establish legal residency in the state in order to file for a speedy divorce. Under the Constitution's "full faith and credit" provision, other states had to honor Nevada divorces.

Divorce lawyers in the 1920s were assailed for the "racket" of helping their clients establish temporary residency in Nevada to obtain a divorce. At the time, most other states allowed divorce under very limited conditions.

WHAT IT MEANS

Each state must respect and honor the state laws and court orders of the other states, even when its own laws are different. For example, if citizens of New Jersey marry, divorce, or adopt children in that state, Florida must recognize those actions as valid, even if the marriage, divorce, or adoption would not have been possible under Florida law. Similarly, if a court in one state orders a person to pay money or stop certain behavior, the courts in other states must recognize and enforce the other state's decision.

Congress also has the power to determine how the states honor each other's acts, records, and court decisions. For example, Congress may pass a federal law that specifies how states must handle child custody disputes when state laws are different or the process by which a person winning a lawsuit in one state can enforce the order in another state.

"The Constitution, in all its provisions, looks to an indestructible Union, composed of indestructible States."

— Chief Justice Salmon P. Chase, *Texas* v. *White* (1869)

FULL FAITH AND CREDIT

Among the ways in which the Constitution united the separate states into a nation was through the "full faith and credit" clause, which requires the courts in one state to recognize the laws, records, and judicial decisions of the other states. The many lawyers at the Constitutional Convention of 1787 were fully aware of the expression "full faith and credit" from Anglo-American common law, and therefore spent little time debating it. For centuries this expression had referred to the respect owed to court decisions and other public records. The Articles of Confederation had contained a similar reference, but the Constitution went a step further and granted Congress the power to enact legislation to implement and enforce the "full faith and credit" provision.

As early as 1790, Congress enacted legislation for authenticating the acts of the various state legislatures and state courts, so that one state's laws and judicial decisions would be recognized in every other state's courts. In 1804, after the purchase of the vast Louisiana Territory, Congress broadened this legislation to include judicial proceedings in the territories as well. While each state's laws are binding only within that state, the full faith and credit provision of the Constitution gives the decisions of each state's courts equal standing across the nation. The "full faith and credit" clause does not require U.S. courts to recognize the decisions of foreign courts, although they can do so independently. In fact, American courts generally recognize and respect the decisions of courts in other lands.

A same-sex couple shows their marriage certificate from California. If one state allows a gay marriage, the Constitution requires other states to recognize the legitimacy of that union, even if their own laws prohibit it.

Article IV
Section 2

Clauses 1–3

[1] The Citizens of each State shall be entitled to all Privileges and Immunities of Citizens in the several States.

[2] A Person charged in any State with Treason, Felony, or other Crime, who shall flee from Justice, and be found in another State, shall on demand of the executive Authority of the State from which he fled, be delivered up, to be removed to the State having Jurisdiction of the Crime.

[3] [No Person held to Service or Labour in one State, under the Laws thereof, escaping into another, shall, in Consequence of any Law or Regulation therein, be discharged from such Service or Labour, but shall be delivered up on Claim of the Party to whom such Service or Labour may be due.]*

This 1775 advertisement offered a reward for the return of a fugitive slave named Titus, who ran away from his owner in New Jersey. Until the ratification of the Thirteenth Amendment, the Constitution required the return of such fugitives.

THE FUGITIVE SLAVE ACTS

For many northerners in the early nineteenth century, the most distasteful portion of the Constitution was the requirement that their states return African Americans who had fled from slavery in the South. William Lloyd Garrison, who published an abolitionist newspaper, *The Liberator*, in Boston, regarded the Constitution as a pact with evil because of its protection of human slavery. Garrison once publicly burned a copy of the Constitution and declared: "So perish all compromises with tyranny!"

Elected officials, however, took an oath to uphold the Constitution, even those portions with which they might disagree. To enforce the Constitution in 1793, Congress passed the Fugitive Slave Act, which allowed slave owners' agents who seized runaways to go before a federal judge to return them to their owners. Abolitionists challenged this law in court, and some northern states passed laws to counteract it, but in *Prigg* v. *Pennsylvania* (1842) the Supreme Court acknowledged that the fugitive slave provision was one of the compromises that had been necessary to ensure the ratification of the Constitution.

As tensions mounted between pro- and antislavery factions over the question of whether to permit or bar slavery in the new western territories, Congress forged the Compromise of 1850. Part of this compromise was a new Fugitive Slave Act that allowed fugitives to be returned to slavery without a court order, and set fines for anyone who tried to obstruct this law.

Instead of calming tempers, the provisions of this compromise outraged public opinion in the North and contributed to the coming of the Civil War. After the Southern states seceded, Congress repealed the Fugitive Slave Act. In 1863 President Abraham Lincoln signed the Emancipation Proclamation, declaring slaves in the states under rebellion to be free, and in 1865 the Thirteenth Amendment abolished slavery entirely.

* Abolished by the Thirteenth Amendment.

American agents James Monroe and Robert Livingston (seated) consider the French foreign minister's proposal to sell the Louisiana Territory to the United States. Many new states would be carved from this territory.

WHAT IT MEANS

States cannot discriminate against citizens of other states. A state must give people from other states the same fundamental rights it gives its own citizens. For example, Arizona cannot pass a law prohibiting residents of New Mexico from traveling, owning property, or working in Arizona, nor can the state impose substantially different taxes on residents and nonresidents. But certain distinctions between residents and nonresidents are permitted, such as giving state residents a right to buy a hunting license at a lower cost.

When any person accused of committing a crime in one state flees to another, the second state is obligated to return the fugitive to the state where the crime was committed. The process used to return fugitives (called extradition) was created by Congress and originally enforced by the governors of each state. Today the state and federal courts enforce the return of accused prisoners. Fugitives do not need to have been charged with the crime in the first state in order to be captured in the second and sent back. Once returned, the state can charge the accused with any crime for which there is evidence. By contrast, when a foreign country returns a fugitive to a state for trial, the state is only allowed to try the fugitive on the charges named in the extradition papers (the formal, written request for the fugitive's return).

The "fugitives from labor" provision gave slave owners a nearly absolute right to recapture runaway slaves who fled to other states, even if slavery was outlawed in those states. This meant that state laws in free states intended to protect runaway slaves were unconstitutional because they interfered with the slave owners' right to their slave's return. After the Civil War, the adoption of the Thirteenth Amendment, which abolished slavery and prohibited "involuntary servitude," nullified this provision.

"Let us then stand by the Constitution as it is, united, and entire: let it be a truth engraven on our hearts and minds, let it be borne on the flag under which we rally, in every exigency, that we have

ONE COUNTRY,

ONE CONSTITUTION,

ONE DESTINY"

— Daniel Webster, speech to the Whig Party in New York City, March 15, 1837

Article IV
Section 3

~

Clauses 1–2

[1]   New States may be admitted by the Congress into this Union; but no new State shall be formed or erected within the Jurisdiction of any other State; nor any State be formed by the Junction of two or more States, or parts of States, without the Consent of the Legislatures of the States concerned as well as of the Congress.

[2]   The Congress shall have Power to dispose of and make all needful Rules and Regulations respecting the Territory or other Property belonging to the United States; and nothing in this Constitution shall be so construed as to Prejudice any Claims of the United States, or of any particular State.

Puerto Rico's El Morro fort was built by the Spanish to protect San Juan harbor. The United States took Puerto Rico as a territory following the Spanish-American War of 1898. The Constitution gives Congress authority to make all rules relating to U.S. territories until such time as they become states or cease being U.S. territories.

CREATING WEST VIRGINIA

The Constitution prohibits one state from being carved out of another, without the original state's consent. The creation of West Virginia in 1863 seemed to fly in the face of this prohibition. The people of the western districts of Virginia were strongly opposed to secession in 1861. They held few slaves and had no desire to become a battlefield in the Civil War. When the Virginia legislature debated secession, those from the Appalachian Mountains region in the west voted to stay with the Union. After Virginia joined the Confederacy, Richmond became the capital of the rebel nation. Pro-Union Virginians then met in Wheeling to declare themselves the legitimate government of the state. Because, as President Abraham Lincoln had argued, states had no right to secede, they asserted that Virginia had never left the Union. With Virginia effectively divided during the war, the pro-Unionist government petitioned Congress to become a separate state. Congress acted and West Virginia joined the Union on June 20, 1863.

Californians held a parade in celebration of the state's admission into the Union in 1850. The Constitution empowered Congress to admit new states.

WHAT IT MEANS

Congress can admit new states into the Union, but a single state cannot create a new state within its boundaries. For instance, the state of New York cannot make New York City a separate state. Nor can two states, nor parts of states such as eastern Oregon and western Idaho, merge to form a new state without the consent of the various state legislatures and Congress. The Constitution does not specify that new states enter into the Union on an equal footing with the other states, but Congress has always granted new states equality with the existing states.

Not all the lands of the United States are states. Some lands are territories, and Congress has the power to sell off or regulate the territories. This includes allowing U.S. territories to become independent nations, which is what happened in the case of the former U.S. territory the Philippines, or regulating the affairs of such current U.S. territories as Guam and Puerto Rico. This provision also gives Congress the power to set rules for lands owned by the United States, such as national park land and national forests. The last sentence of this clause makes sure that nothing in the Constitution will harm the rights of either the federal government or the states in disputes over territory or property.

"I think that the Constitution of the thirteen states was made, not merely for the generation which then existed, but for posterity; undefined, unlimited, permanent, and perpetual— for their posterity, and for every subsequent State which might come into the Union, binding themselves by that indissoluble bond."

— Henry Clay, Senate speech, February 6, 1850

Article IV
Section 4

The United States shall guarantee to every State in this Union a Republican Form of Government, and shall protect each of them against Invasion; and on Application of the Legislature, or of the Executive (when the Legislature cannot be convened) against domestic Violence.

Democratic candidates James K. Polk and George Dallas join hands in support of the Dorr Rebellion in Rhode Island, while the Whig candidates Henry Clay and Theodore Frelinghuysen lament Dorr's defiance of their "Aristocracy." This cartoon from the 1844 Presidential campaign praises Democratic support for expanding the right to vote in Rhode Island.

WHAT IT MEANS

This provision, known as the guarantee clause, ensures that each state is run as a representative democracy, as opposed to allowing a monarchy or dictatorship to control the government. Courts have been reluctant to specify what a republican government means, leaving that decision to Congress.

Congress has the power, and the obligation, to protect the states from invasion by a foreign country or from significant violent uprising within each state. The Constitution authorizes the legislature of each state (or the governor, if the legislature cannot be assembled in time) to request federal help in the event of riots or other violence.

"The government of the Union depends almost entirely upon legal fictions; the Union is an ideal nation, which exists, so to speak, only in the mind and whose limits and extent can only be discerned by the understanding."

—Alexis de Tocqueville,
Democracy in America (1835)

DORR'S REBELLION: A SEVERE TEST OF THE GUARANTEE CLAUSE

The Constitution requires that the states and the federal government operate under a system of representative government, in which public officials are democratically elected to do the public's will. The authors of *The Federalist* explained that while the framers of the Constitution created an executive branch headed by a President, they wanted no part of a monarchy. The powers of the federal government were divided among the three branches to prevent the rise of autocracy or tyranny.

A severe test of this provision occurred in Rhode Island in 1841. There leaders of a popular movement protested that the state disenfranchised half of the men in the state (no women were eligible to vote) because the royal charter, which still served as the state's constitution, allowed only freeholders (landowners) to vote. The established political leadership was therefore known as the Freeholders' Government. Those people who did not own land and were thus unable to vote held their own state convention, wrote a new "People's Con-

stitution," and elected Thomas Wilson Dorr (above) as the state's governor. The Freeholders' Government held its own convention and wrote a new constitution that extended the right to vote—but this was defeated in an election limited to landowners. The Freeholders insisted that they were the

legitimate government, elected by the qualified voters of the state. For a while, two state governments existed.

Both sides called on President John Tyler for help. The President made it clear that he sided with the existing state constitution and would not support Dorr's alternative government. The President also promised federal troops to help the state militia put down Dorr's Rebellion. When Dorr's group tried to seize the state arsenal, the militia defeated them. Dorr was convicted and given a life sentence, but was soon released from prison on an amnesty. By then Rhode Island had adopted a new state constitution that broadened the right to vote. The Supreme Court addressed the issue in *Luther* v. *Bordon* (1849), in which it declared that guaranteeing a republican form of government to the states, as authorized by Article IV, section 4, was a matter for the executive and legislative branches rather than for the judiciary because this was a "political question."

Article V

"Amendments to the Constitution ought to not be too frequently made; . . . [if] continually tinkered with it would lose all its prestige and dignity, and the old instrument would be lost sight of altogether in a short time."

— Andrew Johnson, speech to a crowd gathered at the Capitol in Washington, D.C., on February 22, 1866

WHAT IT SAYS

The Congress, whenever two-thirds of both Houses shall deem it necessary, shall propose Amendments to this Constitution, or, on the Application of the Legislatures of two-thirds of the several States, shall call a Convention for proposing Amendments, which, in either Case, shall be valid to all Intents and Purposes, as Part of this Constitution, when ratified by the Legislatures of three-fourths of the several States, or by Conventions in three-fourths thereof, as the one or the other Mode of Ratification may be proposed by the Congress; Provided that no Amendment which may be made prior to the Year One thousand eight hundred and eight shall in any Manner affect the first and fourth Clauses in the Ninth Section of the first Article; and that no State, without its Consent, shall be deprived of its equal Suffrage in the Senate.

ALEXANDER HAMILTON FORESEES FUTURE AMENDMENTS

Writing in the last Federalist, *the series of articles designed to explain the new Constitution and aid its ratification, Alexander Hamilton addressed the suspicion expressed by some Anti-Federalists that those who gained power under the new Constitution would resist any changes that might restrain their powers. He pointed out that the states retained potential leverage over the national government through the amendment process.*

In opposition to the probability of subsequent amendments it has been urged, that the person delegated to the administration of the national government, will always be disinclined to yield up any portion of the authority of which they were once possessed. For my own part I acknowledge a thorough conviction that any amendments which may, upon mature consideration, be thought useful, will be applicable to the organization of the government, not to the mass of its powers; and on this account alone, I think there is no weight in the observation just stated. I also think there is little weight in it on the other account. The intrinsic difficulty of governing thirteen states at any rate, independent of calculations upon an ordinary degree of public spirit and integrity, will, in my opinion, constantly *impose* on the national rulers the *necessity* of a spirit of accommodation to the reasonable expectations of their constituents. But there is yet a further consideration, which proves beyond the possibility of doubt, that the observation is futile. It is this, that the national rulers, whenever nine states concur, will have no option upon the subject. By the fifth article of the plan the congress will be *obliged,* "on the application of the legislatures of two-thirds of the states (which at present amounts to nine) to call a convention for proposing amendments, which *shall be valid* to all intents and purposes, as part of the constitution, when ratified by the legislatures of three-fourths of the states, or by conventions in three-fourths thereof." The words of this article are peremptory. The congress "*shall* call a convention." Nothing in this particular is left to the discretion of that body. And of consequence, all the declamation about their disinclination to a change, vanishes in air. Nor however difficult it may be supposed to unite two-thirds or three-fourths of the state legislature, in amendments which may affect local interests, can there be any room to apprehend any such difficulty in a union on points which are merely relative to the general liberty or security of the people. We may safely rely on the disposition of the state legislatures to erect barriers against encroachment of the national authority.

WHAT IT MEANS

Realizing that over time the nation would want to make changes to the Constitution, its framers established a process to allow that to happen. Unlike laws and regulations that can be passed by simple majorities in Congress, the Constitution is more difficult to change.

Amendments are offered to the states once two-thirds of the Senate (67 of the 100 senators) and of the House (290 of 435 representatives) vote to approve the change, or when two-thirds of the states (34 of the 50 states), call for a national convention (a gathering of representatives of each state) to propose a change.

Once the amendment is proposed, three-fourths of the state legislatures, or state conventions (38 of the 50 states) must vote to ratify the amendment before it becomes part of the Constitution. One portion of the Constitution is not subject to amendment. There can be no amendment that would deny a state its equal votes in the Senate, without that state's consent.

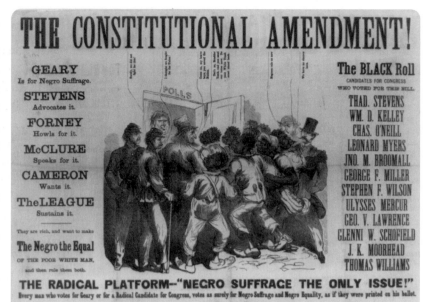

A Democratic campaign poster published in Pennsylvania in 1866 attacks the Thirteenth Amendment for allowing the freedmen to vote and denounces the Republican members of the state's congressional delegation who supported the amendment. The poster accuses them of wanting "to make the Negro the equal of the white man and then rule them both."

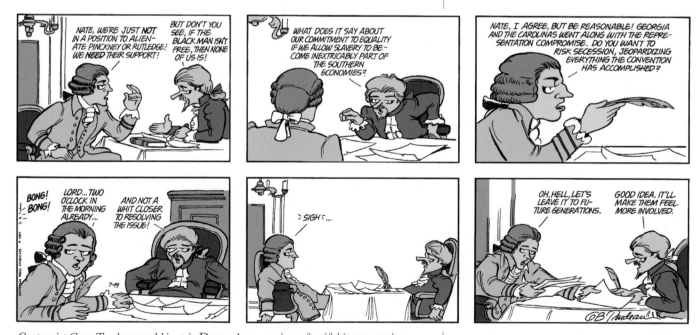

Cartoonist Gary Trudeau used his strip Doonesbury *to give a fanciful interpretation of why the Constitutional Convention failed to resolve the slavery issue. The exhausted delegates understand the problem they face but leave it to future generations to resolve.*

Article VI

Clauses 1–3

On January 3, 1939, members of the House of Representatives took the oath of office at the beginning of the 76th Congress. The Constitution provides that all members of the House stand for election every two years.

WHAT IT SAYS

[1] All Debts contracted and Engagements entered into, before the Adoption of this Constitution, shall be as valid against the United States under this Constitution, as under the Confederation.

[2] This Constitution, and the Laws of the United States which shall be made in Pursuance thereof; and all Treaties made, or which shall be made, under the Authority of the United States, shall be the supreme Law of the Land; and the Judges in every State shall be bound thereby, any Thing in the Constitution or Laws of any State to the Contrary notwithstanding.

[3] The Senators and Representatives before mentioned, and the Members of the several State Legislatures, and all executive and judicial Officers, both of the United States and of the several States, shall be bound by Oath or Affirmation, to support this constitution; but no religious Test shall ever be required as a Qualification to any Office or public Trust under the United States.

The new Constitution recognized that the debts of the previous government under the Articles of Confederation were still valid.

If a state law is in conflict with federal law, federal law must prevail. Referred to as the "supremacy clause," this article declares that the Constitution and the laws and treaties of the federal government are the highest in the land. While state courts rule on state laws, the federal courts can step in and order changes if the state laws go against federal law.

All federal and state officials must take an oath of allegiance to the Constitution. Although state officials have a duty to obey their own state constitutions and laws, their first loyalty must be to the U.S. Constitution. To ensure freedom of religion, public officials cannot be required to practice or pledge allegiance to any particular religion in order to hold office.

SOLEMNLY SWEARING: THE OATH OF OFFICE

While the Constitution specified the precise words that Presidents of the United States take in their inaugural oaths, it left it to Congress to determine the oath that other federal officials would take. The first bill that passed the U.S. Senate in 1789 was the Oath Act, which set out a short oath for members of Congress and civil servants: "I do solemnly swear that I will support the Constitution of the United States."

This oath served its purpose until the secession of the Southern states raised alarming questions about the loyalty of members of Congress and the executive branch to the federal government. Fearing traitors in its midst, Congress in 1862 enacted an Ironclad Test Oath in which people proclaimed their past and future loyalty to the Constitution. This oath required members to swear that they had never voluntarily borne arms against the United States, or aided, recognized, or supported a government hostile to the United States. When the war ended, Radical Republicans in Congress used this oath to prevent former Confederates from taking seats to which they were elected. In 1868, they began to relax this requirement, but did not repeal the so-called Ironclad Test Oath until 1884.

Today, federal officials "solemnly swear (or affirm) that I will support and defend the Constitution of the United States against all enemies, foreign and domestic; that I will bear true faith and allegiance to the same; that I take this obligation freely, without any mental reservation or purpose of evasion; and that I will well and faithfully discharge the duties of the office on which I am about to enter: So help me God."

"The Federal Constitution is a perfect and entire thing, an edifice put together not for the accommodation of a few persons, but for the whole human race; not for a day or a year, but for many years, perhaps a thousand, perhaps many thousands."

— The poet Walt Whitman in an article entitled "The Federal Constitution" (1856)

Article VII

The Ratification of the Conventions of nine States, shall be sufficient for the Establishment of this Constitution between the States so ratifying the Same.

THE ANTI-FEDERALISTS

Ratification of the new Constitution encountered stiff resistance from those who became known as the Anti-Federalists. For the most part, the Anti-Federalists thought that the states, not the national government, should be supreme. Most of the prominent Anti-Federalists, among them such distinguished veterans of the American Revolution as John Hancock, Samuel Adams, and Patrick Henry, had not participated in the Constitutional Convention because they did not want a stronger central government. Two of the Anti-Federalists, Edmund Randolph and George Mason, had been delegates to the convention but came away with strong reservations about the final document. Mason, in particular, raised an objection to the Constitution's lack of a bill of rights.

Many of the Anti-Federalists felt that smaller governments would best preserve a truly "republican" form of government, in which the people would be represented by public officials they elected. They fretted over the emergence of a new "aristocracy" in the national leadership. Other Anti-Federalists were farmers who worried about the new government's ability to tax the import of goods. Some expressed concern that the federal government would maintain a large standing army. They were also troubled by the creation of a national court system that could overrule state courts.

The Anti-Federalists published their complaints about the Constitution in various newspapers, and pressed their concerns in the state ratification conventions. Eventually, they lost their battle but they made their concerns clear enough that the First Congress responded with the ten amendments that became the Bill of Rights.

SIGNERS

Done in Convention by the Unanimous Consent of the States present the Seventeenth Day of September in the Year of our Lord one thousand seven hundred and Eighty seven and of the Independence of the United States of America the Twelfth. In witness whereof We have here unto subscribed our Names,

George Washington, President and deputy from Virginia

New Hampshire
John Langdon
Nicholas Gilman

Massachusetts
Nathaniel Gorman
Rufus King

Connecticut
William Samuel
  Johnson
Roger Sherman

New York
Alexander Hamilton

New Jersey
William Livingston
David Brearley
William Paterson
Jonathan Dayton

Pennsylvania
Benjamin Franklin
Thomas Mifflin
Robert Morris
George Clymer
Thomas Fitzsimons
Jared Ingersoll
James Wilson
Gouverneur Morris

Delaware
George Read
Gunning Bedford Jr.
John Dickinson
Richard Bassett
Jacob Broom

Maryland
James McHenry
Daniel of St. Thomas
  Jenifer
Daniel Carroll

Virginia
John Blair
James Madison Jr.

North Carolina
William Blount
Richard Dobbs
  Spaight
Hugh Williamson

South Carolina
John Rutledge
Charles Cotesworth
  Pinckney
Charles Pinckney
Pierce Butler

Georgia
William Few

Attest: Abraham Baldwin   William Jackson, Secretary

The delegates to the Constitutional Convention signed the Constitution on September 17, 1787, in the Pennsylvania State House, now known as Independence Hall. George Washington, seated on the right of the platform, invested his enormous personal prestige in the venture.

WHAT IT MEANS

Unlike the Articles of Confederation, which needed the unanimous consent of the thirteen states to make changes in the structure of the government, the Constitution required ratification by only nine of the states for the new government to go into effect. All of the original thirteen states, except Rhode Island, held conventions to ratify the Constitution. North Carolina's convention adjourned without voting on the document. On December 7, 1787, Delaware became the first state to ratify the Constitution, followed by Pennsylvania, New Jersey, Georgia, Connecticut, Massachusetts, Maryland, and South Carolina. The ninth ratification, by New Hampshire, occurred on June 21, 1788. Virginia and New York ratified the Constitution shortly afterward. North Carolina and Rhode Island waited to ratify the Constitution until after Congress passed the Bill of Rights and sent it to the states for ratification.

Of the fifty-five delegates who attended the Constitutional Convention, thirty-nine signed the document. Some of the delegates who did not sign supported the new Constitution but were absent at the time of its signing. A few, however, raised objections to the Constitution and refused to sign it. William Jackson was not a delegate but served as the secretary for the convention and authenticated the signatures of the delegates.

"I hold the view that the Constitution is the most revolutionary document . . . ever written, and it should to new countries serve as a source of stimulation and enterprise."

—John F. Kennedy, campaign speech in North Carolina, September 17, 1960

First Amendment

(1791)

—

"If there is a bedrock principle underlying the First Amendment it is that the Government may not prohibit the expression of an idea simply because society finds the idea itself offensive and disagreeable."

—William J. Brennan Jr.,
Texas v. *Johnson* (1989)

—

WHAT IT SAYS

Congress shall make no law respecting an establishment of religion, or prohibiting the free exercise thereof; or abridging the freedom of speech, or of the press; or the right of the people peaceably to assemble, and to petition the Government for a redress of grievances.

THE PENTAGON PAPERS

The First Amendment's guarantee of freedom of the press stands as an essential right if the people are to learn anything beyond the "official" information that the government distributes. Yet government leaders have complained that some information that the media has released (or was about to release) could have jeopardized national security. This was the case in 1971 when first the *New York Times*, and then the *Washington Post* and the *Boston Globe*, published excerpts from the still-classified Pentagon Papers.

The documents were part of a highly secret study conducted by the Defense Department into why and how the United States had gotten involved in the Vietnam War. One of the people who had worked on the project, Daniel Ellsberg, became disillusioned with the war and believed that the public needed to know what the Pentagon Papers contained, despite their classified status. He secretly provided copies to journalists from several major newspapers.

Although the documents dealt with events that occurred before he came to office, Richard Nixon believed that their publication hindered his ability to conduct the war and negotiate the peace. The Nixon administration called on the federal district court to issue an injunction against the newspapers to prevent them from publishing any installments of the Pentagon Papers. The government was seeking "prior restraint"—attempting to stop the newspapers before they published what they had, rather than punishing them afterward. The federal judge who heard the case asked the government's attorneys to select the "ten worst cases" in which classified material would endanger the nation if published. When the government produced its list, the newspapers were able to demonstrate that the information was already public knowledge. When the judge refused to halt publication, the government appealed to the Supreme Court, which in New York Times *Co.* v. *United States* (1971), decided by a 6-to-3 margin that the government had failed to justify prior restraint. "The press was to serve the governed, not the governors," asserted Justice Hugo Black for the majority.

WHAT IT MEANS

The First Amendment may well be the best known of our constitutional protections, and possibly the least understood. The First Amendment's free speech, assembly, and press guarantees allow citizens to express and be exposed to a wide range of opinions. It was intended to ensure a free marketplace of ideas—even if the ideas are unpopular. Freedom of speech encompasses not only the spoken word, but also all kinds of expression (including nonverbal communications, such as sit-ins). Under its provision, the media—newspapers, television, radio, books, art, advertisements, and the Internet—are fit to distribute news, information, ideas, and opinions. The amendment protects not only the speaker but also the person who receives the information. The ability to read, hear, see, and obtain different points of view is a First Amendment right, too.

A congressional clerk sorts through a huge stack of letters and petitions with citizens' views on the Neutrality Act, sent after World War II began in Europe. The First Amendment guarantees Americans the right to petition their government.

The right to free speech is not absolute, however. The government may limit or ban libel (the communication of false statements about people that injures their reputations). The government can further restrict obscenity, "fighting words"—insults intended to provoke a fight—and words that present a "clear and present danger" of causing violence, to use the phrase of Justice Oliver Wendell Holmes Jr. The government can also regulate speech through specific rules limiting the time, place, or manner in which it is made.

The First Amendment also protects the freedom of assembly, which can mean everything from gathering with a group of people to picket or protest to giving people the right to associate with one another in groups for economic, political, or religious purposes without unnecessary government regulation. Related to this is the right to petition the government, which includes everything from signing an actual petition to filing a lawsuit.

The First Amendment protects individuals' freedom of religion in two ways. It allows people to hold whatever religious beliefs they want and to "exercise" these beliefs, as by attending religious services or wearing religiously mandated items of clothing. The free exercise of religion also includes the right not to believe in any religion and not to participate in any religious "exercise." The amendment further prohibits the government from endorsing religion in general or one set of religious beliefs in particular. The free exercise clause and establishment clause sometimes clash, and courts have to help keep the balance between accommodating people's religious freedom and maintaining a neutral approach to religious believers and nonbelievers alike.

As part of their religious culture, Amish children dress in traditional garb. The First Amendment protects the freedom to worship as one chooses.

First Amendment

Editors imprisoned under Alien and Sedition Acts

→ 1798

A U.S. peace treaty with Great Britain angers France, which strikes back by seizing U.S. ships. On the verge of war, the Federalist majorities in Congress enact four bills collectively known as the Alien and Sedition Acts to silence pro-French sentiment in the United States. These acts make it a crime to criticize the federal government and its policies. Under this law, critical newspaper publishers are convicted and imprisoned. In 1800, the Democratic-Republicans win the Presidency and majorities in Congress. The new majority lets the Sedition Act expire, and President Thomas Jefferson pardons all those who had been convicted under it.

Efforts to stifle debate about slavery

→ 1836

As abolitionists develop the tactic of submitting many antislavery petitions to Congress, proslavery members of the U.S. House of Representatives adopt "gag" rules that bar such petitions from being introduced and debated. In 1844, former President John Quincy Adams, then a representative from Massachusetts, leads the effort to repeal these rules.

The Sedition Act punishes critics of World War I

→ 1918

NO WAR TALK!
Attorney General Gregory, says:
"OBEY THE LAW
Keep Your Mouth Shut!"

After the United States enters World War I, the federal government imposes criminal penalties on all forms of expression that are critical of the war mobilization. Some nine hundred people are convicted under the law, and hundreds of noncitizens are deported without a trial. Congress repeals the Sedition Act in 1921.

Prayer not allowed in public schools

→ 1962

New York State's Board of Regents drafted a nondenominational prayer for students to recite voluntarily at the beginning of each school day: "Almighty God, we acknowledge our dependence upon Thee, and beg Thy blessings upon us, our teachers, and our country." Ruling in *Engel v. Vitale* (1962), the Supreme Court rejected the notion that the prayer's lack of reference to any specific religion exempted it from the First Amendment's prohibition against establishing a religion. Any state-sanctioned prayer, the court argued, was an unconstitutional recognition of religion.

Supreme Court places limits on libel

→ 1964

L. B. Sullivan a Montgomery, Alabama, city commissioner, sues the *New York Times* for libel after it publishes a full-page advertisement criticizing anti–civil rights activities in Montgomery. Although the Alabama Supreme Court rules against the newspaper, the Supreme Court reverses that judgment in *New York Times* v. *Sullivan*. The Supreme Court rules that public officials cannot sue for libel unless they prove that a statement was known to be false and made with "actual malice," meaning that it was made "with knowledge that it was false or with reckless disregard of whether it was false or not."

Freedom of Information Act passes

→ 1966

President Lyndon B. Johnson signs the Freedom of Information Act (FOIA), requiring that government records be made available to the public and press upon request. Exceptions are made for documents relating to national security, confidential financial data, and law enforcement. President Johnson notes "a democracy works best when the people have all the information that the security of the nation permits. No one should be able to pull curtains of secrecy around decisions which can be revealed without injury to the public interest."

TOP SECRET
For Your Eyes Only!

TIMELINE

Limits to First Amendment recognized in cases of "clear and present danger"

1919

Supreme Court justice Oliver Wendell Holmes, in his opinion in *Schenck v. United States,* upholds the conviction of Socialist Charles Schenck for distributing antiwar leaflets in violation of the Espionage Act. Although under normal circumstances the First Amendment would have protected such activities, the Court holds that, in wartime, speech that poses a "clear and present danger of inciting imminent, lawless action" can be restricted, comparing it to "falsely shouting fire in a theater and causing a panic."

No religious instruction in public schools

1948

In Illinois, the Champaign Council on Religious Education, composed of Jewish, Catholic, and Protestant groups, offered voluntary religious instruction to students in local public schools. The Supreme Court ruled in *McCollum v. Board of Education Dist.* (1948) that such use of school buildings was unconstitutional because it was "a utilization of the tax-established and tax-supported public school system to aid religious groups and to spread the faith," and therefore violated the establishment of religion clause of the First Amendment.

"Symbolic speech" is protected

1961

In *Garner v. Louisiana,* the U.S. Supreme Court overturns the convictions for disturbing the peace of five African Americans who protested segregation by staging a "sit-in" at an all-white restaurant. Justice John Harlan explains that a sit-in demonstration is "as much a part of the free trade of ideas as is verbal expression." Similarly, in the case of *Tinker v. Des Moines Independent Community School District* (1969), the Supreme Court rules that the Des Moines, Iowa, School Board had been wrong to suspend three students who wore black armbands to school to protest the Vietnam War. The Court bases its decision on the grounds that the students' passive protest posed no risk of disrupting school activities.

Money spent in political campaigns is considered "speech"

1976

When Congress tries to limit expenditures in political campaigns, the U.S. Supreme Court, in *Buckley v. Valeo,* invalidates those provisions that restrict candidates ability to spend their own money on a campaign, limit campaign expenditures by an outside group, and limit total campaign spending. The Court compares restrictions on spending with restrictions on "political speech." The majority reasons that discussion of public issues and political candidates are integral to the American political system under the Constitution. In the Court's opinion, government-imposed limits on the amount of money a person or group can spend on political communication reduces "the quantity of expression by restricting the number of issues discussed, the depth of their exploration, and the size of the audience reached."

Restrictions on religious items displayed around government buildings

1989

The American Civil Liberties Union challenged a Christmas crèche and a Hanukkah menorah displayed at the Allegheny County Courthouse in Pittsburgh, Pennsylvania. In *Allegheny County v. ACLU* (1989) the Supreme Court ruled that while not all religious celebrations on government property violated the First Amendment, anything that clearly expressed official endorsement was unconstitutional. The nativity scene inside the courthouse, with a banner reading "Gloria in Excelsis Deo" ("Glory to God in the Highest") failed the constitutional test, but the menorah erected outside the building to "celebrate the season" was allowed to remain.

Second Amendment

(1791)

Last week, the government came and took this shopkeeper's gun away.

No, it hasn't happened yet. But it's close. Because a bunch of politicians are now pushing an idea called *gun control*. Where the federal government will either register or out-and-out take over the guns held by our country's private citizens. Starting with the small, lightweight, easy-to-use ones.

On the surface, gun control might sound like a good idea. But it has one fearful flaw.

When honest people give up their guns, *the criminals among us aren't going to.* So with gun control, only the thieves, thugs and insane killers will have guns. And that's a real danger. To our country. And to you.

It looks like they're actually going to get it across. Unless we can tell enough people what's happening, fast enough. Unless this ad and others like it can run over and over in national magazines and newspapers and on TV.

Will you help?

We're not saying every store owner should keep a gun under the cash register. Only that you should be *able* to, if you want to. Please send a contribution. As much as you can. As soon as you can.

The gun you save may be your own.

GIVE. SO THIS AD MIGHT LIVE.

TO: FIREARMS FREEDOM FUND
Liberty Park, 12500 N.E. 10th Place
Bellevue, WA 98005

Okay. I'll help spread the word. My contribution of
☐ $15 ☐ $25 ☐ $50 ☐ $100 ☐ $_____
is enclosed. (Check or money order payable to F.F.F.)

name _____

address _____

city _____ state ____ zip _____

Charge the amount indicated above to my bank-card account:
☐ Visa ☐ Mastercard

☐ I pledge the same amount I checked *every month for the next year.* Please send me monthly bills and a progress report.

NATIONAL FIREARMS FREEDOM FUND is a priority project of the Citizens Committee for the Right to Keep and Bear Arms, Alan Gottlieb, Chairman. We guarantee your money will be spent honestly and to good purpose.

A group advocating gun ownership under the Second Amendment's right to "keep and bear arms" ran this advertisement warning merchants that tougher gun control laws would leave them at the mercy of armed criminals. Those opposed to government regulation of firearms have often argued that such efforts would likely lead to gun confiscation and government regulation of gun sales and ownership.

WHAT IT SAYS

A well regulated Militia, being necessary to the security of a free State, the right of the people to keep and bear Arms, shall not be infringed.

THE CONTROVERSY OVER GUN-FREE SCHOOL ZONES

The problem of gun violence at schools gained national attention from several tragic incidents when students and teachers were wounded or killed. School safety has traditionally been the responsibility of state and local government, but these violent acts caused Congress to consider what role the federal government could play. In 1990, the U.S. Congress passed the Gun-Free School Zones Act, making it a federal offense "for any individual knowingly to possess a firearm at a place that the individual knows, or has reasonable cause to believe, is a school zone."

A San Antonio high school student named Alfonso Lopez confronted this law when he brought a concealed handgun to school in his backpack full of books. Tipped off, school authorities found the weapon and charged Lopez with violating the law. A federal district court found Lopez guilty because he had been caught with the concealed weapon inside the school.

Under the commerce clause of the Constitution, Congress has passed numerous laws regulating interstate commerce, that is, business that happens across state lines. Congress has used this provision to pass laws that govern the making and selling of guns bought in more than one state. Yet, Lopez said that his possession of a gun near a school had nothing to do with interstate business and therefore was a matter that only his home state could control. As Texas had no law about guns in schools, he argued that the matter should be dropped because the federal law was unconstitutional.

The case went to the U.S. Supreme Court, which by a 5-to-4 ruling in *United States* v. *Lopez* (1995), found that Congress could not use its commerce clause power to enact laws prohibiting guns in school zones. Decisions about school safety, the justices concluded, must be left to the general police power of each state's government.

WHAT IT MEANS

The principal debate surrounding the Second Amendment concerns whether the right to bear arms applies to individuals or only to a militia. The proliferation of firearms, their use in crimes, and a high rate of deliberate and accidental shootings in the United States has caused many Americans to advocate tighter gun controls. They argue that the Second Amendment applies essentially to militias. Hunters, those who own weapons for self-protection, and other gun enthusiasts insist the Second Amendment prohibits any restrictions on their right to bear arms. Rather than limit the sale of guns, they argue, the government should enact stiffer penalties for those caught using a gun while committing a crime. The courts have held that the right does apply to individuals, but have also recognized certain limits on that right. Recent questions about the Second Amendment have centered around such issues as restrictions on concealed weapons, bans on assault weapons, and mandatory background checks and waiting periods before weapons can be purchased. Both gun rights advocacy groups, such as the National Rifle Association and gun control advocacy groups, such as Handgun Control, Inc., have vigorously lobbied the government to decide these issues.

"To suppose arms in the hands of citizens, to be used at individual discretion, except in private self-defense, or by partial orders of towns, countries or districts of a state, is to demolish every constitution, and lay the laws prostrate, so that liberty can be enjoyed by no man . . ."

—John Adams,
Defence of the Constitutions of Government of the United States of America (1787)

A hunter proudly displays a deer that he shot. Hunters have been among the most vociferous defenders of the Second Amendment's right to bear arms.

Second Amendment

Automatic firearms are regulated
1934

Following an attempt on the life of President-elect Franklin D. Roosevelt with a handgun in 1933, Congress passes the National Firearms Act of 1934. The nation's first federal gun control law taxes the manufacture, sale, and transfer of fully automatic firearms and "gangster-type weapons," including machine guns and sawed-off shotguns. It also requires FBI background checks and local law enforcement notification for people who wish to purchase these weapons.

Federal regulation of gun sales begins
1938

The Federal Firearms Act of 1938 requires gun sellers to obtain a license from the Internal Revenue Service to sell guns and to maintain a record of purchases. The act also prohibits convicted felons from purchasing firearms or ammunition. However, the law makes no provision for criminals who provide false information when they purchase weapons.

Mandatory registration of shotguns is approved
1939

In *United States* v. *Miller,* the U.S. Supreme Court upholds the mandatory registration of sawed-off shotguns under the National Firearms Act as constitutional. Rejecting a challenge that cites the Second Amendment, the Court rules that these types of guns are not part of any ordinary military equipment, that their use cannot contribute to the common defense, and that their possession does not have any relationship to the preservation of a militia.

Government seeks to make school zones gun-free
1990

The Gun-Free School Zones Act makes it a federal crime to knowingly bring a gun within a thousand feet of a school, or to fire a gun within that zone. However, in *United States* v. *Lopez* (1995), the U.S. Supreme Court rules that Congress overstepped its constitutional authority under the commerce clause when it passed this act. The Court finds that the punishment of gun possession and gun use near schools is a matter for each state to regulate on its own.

The Brady Law requires background checks
1994

The Brady Law is named for former Presidential press secretary James Brady, who was seriously wounded during the 1981 assassination attempt on President Ronald Reagan. The law requires federally licensed firearm dealers to perform background checks with law enforcement officials before selling a firearm. During the background check, officials confirm whether the buyer falls within a category of individuals prohibited from owning or possessing a firearm by state law or the 1968 Gun Control Act. In *Printz* v. *United States* (1997) the U.S. Supreme Court holds that the Brady Law's waiting-period requirement is constitutional, but finds that the mandatory background checks required of local authorities are unconstitutional.

Semiautomatic weapons are banned
1994

The Violent Crime Control and Law Enforcement Act of 1994 bans nineteen types of semiautomatic weapons and ammunition clips holding more than ten rounds (except for military or police use). It also bans handgun possession by anyone under age eighteen and increases the requirements for federal gun dealer licenses.

TIMELINE

Congress enacts expanded gun regulations

1968

In 1927, Congress had passed legislation that banned mailing such concealable weapons as cane guns and pen guns, but until 1968 there is no law that regulates the mailing of rifles, shotguns, or handguns. Following the assassination of President John F. Kennedy in 1963 and the handgun-related assassinations of Reverend Martin Luther King Jr. and Senator Robert Kennedy in 1968, Congress enacts the Gun Control Act. The act regulates imported guns, expands licensing and record keeping requirements, bans mail-order sales of guns and ammunition, raises the age at which one can legally buy a gun, and prevents convicted felons, mentally ill people, and illegal drug users from buying guns.

The Bureau of Alcohol, Tobacco, and Firearms is created

1968

Displeased with the lack of vigorous enforcement of federal gun control laws, Congress separates the Bureau of Alcohol, Tobacco, and Firearms (ATF) (since renamed the Bureau of Alcohol, Tobacco, Firearms, and Explosives) from the Internal Revenue Service and forms it as a separate law enforcement organization within the U.S. Department of Justice.

The Firearm Owner's Protection Act is passed

1987

Congress responds to complaints from gun owners by repealing some federal restrictions on the purchase of out-of-state rifles and shotguns with the Firearm Owner's Protection Act. Proponents of the act argue that the laws did little to reduce crime. The act also permits citizens to transport "unloaded and inaccessible" guns from one state to another, regardless of local laws.

Domestic violence offender gun ban is enacted

1996

Despite increasing opposition in Congress to gun control laws, advocates manage to amend an omnibus spending bill to prohibit anyone convicted of a domestic violence offense from owning or possessing a gun.

Smith & Wesson reaches a settlement

2000

In the first settlement of its kind, the gun manufacturer Smith & Wesson reaches a settlement in many of the lawsuits brought against it by municipalities around the country, including Atlanta; Berkeley, California; Bridgeport, Connecticut; Camden, New Jersey; Detroit; Gary, Indiana; Englewood, New Jersey; Los Angeles, Miami-Dade; San Francisco; St. Louis; and Washington, D.C. The settlement binds Smith & Wesson to change the way it designs and distributes its guns. The company is required to install safety mechanisms including child safety locks and "smart gun" technology and sell only to authorized dealers who can prove that the guns they sell are not disproportionately used in crimes.

Third & Fourth Amendments

(1791)

"The test of reasonableness under the Fourth Amendment is not capable of precise definition or mechanical application. In each case it requires a balancing of the need for the particular search against the invasion of personal rights that the search entails."

— Justice William H. Rehnquist, *Bell* v. *Wolfish* (1979)

WHAT IT SAYS

[Third Amendment] No Soldier shall, in time of peace be quartered in any house, without the consent of the Owner, nor in time of war, but in a manner to be prescribed by law.

[Fourth Amendment] The right of the people to be secure in their persons, houses, papers, and effects, against unreasonable searches and seizures, shall not be violated, and no Warrants shall issue, but upon probable cause, supported by Oath or affirmation, and particularly describing the place to be searched, and the persons or things to be seized.

WHAT IT MEANS

The Third and Fourth Amendments are intended to protect citizens' rights to the ownership and use of their property without government intrusion. The men who drafted the Constitution, like many other citizens of their era, were resentful of the pre-Revolutionary laws that allowed British soldiers to use private homes for their barracks. The Third Amendment therefore bars the government from forcing individuals to provide lodging, or quarters, for soldiers in their homes, except under very extreme circumstances when national security may override individuals' right to privacy.

The Third Amendment has never been the subject of a Supreme Court decision and has rarely been addressed in federal court cases. The Third Amendment has instead been cited by courts as evidence that the Constitution created a general right of privacy for individuals, to protect them from government intrusion into their personal affairs.

The Fourth Amendment protects people against unreasonable searches and seizures by government officials. A "search" can mean everything from being "frisked" by a police officer to taking a blood test to having one's home and car examined. A "seizure" refers to the government taking control of something in individuals' possession, including the individuals themselves. Items that are "seized" are often used against a person as evidence at trial.

As a general rule, before police can search anyone's property they must go to the courts for a warrant, which is granted on probable cause of finding evidence of a crime. The Fourth Amendment also suggests that some searches may be reasonable without a warrant. For instance, a car stopped for speeding can be subject to search if the police observe evidence of illegal narcotics. But the courts will not accept evidence seized without a warrant when the police stop cars randomly for safety purposes to check drivers' licenses.

The Fourth Amendment also protects people against arbitrary arrest. The courts will not accept as evidence a confession taken from a person who is being held in custody illegally, nor consider evidence that is collected as a result of unlawful arrest. However, there are certain "special

Police in Utah frisk students suspected of committing a burglary. In Terry v. Ohio *(1968), the Supreme Court recognized the right of the police to stop and frisk someone, without violating the Fourth Amendment, if the police have a "reasonable suspicion" that a crime is being committed.*

needs" for which the courts have allowed searches without warrants, because they meet the constitutional requirement of reasonableness. For instance, prison authorities may search prisoners and their cells for weapons, school authorities may search students and their lockers for drugs, and airport authorities may search passengers and their luggage for explosives.

The invention of electronic eavesdropping equipment in the twentieth century complicated the definition of "search." At first the Supreme Court accepted evidence gathered by wiretapping, declaring it outside the Fourth Amendment's protections, as it involved no physical trespassing of a person's property, and that simply overhearing evidence was not a "seizure." But, Congress, in writing the Federal Communications Act of 1934, specifically prohibited the government from wiretapping without a warrant. And, in later years, the Supreme Court concluded that the Fourth Amendment protections went beyond "physical intrusion" and included evidence collected electronically.

The Fourth Amendment has been frequently cited as evidence that the Constitution recognizes the right to privacy, that is, people have a right to be "secure" from the government with regard to their bodies, homes, papers, and other effects.

On Halloween afternoon in 1963 a Cleveland plainclothes police officer was walking his beat when he spotted two men, Richard Chilton and John Terry, standing on a corner. The men walked a short distance down the road, looked in a store window, and then continued a few feet farther before turning around and returning to the corner, where they held a brief discussion. The two men repeated this pattern twenty-four times as the officer watched them. A third man approached them, talked with them, and then walked away. Chilton and Terry followed this third man, joining him a few blocks away. The officer suspected them of preparing to hold up the store, and approached them, identified himself, and asked for their names. The men only mumbled, fueling the officer's suspicions.

Fearing that the men were armed, the officer frisked the outside of Terry's clothing and found a gun. He then patted down the other two men and found a weapon in Chilton's coat. He brought all three men to the police station, where Terry and Chilton were charged with carrying concealed weapons.

At their trial, Terry and Chilton argued that the weapons had been "seized" as the result of an "unreasonable search" in violation of the Fourth Amendment. They contended that the search was "unreasonable" because the officer lacked "probable cause" to believe that they were carrying guns. Because the search was improper, they argued, the guns should be excluded from the evidence against them. The trial judge rejected this argument, admitted the guns into evidence, and Terry and Chilton were found guilty.

They appealed their convictions, eventually to the U.S. Supreme Court. In *Terry* v. *Ohio* (1968), the Supreme Court agreed that the searches of Terry and Chilton had been "reasonable" under the Fourth Amendment, and upheld their convictions. This type of "stop and frisk" of a suspect is now known to law enforcement officials as a "Terry stop."

Third & Fourth Amendments

The Supreme Court finds that the police conducted an illegal search and seizure

1914

Without a search warrant, the police enter a man's home and take private documents that are then used to convict him of sending lottery tickets through the mail. In *Weeks* v. *United States* (1914) the Supreme Court unanimously rules that the police seizure of Weeks's belongings violated his constitutional rights and that the government further violated the Fourth Amendment when it refused to return his possessions.

States are bound by the Fourth Amendment

1949

Fourth Amendment protections against unreasonable searches and seizures apply to officers of state governments (such as police officers or school officials) as well as to officers of the federal government, the Supreme Court decides in *Wolf* v. *Colorado.*

The "Exclusionary Rule" is applied to the states

1961

In *Mapp* v. *Ohio*, the Supreme Court applies the Fourth Amendment to the states. It holds that evidence obtained in an illegal search and seizure is not admissible at a state trial, as well as a federal court trial. This principle is commonly known as the Exclusionary Rule, because it excludes illegally gathered evidence.

Courts prohibit the eviction of strikers for soldiers

1982

In the only federal court ruling on an alleged violation of the Third Amendment, the U.S. Court of Appeals for the Second Circuit, in *Engblom* v. *Carey,* rules in favor of seventy guards in a New York State prison. The guards had been evicted from their employee residences on the prison grounds while they were on strike, and the state prison had given their houses as temporary quarters to the National Guardsmen called in to keep the peace during the strike. The court saw the guardsmen as equivalent to "soldiers" and ruled that the prison guards enjoyed a right to privacy in their residences, even if the prison owned their housing.

Evidence can be accepted on "good faith"

1984

The Supreme Court recognizes a "good faith" exception to the Exclusionary Rule in *United States* v. *Leon,* allowing police to use evidence that was obtained with a warrant issued in good faith but later found to be invalid.

Aerial surveillance of homes is legal

1986

Acting on a tip and without a warrant, a police officer flew a plane over the backyard of a suspected marijuana dealer and observed and photographed marijuana plants growing in the yard. Attaching his pictures of the yard as evidence, he obtained a warrant for the search of the home. The homeowner argues that the officer's aerial surveillance was an illegal search under the Fourth Amendment, but fails to get the evidence excluded and pleads guilty to the charges. The Supreme Court in *Ciraolo* v. *California* does not find the flight to be an illegal search. Even though the homeowner had erected a ten-foot fence to maintain his privacy, the court concludes that he had no reasonable expectation of privacy when the yard remained "knowingly exposed" to observation by the naked eye from an aerial view.

TIMELINE

A general right to privacy is recognized

1965

Addressing a state law that prohibited married couples from purchasing contraceptives, the Supreme Court, in *Griswold* v. *Connecticut,* rules that the Constitution gives individuals a "zone of privacy." In reaching this decision, the Court lists various constitutional provisions, including the Third, Fourth, and Ninth Amendments, as evidence that the framers intended such a right of privacy to exist, even though the Constitution does not contain a specific reference to that right.

People have a reasonable expectation of privacy

1967

In *Katz* v. *United States,* the Supreme Court rules that a criminal defendant's Fourth Amendment right to be free from unreasonable search and seizure was violated when, without a warrant, police wiretapped a public phone booth used by the defendant. The Court also cites the Third Amendment (along with the First and Fifth) to find that individuals enjoy a general right to be free from government involvement in their private affairs.

Police can search suspects when they have reasonable suspicion

1968

Whenever possible, the police should obtain a warrant before conducting a search of a person or his or her property. In *Terry* v. *Ohio,* the U.S. Supreme Court recognizes an exception to the general rule, allowing that the police may "pat down" the outside of a suspect's clothing and search the immediate area for weapons when they have a "reasonable suspicion" of illegal activity.

U.S.A. Patriot Act is passed

2001

In the aftermath of the terrorist attacks on September 11, 2001, Congress passes the U.S.A. Patriot Act to enable capture of those responsible for the attacks and prevent future attacks. The act provides for a dramatic expansion of the federal government's authority to monitor suspected terrorists' communications (including those made by e-mail and telephone), and to obtain online records such as organization membership lists and individuals' purchases.

Schools may conduct random student drug testing

2002

In *Vernonia School District* v. *Acton* (1995) the Supreme Court finds that a school district's policy requiring students participating in interscholastic sports to consent to random drug testing does not violate the Fourth Amendment. The Court stipulates that the use of random testing requires a balancing of a student's privacy with the school's legitimate interest in protecting students from harm. It expands upon that decision in *Board of Education* v. *Earls* (2002), which finds that an Oklahoma school district's policy of random drug tests for student participants in nonathletic extracurricular activities was also permissible.

The government cannot imprison suspected terrorists indefinitely

2003

The United States detains suspected terrorists at Guantanamo Bay, Cuba. In *Padilla* v. *Rumsfeld,* the U.S. Court of Appeals cites the Third Amendment in its finding that President George W. Bush lacks the authority to keep accused terrorist José Padilla confined indefinitely, reasoning that although the Constitution has a few specific grants of special authority to Congress that allow it to override individual rights—e.g., the Third Amendment's provision for housing soldiers in private homes during war—it makes no such grants of authority to the President.

Fifth Amendment

(1791)

When he testified before the congressional committee investigating the Iran-Contra scandal in 1987, former White House aide Oliver North refused to answer questions that might incriminate him, unless he was granted limited immunity.

WHAT IT SAYS

No person shall be held to answer for a capital, or otherwise infamous crime, unless on a presentment or indictment of a Grand Jury, except in cases arising in the land or naval forces, or in the Militia, when in actual service in time of War or public danger; nor shall any person be subject for the same offenses to be twice put in jeopardy of life or limb; nor shall be compelled in any criminal case to be a witness against himself, nor be deprived of life, liberty, or property, without due process of law; nor shall private property be taken for public use, without just compensation.

WHAT IT MEANS

Rooted in English common law, the Fifth Amendment seeks to provide fair methods for trying people accused of committing a crime. To avoid giving government unchecked powers, grand jurors are selected from the general population, and their work, conducted in secret, is not hampered by rigid rules about the type of evidence that can be heard. Grand jury charges can be issued against anyone except members of the military, who are subject to courts-martial in the military justice system. In the U.S. federal courts and some state courts, grand juries are panels of twelve to twenty-three citizens who serve for a month or more. If the jurors find there is sufficient evidence against individuals accused of crimes, the grand jury will indict them, that is, charge them with a crime.

GRAPPLING WITH THE RIGHT AGAINST SELF-INCRIMINATION

In the midst of the Cold War, the U.S. House of Representatives had a Committee on Un-American Activities (HUAC) that investigated individuals and organizations who were associated with the U.S.Communist Party. In 1949, the committee called Julius Emspak, an official of the Electrical, Radio, and Machine Workers of America Union, to testify. The committee asked him 239 questions about the union and its relationship with the Communist Party. He declined to answer sixty-eight of these questions, citing "primarily the first amendment, supplemented by the fifth." A district court later held that Emspak's statement about his rights was insufficient; he needed specifically to invoke his right against self-incrimination under the Fifth Amendment. He was found

guilty of refusing to testify before a committee of Congress. Emspak appealed that decision to the Supreme Court, which closely analyzed the conditions that needed to be met in order for people to claim their right against self-incrimination and refuse to answer certain questions.The justices decided that witnesses need only state their wish to be protected under the Fifth Amendment in a way that the court could "reasonably be expected to understand." Next the Court addressed the government's claim that Emspak had waived his rights when he answered "no" to a question about whether he thought admitting his knowledge of certain people would lead him to a criminal prosecution and found that the release of constitutional rights cannot be inferred, and that Emspak's "no" was not a defi-

nite release of his right against self-incrimination. The Court decided that Emspak could choose not to answer the questions that the committee asked him, reasoning that if he were to reveal his knowledge of the individuals about whom he was asked he might have uncovered evidence that could have helped prosecute him for federal crimes. Finally, the Court found fault with the House committee for not overruling Emspak's refusal to answer certain questions and instructing him to answer during the hearing. This would have given him a choice between answering or being sentenced for refusal to testify. Accused persons must refuse to answer knowing that they are required to answer. In *Emspak* v. *United States* (1955), the Supreme Court therefore set aside his fine and prison sentence.

Once indicted, defendants stand trial before a petit (from the French word for "small") jury of six to twelve citizens who hear the evidence and testimony to determine whether the accused are guilty or innocent.

The Fifth Amendment protects people from being put in "double jeopardy," meaning they cannot be punished more than once for the same criminal act and that once found innocent of a crime they cannot be prosecuted again for the same crime. The double jeopardy clause reflects the idea that government should not have unlimited power to prosecute and punish criminal suspects, instead getting only one chance to make its case.

The Fifth Amendment's right against self-incrimination protects people from being forced to reveal to the police, a judge, or any other government agents any information that might subject them to criminal prosecution. Even if a person is guilty of a crime, the Fifth Amendment demands that the prosecutors find other evidence to prove their case. If police violate the Fifth Amendment by forcing a suspect to confess, a court may prohibit the confession from being used as evidence at trial. Popularly known as the "right to remain silent," this provision prevents evidence taken by coercive interrogation from being used in court and also means that defendants need not take the witness stand at all during their trials. Nor can the prosecution point to such silence as evidence of guilt. This right is limited to speaking, nodding, or writing. Other personal information that might be incriminating, such as blood or hair samples, DNA samples, or fingerprints, may be used as evidence, with or without the accused's permission.

The right to due process of law protects those accused of crimes from being imprisoned without fair procedures. The due process clause applies to the federal government's conduct. The Fourteenth Amendment, ratified in 1868, contains a due process clause that applies to the actions of state governments as well. Court decisions interpreting the Fourteenth Amendment's due process rights generally apply to the Fifth Amendment and vice versa. Due process applies to all judicial proceedings, whether criminal or civil, that might deprive someone of "life, liberty, or property."

The "taking clause" of the Fifth Amendment strikes a balance between private property rights and the government's right to take property that benefits the public at large. The superior power the government can exert over private property is sometimes referred to as "eminent domain." Government may use eminent domain, for instance, to acquire land to build a park or highway through a highly populated area, so long as it pays "just compensation" to the property owners for the loss.

> *"The Fifth Amendment was designed to protect the accused against infamy as well as against prosecution."*
>
> —Justice William O. Douglas, dissenting opinion, *Ullmann* v. *United States* (1956)

Many homes and businesses were demolished so that the Cross Bronx Expressway could be constructed in New York City. The Fifth Amendment provides that the government cannot take private property for public use "without just compensation."

Fifth Amendment

Seizure of property without full hearing does not violate due process

1856

The federal government seizes property from a man who owes it money. He argues that the lack of a hearing violates his Fifth Amendment right to "due process." The Supreme Court rules in *Murray's Lessee* v. *Hoboken Land and Improvement Co.* that different processes may be legitimate in different circumstances. To determine the constitutionality of a procedure the Court looks at whether it violates specific safeguards in the Constitution and whether similar types of proceedings had been used historically, particularly in England. In this case, because a summary method for the recovery of debts had been used in England, the procedure is constitutional in the United States.

Slaves cannot be taken from their owners by federal law

1857

In *Dred Scott* v. *Sandford,* the Supreme Court decides that Dred Scott, who had moved with his owners to the free state of Illinois, returned to slavery when his owners moved back to Missouri, a slave state. The Court rules that slaves are property and that therefore the Missouri Compromise, which forbids slave owners from taking their property into free states violated the owners' Fifth Amendment rights not to have private property taken from them without just compensation. The Court further declares that slaves are not citizens of the United States entitled to the protection of the Fifth Amendment.

The government can take private property

1876

In *Kohl* v. *United States,* the U.S. Supreme Court upholds the federal government's right to take land in Cincinnati, Ohio, to build a post office. The government's ability to exercise the power of eminent domain contained in the Fifth Amendment is ruled essential to the government's ability to fulfill its duties to the public. This important goal outweighs any inconvenience to individuals living on the land.

Curfew regulations do not violate due process rights

1943

In the wake of Japan's attack on Pearl Harbor, Congress passes a law requiring Japanese Americans to live in restricted areas and obey curfews. In the case of *Hirabayashi* v. *United States,* the U.S. Supreme Court rules that this is not a violation of the Japanese Americans' Fifth Amendment right to due process, as they may have divided loyalties during wartime and their segregation is necessary to protect national security.

Organizations do not have the right against self-incrimination

1944

In *United States* v. *White,* the U.S. Supreme Court rules that a labor union under criminal investigation cannot refuse to turn over its records on the grounds of self-incrimination, explaining that the Bill of Rights was enacted to protect individuals, not organizations, from government control.

A suspect has the right to remain silent

1966

In *Miranda* v. *Arizona,* the U.S. Supreme Court rules that the right against self-incrimination is not limited to in-court testimony, but also applies when a suspect is taken into police custody for questioning. Before any questioning can begin, police must explain that the suspect has the right to remain silent, that any statement he does make may be used as evidence against him, and that he has a right to the presence of an attorney, either retained or appointed. The court refuses to accept as evidence any statements made after the right to remain silent has been invoked. These mandatory statements by police are known as Miranda rights and the process of informing is known as Mirandizing.

TIMELINE

Conviction in both federal and state court is not double jeopardy

1922

A defendant who had been convicted in state court objects to having to stand trial in federal court for the same crime. In *United States* v. *Lanza*, the U.S. Supreme Court rules that the double jeopardy clause was not violated because the state and federal legal systems are different government "units," and that each can determine what shall be an offense against its peace and dignity.

Due process requires a hearing before someone is deported

1922

In *Ng Fung Ho* v. *White*, the U.S. Supreme Court rules that the Fifth Amendment due process clause requires the government to hold a hearing before deporting a U.S. resident who claims to be a citizen, arguing that otherwise the person is deprived of liberty, and possibly in danger of losing property and life.

The right against self-incrimination applies in some civil cases

1924

The U.S. Supreme Court considers the question of whether a debtor who testifies at his own bankruptcy hearing is allowed to refuse to answer questions that might incriminate him. In *McCarthy* v. *Arndstein*, the Supreme Court holds that the Fifth Amendment privilege against self-incrimination applies to defendants in civil cases, not just criminal cases, if criminal prosecution might result from the disclosure.

Double jeopardy applies to state trials

1969

At first the Bill of Rights was seen as a limitation on the federal government's powers, not on the state government. In *Benton* v. *Maryland,* the U.S. Supreme Court rules that the double jeopardy clause represents a fundamental ideal of "our constitutional heritage," and extends double jeopardy protection to defendants in state court trials. The justices also cite the Fourteenth Amendment's prohibition on state governments limiting liberty without due process. Double jeopardy, they rule, violates the due process rights of the accused.

Prior notice and a hearing are required

1993

Four years after police found drugs and drug paraphernalia in a man's home and he pleaded guilty to drug offenses under Hawaiian law, the federal government files a request to take his house and land because it had been used to commit a federal drug offense. Following an ex parte proceeding (in which only the prosecution participates), a judge authorizes the property's seizure without prior notice to the individual. The Supreme Court, in *United States* v. *James Daniel Good Real Property,* rules that the property owner was entitled to advance notice and a full hearing before the government could take his home and land.

A death sentence imposed after retrial is not double jeopardy

2003

A defendant is convicted of first-degree murder, but the jury cannot reach a unanimous decision whether to sentence the defendant to death or to life in prison. By default, a life sentence is imposed. The defendant appeals his conviction and wins a retrial, but at the second trial the jury unanimously hands down a death sentence. In *Sattazahn* v. *Pennsylvania,* the U.S. Supreme Court rules that this second verdict does not violate the double jeopardy clause because the first jury's inability to reach a unanimous verdict means that there was no official finding of the facts regarding what kind of penalty the defendant deserved. As these questions remain open at the time of the second trial, the second jury can look at the facts again.

Sixth
Amendment

(1791)

WHAT IT SAYS

In all criminal prosecutions, the accused shall enjoy the right to a speedy and public trial, by an impartial jury of the State and district wherein the crime shall have been committed, which district shall have been previously ascertained by law, and to be informed of the nature and cause of the accusation; to be confronted with witnesses against him; to have compulsory process for obtaining witnesses in his favor, and to have the Assistance of Counsel for his defence.

THE JURY AS A CROSS SECTION OF THE COMMUNITY

In the early 1980s, Daniel Holland went on trial in Illinois for a variety of charges that stemmed from the 1980 kidnapping, rape, and robbery of a stranded motorist. On the appointed day for jury selection, the prosecution and Holland's counsel were faced with a jury pool made up of twenty-eight whites and just two African Americans. After questioning the potential jurors, the attorneys were permitted to remove, or "strike," a certain number of jurors. Some were to be struck "for cause," meaning that they had expressed some bias or other sentiment that cast doubt on their ability to be fair. The attorneys were permitted to strike a smaller number for no stated reason at all, the so-called peremptory challenge.

The prosecution used its peremptory challenges to strike both African American jurors. Holland's counsel objected on the grounds that Holland, who was white, had the Sixth Amendment right to "be tried by a representative cross section of the community"—words the U.S. Supreme Court had used in its ruling in *Taylor* v. *Louisiana* (1975). Holland's attorney argued that an all-white jury violated that right. The trial judge rejected the argument, an all-white jury was sworn in, and Holland was convicted of virtually all the charges. He was sentenced to sixty years in prison.

Holland appealed the convictions. When the case of *Holland* v. *Illinois* (1990) reached the U.S. Supreme Court, the justices found no Sixth Amendment violation. The Court explained that the guarantee of a jury drawn from a "representative cross section of the community" referred only to the pool from which the jurors are picked, not the composition of the final jury itself. The guarantee was intended to ensure an impartial jury, not a diverse one.

In a vigorous dissent, Justice Thurgood Marshall disagreed with the majority's view that jury fairness was the only reason for the "fair cross section" requirement. Justice Marshall argued, instead, that there was a larger goal: making sure that a jury's verdict reflects the "common sense judgment of the community." That goal was not met, he reasoned, when any group was excluded from the jury process, at either the jury pool stage *or* the jury selection stage.

The practical result of the Supreme Court's ruling in this case was to make it easier for prosecutors to challenge potential jurors for any reason.

The Sixth Amendment further specifies the protections offered to people accused of committing crimes. It allows the accused to have their cases heard by an impartial jury made up of people from the surrounding community who have no connection to the case. In some instances when there has been a significant amount of news coverage of the crime, jury members may be picked from outside the place where the crime took place.

Without the Sixth Amendment's right to a speedy trial, criminal defendants could be held indefinitely, under a cloud of unproven accusations. A speedy trial is also critical to a fair trial, because if a trial takes too long to occur witnesses may die or leave the area, their memories may fade, and physical evidence may be lost. The public trial guarantee protects defendants from secret proceedings that might encourage abuse of the judicial system. Criminal defendants can voluntarily give up their right to a public proceeding—such a renunciation is called a waiver—and judges may limit public access to trials in certain circumstances, such as to protect witnesses' privacy or to keep order in the court.

A speedy, public trial heard by an impartial jury would be meaningless if a defendant did not know what crime he or she was being charged with and why. Criminal defendants further have the right to face their accusers, which requires that prosecutors put their witnesses on the stand to testify under oath. The defendant's counsel may then cross-examine the witnesses, which may reveal their testimony as unreliable.

The Sixth Amendment guarantees a criminal defendant the right to have an attorney. That right does not depend on the defendant's ability to pay an attorney. If a defendant cannot afford one, the government must provide one. The right to an effective defense does not guarantee a successful defense. A defendant can receive effective legal assistance and still be convicted.

> *"The right of a speedy trial is necessarily relative. It is consistent with delays and depends upon circumstances."*
>
> — Justice Joseph McKenna,
> majority opinion,
> *Beavers* v. *Haubert* (1905)

The 1957 Hollywood movie Twelve Angry Men *dramatically demonstrated how a single juror could persuade other jurors to reconsider their "guilty" vote in a murder trial. By raising reasonable doubts about the evidence and testimony, and by confronting personal prejudices, the lone hold-out (Henry Fonda, far left) convinced each of the others, one by one, to vote "not guilty."*

Sixth Amendment

Defendants can give up the right to a jury trial

1930

In *Patton* v. *United States,* the U.S. Supreme Court decides that defendants can give up their right to a jury trial, and choose to have the judge alone decide their guilt or innocence. This choice must be made with the understanding of what they are giving up (that is, it must be an "intelligent" or "knowing" choice). In the federal courts and in some state courts, the prosecution and the judge also must agree not to have a jury.

The Supreme Court reverses the conviction of the "Scottsboro Boys"

1932

In Scottsboro, Alabama, nine African Americans known as the "Scottsboro Boys" have been convicted of rape and sentenced to death. The U.S. Supreme Court overturns their convictions in *Powell* v. *Alabama* because their attorney had been appointed on the morning of the trial and had no opportunity to investigate the case or put on a meaningful defense. In a second trial, the nine men again are convicted, despite testimony by one of the alleged victims there has been no rape. Once again the Supreme Court reverses their convictions because of the exclusion of African Americans from the jury. At a third trial, four of the men are again convicted, while a fifth pleads guilty. Charges against the other four are dropped.

The Supreme Court rejects secret trials

1948

A Michigan law allows judges to hold secret grand jury proceedings. Grand jury proceedings historically have been conducted in private, but a grand jury only has the power to indict someone to stand trial. However, in this case, the grand jury goes further, deciding the defendant's guilt, and sending him to jail. The U.S. Supreme Court in *In re Oliver,* overturns the conviction of a Michigan man who has been convicted and sentenced after such a secret hearing.

> GRAND JURY SUBPOENA
>
> **US DISTRICT COURT**
>
> You are hereby commanded to appear before the GRAND JURY – to testify against your friends.
>
> Rules of the Grand Jury:
> • Secret hearings – no lawyers or press allowed
> • Silence punished by 18 months in jail
> • There is no limit to what we can ask

The exclusion of jurors based on race is unconstitutional

1965

In *Swain* v. *Alabama,* the U.S. Supreme Court holds that prosecutors cannot use peremptory challenges to exclude jurors of a particular race (as it had ruled earlier about ethnic groups). The Court sets rules for proving that jurors have been stricken because of their race. Having few or no minority jurors is not proof enough. It is necessary to show that minority jurors in a certain community have been excluded over a series of trials or over a period of years before a constitutional violation can be found. The Court's ruling in *J.E.B* v. *Alabama* (1994) extends this provision to gender as well as race.

Reservations about the death penalty should not bar one from a jury

1968

A person who expresses reservations about the death penalty is not necessarily unfit to serve on a jury, the Supreme Court rules in *Witherspoon* v. *Illinois.* The Court holds that a prosecutor can "strike" a person from the jury "for cause" (that is, because of indications that the person cannot be fair) only if the potential juror cannot make an impartial decision about imposing the death penalty.

The Supreme Court relaxes the requirement of a twelve-member jury

1970

Although it is not specified in the Constitution, the Supreme Court in *Thompson* v. *Utah* (1898) rules that, just as in England, a jury must have twelve people when trying someone charged with a serious crime. However in *Williams* v. *Florida* (1970), the Supreme Court calls a twelve-member jury a "historical accident" and decides that what matters is if the jury's size will allow it to reach a fair decision. The Court finds that it makes sense to determine the jury's size by the seriousness of the crime.

TIMELINE

The Judicial Power—the Judiciary.

A court of justice.

Exclusion of ethnic groups from a jury is unconstitutional

1954

In *Hernandez* v. *Texas,* the U.S. Supreme Court rules that the exclusion of Mexican Americans from a jury, through the prosecutor's use of peremptory challenges (objections to certain potential jurors serving on a jury without any specific reason), violates the Fourteenth Amendment's requirement that all people be treated equally.

Pretrial publicity can jeopardize the right to an impartial jury

1961

If there has been an excessive amount of press coverage or other publicity before a defendant goes to trial, it may not be possible to find people to serve on a jury who have not prejudged the case. In *Irwin* v. *Dowd,* the U.S. Supreme Court rules that a criminal defendant is entitled to have a trial relocated to another community to make sure that the jury will be impartial.

The right to counsel is not dependent on the ability to pay

1963

Since 1938 the Supreme Court has ruled that the government has to provide counsel for defendants in federal court trials who cannot afford to pay for one. But the court does not extend this right to state trials until the landmark case of *Gideon* v. *Wainwright.* In *Argersinger* v. *Hamlin* (1972) the Court extends its *Gideon* ruling by specifying that a defendant found guilty, whether of a misdemeanor or a felony, cannot be sentenced to jail time unless offered an attorney at trial.

Jury trials are not required for juvenile offenders

1971

Although previous U.S. Supreme Court decisions afforded juvenile defendants many of the same constitutional protections as adults, in *McKeiver* v. *Pennsylvania,* the Court rules that juveniles do not have a Sixth Amendment right to a jury if tried in juvenile court.

Information in public court documents may be published

1975

In *Cox Broadcasting Corp.* v. *Cohn,* the U.S. Supreme Court rules that a state cannot prevent the news media from publishing or broadcasting the name of a rape victim in a criminal case, when the name has already been included in a court document available to the public.

Presidential order permits military trials of suspected terrorists

2001

Following the terrorist attacks on September 11, 2001, President George W. Bush signs a military order authorizing the government to detain noncitizens suspected of terrorism, and to try them before military tribunals. Civil liberties groups criticize the order, fearing that the accused might be held indefinitely without receiving a trial, and that trials could be held in secret, without the usual rules about the kind of evidence that is admissible.

Seventh & Eighth Amendments

—

(1791)

WHAT IT SAYS

[Seventh Amendment] In suits at common law, where the value in controversy shall exceed twenty dollars, the right of trial by jury shall be preserved, and no fact tried by a jury, shall be otherwise reexamined in any Court of the United States, than according to the rules of the common law.

[Eighth Amendment] Excessive bail shall not be required, nor excessive fines imposed, nor cruel and unusual punishments inflicted.

Henry Wirz, the Confederate officer who commanded the Andersonville prison camp, where thousands of Union army soldiers died, was tried by a military commission and hanged in Washington, D.C., on November 10, 1865. At that time, death by hanging was not considered "cruel and unusual punishment."

WHAT IT MEANS

The Seventh and Eighth Amendments add to the Constitution's protections for individuals in the judicial system. The Seventh Amendment guarantees a jury trial in common law—consisting of centuries of judicial precedents—civil cases such as personal injury cases arising from car accidents, disputes between corporations for breach of contract, or discrimination and employment cases. The parties in a federal civil trial have the right to have their case decided by a jury of their peers. In a civil case a plaintiff (who brings the suit) may obtain money damages or a court order preventing the defendant from engaging in certain conduct, but civil cases cannot send a defendant to jail. The Seventh Amendment has not been extended to the states, which may choose not to employ juries in civil cases.

In addition to defining what kinds of cases require a jury, the Seventh Amendment highlights the jury's role as "fact finder," and it imposes limits on the judge's ability to override the jury's conclusions. Under the common law, the jury hears the facts and decides the verdict, and the judge sets the penalty based on the jury's findings.

The Eighth Amendment deals with bail, the money that defendants pay in exchange for their release from jail before trial. This money is returned to the defendants when they appear at trial, but the government keeps the money if a defendant does not appear. Bail is an incentive for a defendant to remain in the area and participate in the trial. Bail also promotes the ideal of being "innocent until proven guilty," in that defendants are not punished with jail time prior to conviction and sentencing.

The Eighth Amendment ensures that bail cannot be excessive, set so high that only the richest defendants can afford it. However, the Supreme Court has identified certain circumstances in which courts can refuse bail entirely, such as when a defendant shows a significant risk of fleeing or poses a danger to the community.

The better-known component of the Eighth Amendment is its prohibition against "cruel and unusual" punishment. The phrase was originally intended to outlaw gruesome methods of punishment, such as torture or burning at the stake, but the courts have broadened it over the years to protect against punishments that are deemed too harsh for the particular crime. Eighth Amendment challenges to the death penalty have often focused on whether certain offenders, such as juveniles or the mentally retarded, should be subject to a sentence of death, and whether death sentences have been decided fairly or have been tainted by racial bias. The "cruel and unusual" provision has also been used to challenge grossly unsanitary or otherwise deficient prison conditions.

A JURY TRIAL FOR LANDLORDS

In 1969, a social worker in Wisconsin found an apartment for one of her clients, an African American woman named Julie Rogers. However the landlords, Leroy and Mariane Loether and Mrs. Anthony Perez, refused to rent to Rogers. Rogers believed they rejected her because she was African American. She brought a lawsuit under the newly enacted 1968 Fair Housing Act (FHA), a federal statute that makes it illegal to refuse to rent a home to someone because of that person's race, sex, familial status, or national origin.

The landlords asked the federal district court to grant them a jury trial in the case, but the court denied the request. The judge tried the case himself, and ruled that the defendants had violated the FHA and awarded Rogers $250 in punitive damages. The Court of Appeals for the Seventh Circuit reversed this ruling, and Rogers appealed to the U.S. Supreme Court. Because Rogers had in the meantime married and had taken her husband's last name, Curtis, the case is known as *Curtis* v. *Loether*.

The Supreme Court ruled unanimously that the landlords' request for a jury trial should have been granted. In an opinion written by Justice Thurgood Marshall, the Court reexamined the text of the Seventh Amendment, and considered what "common law" really meant. The justices rejected Mrs. Curtis's argument that the phrase excluded lawsuits brought under statutes. Instead, the Supreme Court found that the FHA's ban on housing discrimination was a rule against inflicting personal injury, which is a "legal" kind of claim, allowable at "common law." The Court additionally found that the monetary damages sought by the plaintiff were also "legal" in nature. Therefore, the Seventh Amendment's protections applied, and either party in an FHA case could demand a jury trial.

The *Curtis* decision required courts to take a close look at a statute's goals and then compare them to the kinds of claims over the years for which the right of trial by jury has been preserved.

Seventh & Eighth Amendments

Bail required for all criminal defendants

1789

Through the Judiciary Act of 1789, Congress establishes the federal judicial system. One of its provisions states that whenever an arrest occurs in a criminal case, bail *shall* be available, except if the crime is punishable by death. In those cases, bail *may* be available, if a judge decides that it is appropriate under the circumstances.

Execution by electrocution is not "cruel and unusual" punishment

---
1890

When New York State allows the use of the newly invented electric chair for executions, the U.S. Supreme Court, in *In re Kemmler*, rules that it is constitutional. Only if the chosen method of execution involves "torture or a lingering death" does it violate the Eighth Amendment.

Punishment must be appropriate to the crime

1910

An American officer in the government of the Philippines (then a U.S. territory) is found guilty of falsifying an official document and is sentenced to fifteen years in prison, hard labor, lifetime surveillance, and the loss of his civil rights. In *Weems* v. *United States,* the U.S. Supreme Court finds that this sentence amounts to "cruel and unusual" punishment because its length and harshness are out of proportion to the crime committed.

The death penalty is reinstated

1976

In three cases known together as *Gregg* v. *Georgia,* the U.S. Supreme Court rules that death penalty laws are constitutional when they include limitations on jury discretion, such as sentencing guidelines, "bifurcated" trials (meaning that the guilt versus innocence and sentencing phases of the trial are held separately), and a process for immediate appeal of a sentence of death. The ruling upholds many of the newly passed state death penalty laws and permits executions to resume.

The Eighth Amendment does not cover corporal punishment of students

---
1977

In *Ingraham* v. *Wright,* the U.S. Supreme Court refuses to find that the Eighth Amendment bars punishment of schoolchildren by "paddling." Based on the amendment's history and its language, the Court concludes that the amendment applies only to punishment of *criminal* offenses, not civil offenses such as breaking school rules.

Isolating prisoners can be "cruel and unusual" punishment

1978

Arkansas has a practice of placing prisoners in isolation cells for thirty-day periods as punishment for breaking prison rules. In *Hutto* v. *Finney,* the U.S. Supreme Court rules that it is "cruel and unusual" punishment. The Court bases its ruling not on the length of time that prisoners are isolated, but on the overall conditions in the prisons.

TIMELINE

Trial judges cannot make retrials conditional

> 1935

Seventh Amendment does not prevent "directed verdicts"

> 1943

Most death penalty statutes are declared unconstitutional

> 1972

A person is injured in an automobile accident in Massachusetts and brings suit against the other driver for negligence. At a jury trial he is awarded $500. Disappointed with that amount, he asks for a new trial on the grounds that the verdict was inadequate. The trial judge agrees to order a new trial, unless the other driver will consent to an increase in the damages to $1,500. When the second driver agrees, the judge denies another trial. The injured party then appeals. In the case of *Dimick* v. *Schiedt* (1935), the Supreme Court holds that, under the Seventh Amendment and the common law, the trial court lacked the power to make a new trial conditional on the consent of the defendant to an increase in the payment for damages.

In *Galloway* v. *United States,* the U.S. Supreme Court rules that federal judges can reject the verdict of the jury and direct that another verdict be entered (known as a "directed verdict") if the judge concludes that there is insufficient evidence to support the jury's decision. The minority angrily dissent from this ruling, arguing that it erodes a major portion of the Seventh Amendment's guarantee of a jury verdict.

The U.S. Supreme Court decides three cases known as a group by the name of *Furman* v. *Georgia,* finding that Georgia's death penalty statute, which gives juries complete discretion in sentencing, violates the Eighth Amendment, arguing that death penalties had been rendered in an arbitrary and discriminatory manner. This ends Georgia's death penalty and those in forty other states. Thirty-five states draft new death penalty laws to meet the Supreme Court's concerns. Some create sentencing guidelines for judges and juries. Some create a specific list of crimes for which the death penalty is mandated, and others draft a list of "aggravating" and "mitigating" factors to help judges and juries decide the appropriateness of the penalty in each case.

"Preventive detention" is found constitutional

> 1987

Jury trials are extended to copyright disputes

> 1998

Death penalty ruled out for juvenile offenders

> 2005

Concerned about an increase in crime, Congress passes the Bail Reform Act of 1984, which for the first time allows suspects to be detained solely on an appearance of dangerousness. In *United States* v. *Salerno,* the U.S. Supreme Court upholds the Bail Reform Act of 1984, finding that it does not violate the Eighth Amendment's prohibition against "excessive" bail. The Court rejects the defendant's argument that the only consideration in setting bail should be figuring out how much money will be enough to prevent a defendant from fleeing before trial. Instead, the Court finds that protection of the public also can be a basis for determining the level of bail, or even for denying bail entirely.

When a local television station owner falls behind in payments to broadcast such programs as *Who's the Boss?* and *T. J. Hooker,* Columbia Pictures ends its agreement with him. The station owner continues to show the programs, and Columbia sues for copyright infringement. Columbia wins this case and seeks payment for damages. The judge denies the station owner's request for a jury trial and conducts a bench trial (a trial heard by a judge without a jury).

Columbia is awarded the damages it seeks. The station owner appeals, and in *Feltner* v. *Columbia Pictures Television, Inc.* (1998), the Supreme Court rules that the station owner is guaranteed the right to a jury trial under the Seventh Amendment.

The Supreme Court, in *Roper* v. *Simmons,* strikes down state death penalty laws for those seventeen and younger as "cruel and unusual" punishment. The majority cites changing public opinion and notes that the United States stands "alone in a world that has turned its face against the juvenile death penalty." The decision will result in a new sentence for Christopher Simmons and likely new sentences for seventy-two juvenile offenders on state death rows at the time of the ruling.

Ninth
& Tenth
Amendments

(1791)

WHAT IT SAYS

[Ninth Amendment] The enumeration in the Constitution, of certain rights, shall not be construed to deny or disparage others retained by the people.

[Tenth Amendment] The powers not delegated to the United States by the Constitution, nor prohibited by it to the States, are reserved to the States respectively, or to the people.

A "death with dignity" campaign in Oregon resulted in a 1994 state law that enabled people with terminal illnesses to determine when to medically end their lives. Challenges to that law raised issues of states' rights under the Tenth Amendment.

WHAT IT MEANS

The Ninth Amendment offers a constitutional safety net, intended to make it clear that Americans have other fundamental rights beyond those listed in the Bill of Rights. The amendment was added out of concern that it would be impossible to mention every fundamental right, and dangerous to list just some of them for fear of suggesting that the list was complete. Because the rights protected by the amendment are not specified, they are referred to as "unenumerated" rights, as opposed to those enumerated in the Constitution. It is up to the courts to interpret through their decisions exactly what rights the amendment does and does not protect.

The Tenth Amendment was included in the Bill of Rights to preserve the balance of power between the federal government and the states. The amendment limits the federal government's power to just what is written in the Constitution. Those powers not listed are left to each of the states. The Tenth Amendment does not specify what those "powers" are, however, leaving room for dispute between the federal and state government and need for interpretation by the courts. At different times in American history the courts have been more or less restrictive in deciding what the federal government can do and what responsibilities fall to the states.

"This right of privacy, whether it is founded in the Fourteenth Amendment's concept of personal liberty and restrictions upon state action, as we feel it is, or . . . in the Ninth Amendment's reservation of rights to the people, is broad enough to encompass a woman's decision whether or not to terminate her pregnancy."

— Justice Harry A. Blackmun, *Roe* v. *Wade* (1973)

IS THERE A CONSTITUTIONAL RIGHT TO PRIVACY?

In November 1961, the executive director of the Planned Parenthood League of Connecticut, Estelle Griswold, was arrested along with a doctor from the one of the league's clinics for giving medical advice about contraceptives to married couples. They were charged under a Connecticut law that made it a crime to help someone to use contraceptives or to use contraceptives oneself.

They did not deny their guilt and were convicted and fined $100. But they appealed their convictions on the ground that the law violated the constitutional rights of the married couples whom they counseled. Griswold argued that married couples' right to "liberty" under the Fourteenth Amendment's due process clause should include the right to decide whether to use contraceptives to prevent pregnancy until they were ready to have children.

In *Griswold* v. *Connecticut* (1965), the U.S. Supreme Court found that there was a "right to privacy" within the Constitution, and that the ban on contraceptives for married couples violated

that right. Yet, nowhere in the Bill of Rights or any other amendments does the word "privacy" appear. Instead, the Court looked at the rights that *were* listed in the First, Third, and Fourth Amendments and concluded that privacy was a common theme running through many of them.

The Supreme Court agreed that the right of marital privacy fell within the "penumbra," or zone, of the guarantees that are included in the Bill of Rights collectively. The Court added that the Ninth Amendment specified that the Constitution's mention of specific rights did not "deny or disparage others retained by the people." In a concurring opinion, Justice Arthur Goldberg noted that the Ninth Amendment served as a reminder to the justices that they could not limit Americans' rights to only those explicitly listed in the Constitution. "The fact that no particular provision of the Constitution explicitly forbids the State from disrupting the traditional relation of the family—a relation as old and as fundamental as our entire civi-

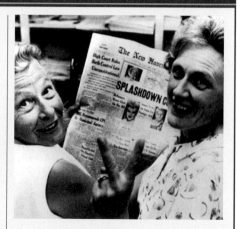

Estelle Griswold (left) and Cornelia Jahncke, President of the Planned Parenthood League of Connecticut, celebrate their victory in Griswold v. Connecticut.

lization—surely does not show that the Government was meant to have the power to do so," wrote Justice Goldberg. "Rather, as the Ninth Amendment expressly recognizes, there are fundamental personal rights such as this one, which are protected from abridgment by the Government though not specifically mentioned in the Constitution."

Ninth & Tenth Amendments

State resolutions seek to void federal laws

1798

Congressional passage of the Alien and Sedition Acts in 1798 dramatically increases the federal government's authority. In protest, Thomas Jefferson writes the Kentucky Resolutions, which are adopted by the Kentucky State Legislature. These resolutions argue that the states have the right to void federal legislation that they consider to go beyond the scope of Congress's constitutional authority. In 1799, the Virginia legislature enacts similar resolutions, known as the Virginia Resolutions, that were authored by James Madison.

The Supreme Court interprets federal powers broadly

1819

Under the leadership of Chief Justice John Marshall, the Supreme Court rules, in *McCulloch* v. *Maryland,* that Congress has the authority to charter a national bank, even though no such "power" is specifically delegated in the Constitution. With this broad interpretation of the federal government's authority, the Supreme Court sharply restricts the rights that were reserved to the states by the Tenth Amendment.

Federal power to regulate interstate commerce is interpreted narrowly

1918

A federal statute seeks to end child labor by prohibiting the interstate shipment of goods that child laborers had produced. In *Hammer* v. *Dagenhart,* known as the Child Labor Case, the U.S. Supreme Court rules that the statute goes beyond the powers the Constitution "delegated" to the federal government. The Court finds that under the Tenth Amendment, it is the right of the individual states to decide how to regulate the use of child labor in manufacturing.

Ninth Amendment supports a constitutional right to privacy

1965

In *Griswold* v. *Connecticut,* the U.S. Supreme Court strikes down a Connecticut law forbidding the use of contraceptives because it restricts the right of marital privacy. Although the Bill of Rights does not actually mention privacy, the Court concludes that it is a natural extension of the rights mentioned in the First, Third, and Fourth Amendments. The Court points to the Ninth Amendment as further evidence that a right does not need to be spelled out in the Constitution to be considered fundamental.

Abortion is included within the constitutional right to privacy

1973

In *Roe* v. *Wade,* the U.S. Supreme Court rejects a Texas law that outlaws abortion because it restricts the right to privacy. As in the *Griswold* case, the Court finds that even though the right to privacy is not specifically listed in the Bill of Rights, the Ninth Amendment allows "unenumerated" rights to be recognized as well.

The Ninth Amendment supports a right to attend criminal trials

1980

In *Richmond Newspapers, Inc.* v. *Virginia,* the U.S. Supreme Court holds that the public's right to attend criminal trials is guaranteed by the First and Fourteenth Amendments. Although that right is not specifically listed in the Constitution, the Court finds the history of the Bill of Rights makes its ruling proper.

TIMELINE

A CHILD LABOR REVOLUTION
NEWSPAPERS IN THE MINING REGION TELL OF THE NEW LAW'S RESULTS

Key New Deal legislation ruled unconstitutional

1935

To combat the Great Depression, Congress and the administration of Franklin D. Roosevelt establish the National Industrial Recovery Administration (known as the NRA). One of the New Deal's key programs, the NRA's provisions include requirements for minimum wages and maximum hours, and certain price controls. In *Schechter Corporation* v. *United States,* the U.S. Supreme Court rules that the NRA exceeds Congress's power to regulate interstate commerce and invades the states' rights to regulate manufacturing. Even an economic emergency such as the depression does not justify the federal government interference with the states' economic activities.

The Ninth Amendment does not limit government's rights

1936

Private individuals challenge a contract between the federal government and a local power company for construction of a dam. In *Ashwander* v. *Tennessee Valley Authority,* the U.S. Supreme Court supports the contract as constitutional because the government has acted within the scope of its war and commerce powers under the Constitution. The Court holds that the Ninth Amendment does not give to the people rights that were specifically given to the government elsewhere in the Constitution.

Tenth Amendment is no barrier to enacting labor laws

1941

In a switch from its earlier pro–states' rights rulings, particularly *Hammer* v. *Dagenhart,* the U.S. Supreme Court rules unanimously in *United States* v. *Darby* that the federal government acted within its authority in passing the Fair Labor Standards Act (FLSA). The Court finds that the law, which establishes numerous minimum wage and maximum labor standards nationwide, falls within Congress' authority to regulate interstate commerce.

Gun-Free School Zones Act is found unconstitutional

1995

In *United States* v. *Lopez,* the U.S. Supreme Court grants the states more rights. It rules that Congress overstepped its authority under the commerce clause when it passed the 1990 Gun-Free School Zones Act. To uphold a law that determined the punishment for gun possession and gun use near schools, the Court rules, would convert the commerce clause authority into general police power held only by the states under the Tenth Amendment.

Mandatory background checks are invalidated

1997

A federal gun control law, known as the Brady Law, imposes on local authorities the obligation to perform mandatory background checks of potential gun buyers. In *Printz* v. *United States,* the U.S. Supreme Court holds that the law violates the Tenth Amendment. The federal government cannot issue directives requiring the states to address particular problems, or command state officials to enforce a federal regulatory program. The Court reasons that such commands are "fundamentally incompatible with our constitutional system of dual sovereignty."

Violence against Women Act exceeds Congressional authority

2000

Legislation about domestic violence and family law had traditionally been left to the states. In *United States* v. *Morrison,* the U.S. Supreme Court strikes down a provision in the federal Violence against Women Act because it exceeds Congress's authority under the commerce clause and impinges on state control. A provision that permits victims of gender-based violence to bring federal lawsuits against their attackers is found to invade states' police power.

Eleventh Amendment

(1795)

The Judicial power of the United States shall not be construed to extend to any suit in law or equity, commenced or prosecuted against one of the United States by Citizens of another State, or by Citizens or Subjects of any Foreign State.

A REVOLUTIONARY WAR CLAIM

During the Revolutionary War, the British took Gideon Olmstead and four other American seamen prisoner. While onboard a British ship carrying a cargo of arms, Olmstead and the others seized their British captors and gained control of the ship. Later, stopped by a ship belonging to the Commonwealth of Pennsylvania, Olmstead and the British ship were brought to Philadelphia. Both Olmstead and Pennsylvania claimed they should get the British ship and its cargo. These conflicting claims sparked a dispute over which court—a state admiralty court or a federal appeals court—should decide the case.

A state admiralty court, after a jury trial, awarded the cargo to Pennsylvania. But a federal appeals court ordered that the cargo be sold and the money given to Olmstead. The state admiralty judge then ordered that the cargo be sold, but refused to give the money to Olmsted. Instead, the judge gave some of the money to David Rittenhouse, as treasurer of the state of Pennsylvania, who pledged to repay the money to the state court if ordered to do so when the dispute was settled.

After Rittenhouse died, Olmstead sued his estate. In a federal admiralty court, Judge Richard Peters found in favor of Olmstead. But then the state of Pennsylvania passed a law that claimed the money for itself and declared the federal ruling invalid. The state argued that the federal court could not rule on the case as the state was immune from suit under the Eleventh Amendment. Olmstead then sought a court order to carry out Judge Peters's ruling. In the case of *United States* v. *Peters,* the Supreme Court disagreed. Writing for the Court, Chief Justice John Marshall (above right) held that a state statute could not override the federal order. He ruled that the federal lawsuit, between Olmstead and Rittenhouse's heirs, did not involve the state and that the Eleventh Amendment did not bar the result.

But Marshall's decision did not end the matter. The ruling sparked an armed confrontation between Pennsylvania and the federal government. Pennsylvania governor Simon Snyder ordered the Pennsylvania militia to protect the Rittenhouse heirs and prevent the federal marshals from enforcing the Supreme Court's order to seize the money. When the federal marshal saw the guards in front of the heirs' home (known locally as Fort Rittenhouse) he climbed a back fence, entered the house from the rear, and seized the money. The general of the Pennsylvania militia was later indicted and convicted of obstructing justice (though President James Madison soon pardoned him) and Olmstead, at long last, received his money.

WHAT IT MEANS

After the U.S. Supreme Court ruled in 1793 that two South Carolina men could sue and collect debts from the state of Georgia, states'-rights advocates in Congress proposed what became the Eleventh Amendment. This amendment specifically prohibits federal courts from hearing cases in which a state is sued by individuals from another state or country. Protecting states from certain types of legal liability is known as "sovereign immunity."

As initially interpreted, the Eleventh Amendment did not bar suits against the states when a matter of federal law was at issue, nor did it prevent suits against a state by its own citizens. Over time, the Supreme Court has expanded its interpretation of the amendment to reflect a broader view that states were immune from all suits in federal courts without their agreement, which seemed unlikely.

The Eleventh Amendment refers to suits "in law or equity." In those cases where neither party in the suit has broken the law they can seek resolution through equity, by which the courts measure the fairness and justice of their claims.

> *"The sooner the limits which separate the two governments [federal and state] are marked by those authorities [the courts], which can define and establish them, the less danger there will be of serious, if not fatal collisions hereafter."*
>
> —Justice Bushrod Washington, *Golden* v. *Prince* (1814)

British naval vessels in combat off the coast of Portugal in 1780 took Gideon Olmstead prisoner. He was rescued by a ship from Pennsylvania. Later both Olmstead and the state of Pennsylvania sued to get the cargo of the captured ship; the Supreme Court ruled in United States v. Peters *that the Eleventh Amendment did not bar the federal courts from hearing the case.*

Eleventh Amendment

Federal courts have jurisdiction where state and federal laws conflict

1821

Two brothers from Norfolk, Virginia, sell tickets in their hometown for a lottery in Washington, D.C. Congress had set up the lottery only for people in Washington, and Virginia had a law banning some gaming. The Virginia Supreme Court rules that the Cohen brothers violated Virginia law by selling the tickets. When the brothers appeal and the case goes before the U.S. Supreme Court, Virginia argues that the federal courts have no power to review the conviction. The high court disagrees on the grounds that state laws or actions can violate federal laws or U.S. constitutional provisions and therefore can be reviewed in federal courts, but rules that the Virginia court decision was correct.

Eleventh Amendment does not protect state officials

1824

The state of Ohio passes a law that taxes the Bank of the United States when it does business within the state, but the U.S. Supreme Court finds that the tax is unconstitutional and orders that it cannot be enforced. A persistent state auditor, Ralph Osborn, goes ahead and collects the tax by seizing $100,000 from the federal bank. In *Osborn* v. *Bank of the United States*, the U.S. Supreme Court holds that Osborn can be ordered to return the money to the federal bank and that public officials acting on behalf of the state who knowingly committing an illegal act do not have the same constitutional protection enjoyed by states under the Eleventh Amendment.

Federal court cannot decide ownership of seized slaves

1828

A Spanish slave vessel, the *Isabelita*, owned by Juan Madrazo, is captured by a pirate ship and carried to Amelia Island off the Georgia coast. William Bowen buys the slaves and intends to take them to East Florida, then a province of Spain. But Georgia officials seize the slaves on the grounds that the law prohibits the importation of slaves. The governor of Georgia asks the federal district court for permission to sell the slaves, but the court of appeals rules against Georgia. Before the Supreme Court, Georgia argues that the federal court cannot award the money and slaves to Madrazo because the Eleventh Amendment bars the federal court from deciding a case in which a state is a party. The Supreme Court agrees and Georgia keeps the money and slaves and Madrazo keeps his ship.

A foreign country cannot sue a state in federal courts

1934

In the early 1830s, a number of Mississippi citizens purchase bonds from their home state. The heirs of the original bondholders, who are unable to collect on the bonds, give them, as a gift, to the Principality of Monaco. Although worthless to the Mississippi residents, they think that Monaco, as a foreign country, might be able to go to federal court to collect on the long overdue debt. Mississippi refuses to pay and argues that under the Eleventh Amendment the federal courts have no jurisdiction to hear the case. In *Principality of Monaco* v. *Mississippi,* the Court finds that the doctrine of sovereign immunity protects Mississippi from suits by foreign countries unless the state specifically consents to such a suit. No such consent is given.

States retain sovereign immunity when participating in welfare programs

1974

A group of people eligible for a welfare program administered by both the federal and state governments ask a federal court to order Illinois to comply with federal time limits in handing out grants. The lower courts ordered Illinois to comply with the federal time limits and to pay out grants that have been wrongfully withheld from recipients. Illinois appeals, claiming that its sovereign immunity under the Eleventh Amendment means that the federal courts cannot order it to pay the grants. In *Edelman* v. *Jordan,* the Supreme Court agrees that the state has not waived its immunity by participating in the joint federal-state welfare program.

State officials are ordered to turn over sunken treasure

1982

In 1622 the *Nuestra Senora de Atocha* sank forty nautical miles west of Key West, Florida. When a salvage company locates the wreck in the spring of 1971, Florida claims that the ship belongs to the state under Florida law. The U.S. Supreme Court rules that the boundary of Florida does not extend as far as the state asserts, and the federal government claims ownership of the salvaged property. The state argues that it cannot be sued for it due to the Eleventh Amendment. In *Florida Department of State* v. *Treasure Salvors,* the U.S. Supreme Court disagrees that the Eleventh Amendment prevents a direct action against the state, because the suit is directed only at state officials, who have no rightful ownership of the salvaged property.

TIMELINE

Citizens cannot take cases against their own states to federal court

The Supreme Court can resolve cases involving the federal government

States can be sued in federal courts over constitutional principles

1890 — 1892 — 1908

A Louisiana man buys bonds issued by the State of Louisiana in 1874. Six years later, when he goes to collect payments that he claims are owed to him, the state refuses to pay. Louisiana officials argue that a state law passed in the interim has nullified the state's obligation to pay the debt. In *Hans* v. *Louisiana,* the bondholder takes the case to federal court. The U.S. Supreme Court rules that a lawsuit against a state by one of its own citizens cannot be heard in federal court.

An 1821 treaty between the United States and Spain sets the boundary between the U.S. and Spanish territories. In 1845 Congress accepts Texas as a state if it meets certain conditions, including the designation of specific boundary lines. The Texas legislature and a federal land commission disagree over approximately 1.5 million acres on the southern border. The U.S. government brings suit against Texas in federal court. Texas argues that the Eleventh Amendment bars the U.S. courts from resolving the dispute. In *United States* v. *Texas,* the Supreme Court holds that the federal courts have jurisdiction in cases in which the U.S. government is a party.

The Minnesota legislature passes laws that reduce the rates that railroad companies can charge to carry passengers and cargo. Stockholders of the railroads file nine lawsuits in federal court against Minnesota officials, challenging the new rate schedules. In one of these cases, *Ex Parte Young,* the Supreme Court holds that it is proper to hear the case in federal court because it involves a federal question: whether the high fines deny the railroad stockholders due process of law (for taking property without a fair procedure in place). In such circumstances, the state is not immune from suit.

Residents may not sue their own state unless the state agrees to be sued

States are immune from charges filed with federal administrative agencies

1987 — 2002

Texas highway worker Jean Welch is injured while working on a ferry dock. She sues her employer, the state of Texas, in federal court. The U.S. Supreme Court rules, in *Welch* v. *Texas Department of Highways and Public Transportation,* that citizens cannot sue their own states in federal courts unless the state has passed a law allowing for citizens to sue. As no specific state law grants consent to sue, the worker's case is dismissed.

A gambling cruise asks South Carolina authorities for permission to dock in the state. South Carolina denies the request and the ship's owners file a complaint with the Federal Maritime Commission, which finds that states have immunity from prosecution in federal courts, but not executive branch agencies. Upon appeal, in *Federal Maritime Commission* v. *South Carolina State Ports Authority,* the U.S. Supreme Court reverses the commission's ruling. The Court holds that federal administrative agencies face the same restraints as the federal courts under the Eleventh Amendment.

Twelfth Amendment

(1804)

—

"I know indeed that some honest men fear that a Republican Government cannot be strong; that this Government is not strong enough. . . . I trust not. I believe this, on the contrary, the strongest Government on earth."

— President Thomas Jefferson,
first inaugural address, 1801

—

WHAT IT SAYS

The electors shall meet in their respective states, and vote by ballot for President and Vice-President, one of whom, at least, shall not be an inhabitant of the same state with themselves; they shall name in their ballots the person voted for, as President, and in distinct ballots the person voted for as Vice-President, and they shall make distinct lists of all persons voted for as President, and of all persons voted for as Vice-President, and of the number of votes for each, which lists they shall sign and certify, and transmit sealed to the seat of the government of the United States, directed to the President of the Senate;—The President of the Senate shall, in the presence of the Senate and House of Representatives, open all the certificates and the votes shall then be counted;—The person having the greatest Number of votes for President, shall be the President, if such number be a majority of the whole number of Electors appointed; and if no person have such majority, then from the persons having the highest numbers not exceeding three on the list of those voted for as President, the House of Representatives shall choose immediately, by ballot, the President. But in choosing the President, the votes shall be taken by states, the representation from each state having one vote; a quorum for this purpose shall consist of a member or members from two-thirds of the states, and a majority of all the states shall be necessary to a choice. [And if the House of Representatives shall not choose a President whenever the right of choice shall devolve upon them, before the fourth day of March next following, then the Vice-President shall act as President, as in the case of the death or other constitutional disability of the President.]* The person having the greatest number of votes as Vice-President, shall be the Vice-President, if such number be a majority of the whole number of Electors appointed, and if no person have a majority, then from the two highest numbers on the list, the Senate shall choose the Vice-President; a quorum for the purpose shall consist of two-thirds of the whole number of Senators, and a majority of the whole number shall be necessary to a choice. But no person constitutionally ineligible to the office of President shall be eligible to that of Vice-President of the United States.

Senate pages carry the electoral ballots to the House chamber where the ballots will be counted at a joint session of Congress. If no candidate receives a majority of electoral votes, the House chooses the President and the Senate selects the Vice President.

* Superseded by the Twentieth Amendment, Section 3.

WHAT IT MEANS

As the Electoral College was originally constituted, the candidate who received the most electoral votes became President and the runner-up became Vice President. With the rise of a two-party system, this meant that the President and Vice President might be chosen from different parties. This occurred in the election of 1796, when John Adams, a Federalist, received the most electoral votes, and his opponent, Thomas Jefferson, a Democratic-Republican, received the second largest electoral vote and became Vice President. In 1800, Jefferson ran for President on the Democratic-Republican ticket with Aaron Burr. They won, but both received the same number of electoral votes. With the Electoral College unable to cast a majority of votes for either of them, the election was thrown into the House of Representatives, where the Federalist Party still had a majority. After numerous attempts to reach a majority, the House finally elected Jefferson President and Burr Vice President.

The turmoil of the 1800 election urged the passing of the Twelfth Amendment, which solved this problem by allowing for separate Electoral College votes for President and Vice President, and by allowing the parties to nominate a team for President and Vice President. The Twelfth Amendment strongly suggests that the President and Vice President not be from the same state, as electors from that state cannot vote for both offices.

If the Electoral College fails to elect a President, the House of Representatives will select the new President from the top three candidates. The vote within the House is by state, not by representatives. Lastly, the Twelfth Amendment extends all the eligibility requirements for the President (a natural-born citizen, at least thirty-five years of age, who has resided in the United States for fourteen years) to the Vice President.

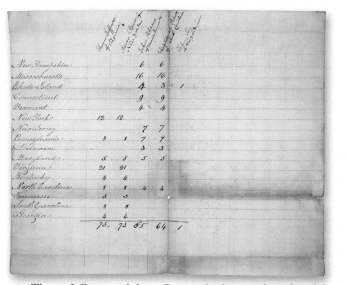

Running mates Thomas Jefferson and Aaron Burr received an equal number of electoral votes in 1800. The Federalist majority in the House of Representatives cast thirty-six ballots trying to choose between these two Democratic-Republican candidates until they finally elected Jefferson President and Burr Vice President. The Twelfth Amendment then revised the system of casting electoral ballots to prevent another tie vote.

THE ELECTORAL CRISIS OF 1876

The Presidential election of 1876 took place as the post–Civil War Reconstruction of the South was coming to an end. As federal troops withdrew from the South, Democrats replaced the Republicans, who had gained office in the South during Reconstruction. In three states, the secretaries of state of the outgoing Republican governments and the incoming Democratic governments each filed election certificates informing the federal govenment that their Presidential candidate had carried the state.

Although the Democratic candidate, Samuel J. Tilden, had won the popular vote, Republicans charged that many African Americans in the South had been kept from the polls by intimidation, and they refused to concede the election. Further complicating the process, Republicans held a majority in the Senate, while Democrats held a majority in the House. The Vice President had died, so the president pro tempore of the Senate, a Republican, would open the ballots. Republicans wanted him to count the Republican ballots, but Democrats objected. To break this stalemate, early in 1877, both parties agreed to an extra-constitutional compromise. They created a joint electoral commission composed of five senators, five representatives, and five Supreme Court justices to hear evidence and determine which electoral ballots to count. Seven commissioners were Republican, seven were Democrats, and one, a Supreme Court justice, was known to be independent. At the last minute, the independent justice resigned and the Supreme Court replaced him with a Republican justice.

The commission voted 8 to 7 to award all the disputed electoral ballots to the Republican candidate. The House and Senate then met in joint session, counted the ballots, and declared Rutherford B. Hayes President of the United States. Democrats reluctantly accepted the outcome on the understanding that Hayes had agreed to withdraw the rest of the federal troops from the southern states and end Reconstruction.

Twelfth Amendment

The Constitution establishes the Electoral College

1787

Rather than being elected directly by the people, Article II of the Constitution specifies that the President and Vice President will be elected by the Electoral College. Electors assemble in their states in January following the November election and vote for the Presidential candidate who won the majority of votes in their state. The candidate who receives the highest vote in the Electoral College becomes the President and the person with the next highest number of votes becomes the Vice President.

George Washington is unanimously elected President

1789

In the first Presidential election, General George Washington of Virginia receives one vote from each of the sixty-nine electors, making him the only President to achieve a unanimous vote in the Electoral College. As each elector casts two ballots without designating which is for President or Vice President, John Adams of Massachusetts, receiving the next highest number of electoral votes, is elected as Vice President. There are not yet any formal political parties.

Candidates from two parties are elected

1797

John Adams, running as a Federalist, receives the largest number of votes and is elected President. Thomas Jefferson, who ran against Adams as the Democratic-Republican candidate, receives the next highest vote and is elected Vice President. The two rivals disagree strongly over federal policies.

Jackson defeats Adams

1828

Galvanized by their anger over the previous presidential election, Jackson and his supporters mount an intense campaign against President John Quincy Adams, who is defeated for reelection. This time, in a two-person race, Jackson wins both the majority of the popular and electoral votes and ousts Adams from the Presidency.

FIRST CAPITOL INAUGURATION · 1829

The Senate elects a Vice President

1837

A number of Democrats oppose the choice of Richard Mentor Johnson to run for Vice President on the ticket with Martin Van Buren. When the members of the Electoral College cast their ballots, Van Buren receives 170 electoral votes and is duly elected President. But Johnson receives only 147 electoral votes, more than his closest contender, but one less than the majority needed for his election. Under the Constitution, the Vice Presidential election then goes to the U.S. Senate. With forty-nine of the fifty-two senators present and voting along party lines, Johnson receives 33 votes, which is enough for the Senate to declare that he has been elected Vice President of the United States.

An electoral commission decides the Presidential election

1877

On Election Day, Democrat Samuel Tilden wins the popular vote by a margin of less than 250,000 votes (out of 8.5 million votes cast) against Republican Rutherford B. Hayes. But, Tilden's 184 electoral votes are 1 short of the necessary majority, while Hayes's 165 electoral votes leave him 20 votes shy of winning the Presidency. Several of the southern states, under Reconstruction rule, submit two slates of electors, one for Tilden and the other for Hayes. Because Republicans control the Senate and Democrats hold the majority in the House, they cannot reach agreement on which ballots to count. They establish an Electoral Commission, composed of senators, representatives, and Supreme Court justices. Voting on party lines, the commission awards all the disputed electors to Hayes, giving him a one-vote victory in the Electoral College, and the Presidency.

TIMELINE

VOTERS HERE ↓

The House of Representatives votes to break an electoral tie

1801

In the Presidential election of 1800, Thomas Jefferson runs for President and Aaron Burr for Vice President on the Democratic-Republican ticket. Both get 73 votes in the Electoral College. This forces the election into the House of Representatives, where the Federalist Party holds the majority. Opposition to Jefferson causes many Federalists to vote for Burr. Repeatedly casting ballots, the House is unable to reach a majority for any candidate until former treasury secretary Alexander Hamilton intervenes with Federalists and persuades them to vote for Jefferson on the thirty-seventh ballot. This event spurs demand for the Twelfth Amendment.

An elector changes his vote

1820

During the Era of Good Feelings, when only one political party exists, President James Monroe runs unopposed for reelection in 1820. Former senator William Plumer of New Hampshire casts his electoral vote for John Quincy Adams rather than for Monroe, to whom he is pledged. Otherwise, Monroe would have received a unanimous vote in the Electoral College. Plumer says he feels that only George Washington deserves a unanimous election.

The popular vote is overridden by the Electoral College

1824

For the first time the winner of the popular vote does not become the President. In a multiple candidate race, Andrew Jackson receives 41 percent of the popular vote, more than his opponents but less than a majority. Four candidates receive electoral votes, but none has enough to constitute a majority. The House of Representatives then meets to decide the winner. House rules call for a vote on the top three contenders from the Electoral College, Speaker Henry Clay, who comes in fourth, is removed from consideration. Clay throws his support to John Quincy Adams, who has come in second to Jackson. When the House picks Adams as President, Adams appoints Clay secretary of state. Jackson and his supporters call this a "corrupt bargain."

The electoral college reverses the popular vote

1888

Running for reelection, the Democratic incumbent President Grover Cleveland wins the popular vote by 90,596 votes (out of 11.3 million votes cast). But Cleveland loses the Electoral College vote to the Republican candidate Benjamin Harrison. Cleveland accepts the outcome, but comes back to defeat Harrison in 1892.

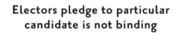

Electors pledge to particular candidate is not binding

1952

In the case of *Roy* v. *Blair,* the United States Supreme Court holds that a state cannot constitutionally require its electors to vote for the candidates to whom they are pledged. There have been at least four instances in which individual electors failed to vote for their party's candidate. The first occurred after the 1820 election, then 1956, 1960, and 1968, each peculiar to the wishes of an individual elector. None of these instances affected the election's outcome.

Presidential election of 2000 is disputed

2000

Vice President Al Gore, the Democratic candidate for President, wins the popular vote by a half-million vote margin, but the outcome of the Electoral College vote depends on the state of Florida, which gives a slim margin to the Republican candidate, Texas governor George W. Bush. A machine recount confirms Bush's lead, but Gore protests significant voting irregularities and calls for more extensive recounting by hand. The Florida Supreme Court supports Gore's position, but the U.S. Supreme Court overturns that decision, clearing the way for Bush to become President.

Thirteenth Amendment

(1865)

"I do order and declare that all persons held as slaves within said designated States, and parts of States, are, and henceforward shall be free; and that the Executive government of the United States, including the military and naval authorities thereof, will recognize and maintain the freedom of said persons."

— Abraham Lincoln,
Emancipation Proclamation
(1863)

WHAT IT SAYS

Section 1. Neither slavery nor involuntary servitude, except as a punishment for crime whereof the party shall have been duly convicted, shall exist within the United States, or any place subject to their jurisdiction.

Section 2. Congress shall have power to enforce this article by appropriate legislation.

THE CONSTITUTION PROPELS THE CIVIL RIGHTS MOVEMENT

Joseph Lee Jones and his wife, Barbara Jo, were employees of the Veterans Administration. In 1966 they wanted to purchase a new home in the Paddock Woods subdivision in St. Louis County, Missouri. Paddock Woods was being developed by the Alfred H. Mayer Company, which planned to divide the land into one hundred lots and build homes on them.

The Joneses visited Paddock Woods, toured a model house, and informed the real estate agent handling the offering that they wanted to buy one of the houses. But because Mr. Jones was an African American, the agent refused to consider his purchase offer. The Joneses sued the company, charging that it had taken its actions solely on the basis of race. This violated the 1866 Civil Rights Act, which made it illegal to refuse to sell property to people because of the color of their skin. They did not seek money damages, just a court order that the real estate developer could not refuse to sell them a house.

Missouri and other southern states had passed laws that made it difficult for African Americans to buy property, and the question was whether the Fourteenth Amendment had made these laws unconstitutional. A lower court dismissed Jones's lawsuit on the grounds that there were no precedents for applying constitutional restrictions on government actions to private conduct. Nor did the federal law prohibit a private company from refusing to sell its property to African Americans. However, in *Jones* v. *Alfred H. Mayer*, the Supreme Court reversed this ruling. The justices pointed out that nothing in the language of the Civil Rights Act said that the federal law only applied to government actions, and that nothing in the history of the passage of the law suggested that Congress intended it to contain an exception for private property owners.

Moreover, the Supreme Court found that the Thirteenth Amendment had granted Congress the power to pass the Civil Rights Act. The amendment specifically abolished slavery and involuntary servitude and gave Congress the power to pass all laws necessary to enforce the amendment. One of the factors that separated slaves from free people was that slaves were not allowed to own property, because they themselves were considered property. The Supreme Court concluded that the Civil Rights Act was intended to remove such badges of slavery. As long as African American citizens who wanted to buy or rent a home could be turned away simply because they were not white, the Supreme Court declared they "cannot be said to enjoy the same right as is enjoyed by white citizens to purchase and lease real and personal property."

WHAT IT MEANS

In 1863, President Abraham Lincoln issued the Emancipation Proclamation based on his war powers. It freed the slaves held within the Southern states that were in rebellion against the United States. The proclamation did not address the issue of slaves held in the border states that remained within the Union. Following the end of the war, Congress passed a constitutional amendment to end slavery throughout the United States. Submitted to the states, it was speedily ratified.

Although the Supreme Court initially had doubts over whether the amendment covered anyone other than African Africans who had been enslaved, it later held, in the Slaughterhouse Cases (1872), that it would apply to "Mexican peonage or the Chinese coolie labor system" or any other system of forced labor. The courts have also ruled that the Thirteenth Amendment forbids "peonage," the practice of forcing people to work to pay off their debts against their will. But the Supreme Court has rejected claims that mandatory community service, taxation, and the military draft are involuntary servitude under the Thirteenth Amendment.

President Lincoln's secretary, John G. Nicolay, sent him this telegram in January 1865 announcing that the House had just voted in favor of the Thirteenth Amendment, ending slavery. Constitutional amendments require two-thirds vote of approval in both houses of Congress.

When the U.S. House of Representatives passed the Thirteenth Amendment in 1865, ending slavery, cheers erupted in the chamber. The Emancipation Proclamation had freed only some of the slaves; the Thirteenth Amendment freed them all.

Thirteenth Amendment

President Lincoln issues the Emancipation Proclamation

1863

During the Civil War, President Lincoln issues the Emancipation Proclamation, declaring that all persons held as slaves in areas under rebellion are free from that point forward. The proclamation does not cover areas loyal to the Union. Lincoln uses his war powers as President to issue the proclamation, but members of Congress call for a constitutional amendment.

Congress passes the Peonage Act

1867

The Peonage Act is written to enforce the Thirteenth Amendment's ban on "involuntary servitude." Under this law, no one in the United States can be forced to work against his or her will even if one person is indebted to another. In addition to physically restraining or harming someone, the use of threats to get someone to work is also illegal. This law does not apply to prisoners convicted of a crime.

Civil Rights Act of 1875 declared unconstitutional

1883

The U.S. Supreme Court strikes down the Civil Rights Act of 1875, which makes it a crime for the operators of hotels, theaters, and other public accommodations to discriminate on the basis of race. The Court holds that Congress does not have the power to enact this broad ban on the actions of a private person or business. The law cannot be justified under the Thirteenth Amendment because the amendment only bars slavery and involuntary servitude. The Court reasons that refusing to allow blacks to use hotels, restaurants, or other public accommodations is not a "badge of slavery."

The military draft is not involuntary servitude

1918

In several consolidated cases, known as *Arver* v. *United States,* men who have been drafted into the military during the First World War challenge the government's action as a violation of the Thirteenth Amendment. The Supreme Court finds that the Thirteenth Amendment does not protect citizens from mandatory military service in times of war.

Striking workers can be made to return to work

1949

In *UAW* v. *Wisconsin Employment Relations Board,* the Supreme Court decides that court orders requiring striking workers in labor disputes to return to work do not violate the Thirteenth Amendment. The Court finds that as workers have the right to quit their jobs, no involuntary servitude exists.

Thirteenth Amendment is used to protect against racial discrimination

1968

In *Jones* v. *Mayer,* the Supreme Court upholds an 1866 law that gives all persons regardless of race the right to buy and sell property. The Court holds that Congress has the power under the Thirteenth Amendment to prohibit private businesses from discriminating against people of color. The Court declares that The freedom that Congress is empowered to secure under the Thirteenth Amendment includes the freedom to buy whatever a white man can buy, the right to live wherever a white man can live. If Congress cannot say that being a free man means at least this much, then the Thirteenth Amendment made a promise the nation cannot keep.

TIMELINE

Labor contracts are not considered involuntary servitude

1897

Sailors working on the commercial ship the *Arago* in California find themselves in jail when they try to quit. Local marshals bring them back to the ship and force them back to work. The sailors sue, claiming that the forced labor is a violation of the Thirteenth Amendment's ban on involuntary servitude. But, in *Robertson* v. *Baldwin,* the Supreme Court rules that there has not been a Thirteenth Amendment violation. The men had all signed employment contracts, so their labor is not "forced" and they have an obligation to complete the work they have contracted to do.

Laws allowing forced labor are found unconstitutional

1903

In a series of cases known as the Peonage Cases, the Supreme Court declares unconstitutional an Alabama law that allows landowners to force farmers to work off their debts or face criminal charges and possible prison. A number of sharecroppers (farmers who rent the land they farm) who have fallen behind in their payments to the landowners challenge the law as a violation of the Thirteenth Amendment. The Supreme Court agrees that this is involuntary servitude because the farmers are prevented from seeking other employment and thereby finding alternative ways of paying the debt.

Obligating convicts to work off fines is involuntary servitude

1914

In *United States* v. *Reynolds,* the Supreme Court finds unconstitutional an Alabama law that allows people to pay off the fines of someone convicted of a misdemeanor, thus freeing the convict from jail, on the condition that the convict works to pay off the debt. Finding that the law allows for "involuntary servitude," the Court notes that the work required to pay the debt can be harsher than if the convict had been sentenced to imprisonment at hard labor in the first place.

A baseball player sues over being traded without his consent

1972

Curt Flood, one of baseball's top players, is traded to the Philadelphia Phillies without his consent and is not allowed to shop his talents to other teams in the league. Because Flood had the option to quit playing baseball altogether, the Supreme Court in *Flood* v. *Kuhn* denies his claim that the trade violates the Thirteenth Amendment's prohibition on involuntary servitude.

Mandatory "community service" in schools is not involuntary servitude

1993

In *Steirer* v. *Bethlehem Area School District,* a U.S. court of appeals rules that a high school community service requirement does not constitute involuntary servitude prohibited by the Thirteenth Amendment. Growing numbers of school districts thereafter add community service to the requirements needed for a high school diploma.

Bush signs national security directive against human trafficking

2003

Calling human trafficking "a modern day form of slavery," President George W. Bush signs a directive to crack down on those who deal in the buying and selling of people (usually in the sex trade industry) both here and abroad. The executive order establishes the cabinet-level President's Interagency Task Force to Monitor and Combat Trafficking in Persons.

Fourteenth Amendment

(1868)

The Charleston Mercury *distributed this broadside announcing that South Carolina had seceded from the Union in December 1860. The Constitution did not provide for secession, and the Northern states fought to preserve the Union.*

WHAT IT SAYS

Section 1. All persons born or naturalized in the United States and subject to the jurisdiction thereof, are citizens of the United States and of the State wherein they reside. No State shall make or enforce any law which shall abridge the privileges or immunities of citizens of the United States; nor shall any State deprive any person of life, liberty, or property, without due process of law; nor deny to any person within its jurisdiction the equal protection of the laws.

Section 2. Representatives shall be apportioned among the several States according to their respective numbers, counting the whole number of persons in each State, excluding Indians not taxed. But when the right to vote at any election for the choice of electors for President and Vice-President of the United States, Representatives in Congress, the Executive and Judicial officers of a State, or the members of the Legislature thereof, is denied to any of the male inhabitants of such State, being twenty-one years of age, and citizens of the United States, or in any way abridged, except for participation in rebellion, or other crime, the basis of representation therein shall be reduced in the proportion which the number of such male citizens shall bear to the whole number of male citizens twenty-one years of age in such State.

Section 3. No person shall be a Senator or Representative in Congress, or elector of President and Vice President, or hold any office, civil or military, under the United States, or under any State, who, having previously taken an oath, as a member of Congress, or as an officer of the United States, or as a member of any State legislature, or as an executive or judicial officer of any State, to support the Constitution of the United States, shall have engaged in insurrection or rebellion against the same, or given aid or comfort to the enemies thereof. But Congress may by a vote of two-thirds of each House, remove such disability.

Section 4. The validity of the public debt of the United States, authorized by law, including debts incurred for payment of pensions and bounties for services in suppressing insurrection or rebellion, shall not be questioned. But neither the United States nor any State shall assume or pay any debt or obligation incurred in aid of insurrection or rebellion against the United States, or any claim for the loss or emancipation of any slave; but all such debts, obligations and claims shall be held illegal and void.

Section 5. The Congress shall have power to enforce, by appropriate legislation, the provisions of this article.

WHAT IT MEANS

Although it was created primarily to deal with the civil rights issues that followed the abolition of slavery, the Fourteenth Amendment has affected a broad range of American life, from business regulation to civil liberties to the rights of criminal defendants. Over time, the Supreme Court has interpreted the amendment to apply most of the guarantees of the Bill of Rights to the states as well as the federal government. The amendment contained three new limitations on state power: states shall not violate citizen's privileges or immunities or deprive anyone of life, liberty, or property without due process of law, and must guarantee all persons equal protections by the law. These limitations on state power dramatically expanded the reach of the U.S. Constitution.

Fulfilling its original purpose, the Fourteenth Amendment made it clear that everyone born in the United States, including a former slave, was a citizen. This voided the Supreme Court's ruling in *Dred Scott* v. *Sandford* (1857), which had asserted that African Americans were not citizens, and therefore were not entitled to constitutional rights. Yet, for a century after the ratification of the Fourteenth Amendment, the Supreme Court believed that racial segregation did not violate the "equal protection of the laws" provision in the amendment as long as equal facilities were provided for all races. This attitude changed dramatically in 1954 when the justices concluded that the intent of the Fourteenth Amendment made racially segregated schools unconstitutional. The Court has gradually adopted a much broader interpretation of the amendment that extends greater protection to women, minorities, and noncitizens.

Black delegates participated in the convention that drafted a new constitution for Virginia after the Civil War. The Reconstruction Act of 1867 required that all former Confederate states write new constitutions.

"Due process has not been reduced to any formula; its content cannot be determined by reference to any code. The best that can be said is that through the course of this Court's decisions it has represented the balance which our Nation built upon postulates of respect for the liberty of the individual, has struck between that liberty and the demands of organized society."

— Justice John Marshall Harlan,
dissenting opinion,
Poe v. *Ullman* (1961)

The Fourteenth Amendment also specified that all adults must be counted for purposes of apportioning the House of Representatives, thereby voiding the "three-fifths" clause of the original Constitution. Ironically, this provision increased the number of representatives for the former Confederate states when they reentered the Union. By the twentieth century, this provision also justified the Supreme Court's insistence that state legislative bodies and the U.S. House of Representatives be apportioned equally. The amendment also addressed concerns about the number of Confederates seeking to serve in Congress after the Civil War. Former Confederate federal and state officials and military personnel were required to take an oath of loyalty to the United States. The former Confederate states were also prohibited from repaying the Confederate debts or compensating former slave owners for the property they lost with the abolition of slavery.

Finally, the last section of the amendment gave Congress the power to enforce all the provisions within the whole amendment. Under this provision, Congress passed the Civil Rights Act of 1964, the Voting Rights Act of 1965, sections of other civil rights legislation that protect women's rights, and the Americans with Disabilities Act, affording equal treatment for disabled people.

Over time, the Supreme Court has interpreted the Fourteenth Amendment's due process clause to incorporate (or apply) many of the guarantees of the Bill of Rights to the states, as well as to the federal government. The concept of incorporation has dealt mostly with such "fundamental" rights as freedom of speech, press, religion, assembly, and petition. Because the Court has not held the states subject to some of the other provisions of the Bill of Rights, such as the right to bear arms or the right to a trial by jury in civil cases, its approach has been called "partial incorporation."

Accompanied by other woman suffrage advocates, Victoria Woodhull advocated their cause before members of the House Judiciary Committee on January 11, 1871. Woodhull, the editor of a weekly newspaper that promoted equal rights, argued that the Fourteenth Amendment's guarantee of the privileges of citizenship should include women's right to vote. The next year the Equal Rights Party nominated Woodhull for president, but she was stopped when she tried to cast a ballot.

EQUAL PROTECTION OF THE LAW

As Congress contended with President Andrew Johnson over the post–Civil War Reconstruction of the South, it created a Joint Committee on Reconstruction to consider legislation that would protect the "freedmen," as newly freed African Americans were called. Members of the joint committee considered various options, among them stripping political rights from former Confederate leaders and giving southern blacks the right to vote. They felt they needed to act promptly as the abolition of slavery had voided the Constitution's "three-fifths compromise" and would increase the South's representation in the House and its weight in the Electoral College. Some northerners feared that the South would rally to elect Robert E. Lee as President.

The joint committee considered a constitutional amendment that would have excluded anyone denied the right to vote because of race from being counted for purposes of congressional representation. But they soon realized that states could get around this formula by instituting literacy tests, poll taxes, and other discriminatory devices that could be presented as "race neutral." Representative John A. Bingham, a member of the joint committee, then drafted another proposal to extend the "equal protection of life, liberty, and property" to all citizens. This was the seed of the Fourteenth Amendment, which was expanded, debated, and revised until passed by the House and Senate.

Woman suffrage advocates were upset with the Fourteenth Amendment's reference to "male inhabitants," marking the first time that the distinction "male" appeared in the Constitution. They believed that gender equality was being sacrificed for racial equality. But, others perceived that the amendment had broader implications than its obvious intention of protecting the freedmen. They believed that the amendment's equal protection clause would apply to women as well as to men, to Indians, and to immigrants. They also believed that the amendment would at last apply the guarantees of the Bill of Rights to the states as well as to the federal government. They left the ultimate interpretation to the federal courts, however, and it would take another century before the courts embraced such an expansive view of the Fourteenth Amendment.

Fourteenth Amendment

The Bill of Rights applies only to the federal government

1833

Although one of James Madison's original amendments would have applied the Bill of Rights to the states, the Senate rejected it on the grounds that the states protect rights in their own constitutions. In the case of *Barron* v. *Baltimore* (1833), the Supreme Court reiterates this by arguing that the Fifth Amendment and other portions of the Bill of Rights apply only to the federal government.

State regulation of business does not violate the Fourteenth Amendment

1873

A group of butchers in New Orleans sue when the state gives monopoly rights to a single slaughterhouse. In a 5-to-4 decision, the justices rule in the Slaughterhouse Cases that the due process and equal protection provisions of the amendment do not limit state powers to regulate business. The dissenters on the Court argue for a broader interpretation of the Fourteenth Amendment as a safeguard against state violations of personal rights and due process.

The interpretation of the Fourteenth Amendment is broadened

1882

Concerned about increasing state regulation, corporations seek to overturn the Supreme Court's decision in the Slaughterhouse Cases. Former U.S. senator Roscoe Conkling, who had been one of the authors of the Fourteenth Amendment, argues in *San Mateo County* v. *Southern Pacific Railroad Company* that the Amendment's phrase "any person" also applies to a corporation. Therefore, the county's efforts at regulation violate the railroad's right to "substantive due process." The Court accepts this line of reasoning, frustrating state and federal governments' efforts to regulate business practices for the next half century.

Equal protection guarantees one person, one vote

1962

In many state legislatures, rural districts have far fewer voters than densely packed urban districts, yet each district has the same number of representatives. In *Baker* v. *Carr,* the U.S. Supreme Court orders federal courts to consider suits that challenge the apportionment of state legislatures, arguing that legislative bodies that are not apportioned equally violate the equal protection clause of the Fourteenth Amendment. All legislative bodies (except the U.S. Senate) are held to a standard of one person, one vote, so that all districts in a legislative body must represent roughly the same number of constituents.

The Supreme Court broadens the incorporation doctrine

1963

When a man in Florida is convicted after being denied an attorney—because he cannot afford to hire one—he petitions the Supreme Court. The case *Gideon* v. *Wainwright* (1963) results in a ruling in which the Court asserts that the Fourteenth Amendment embraces the fundamental principles of liberty and justice that lie at the base of all our civil and political institutions. Writing for the majority, Justice Hugo Black reasons that the due process provisions of the Fourteenth Amendment mean that the states are not immune from the Bill of Rights.

The Fourteenth Amendment protects a right to privacy

1964

In striking down a Connecticut law that prohibits the sale of contraceptives, the U.S. Supreme Court, in *Griswold* v. *Connecticut,* cites the Fourteenth Amendment as one of the amendments supporting its decision that the Constitution gives Americans a right to privacy.

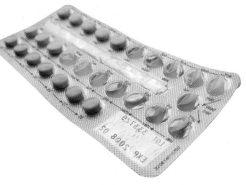

TIMELINE

Jim Crow laws are accepted as constitutional

1896

In response to efforts in the southern states to segregate people by race—"Jim Crow" laws and practices—Congress passes the Civil Rights Act of 1875, which guarantees equal rights to all citizens in all public places. When African Americans are denied equal accommodations they sue, but in 1883 the Supreme Court rules that the Fourteenth Amendment deals with discrimination by the states, not by individuals. Then in *Plessy* v. *Ferguson,* the Court upholds a Louisiana law that segregates railroad cars, reasoning that if the law provides equal accommodations it does not violate the Fourteenth Amendment.

The Supreme Court upholds minimum wage laws

1937

For decades, the Supreme Court strikes down reforms designed to aid women and children workers on the grounds that these laws impair the freedom of contract under the Fourteenth Amendment. After California enacts a minimum wage for women workers, Elsie Parrish sues a hotel company for paying her less than this minimum wage. The Supreme Court upholds the state law by noting that the Constitution does not mention the freedom of contract, that all liberties are subject to due process, and that employers and employees are not equally free when it comes to negotiating work agreements.

School segregation is found unconstitutional

1954

Since *Plessy* v. *Ferguson,* the courts have accepted racial segregation as long as all races are treated equally. In many states, schools for whites and African Americans are separate but far from equal in funding and equipment. In  *Brown* v. *Board of Education of Topeka, Kansas,* the Supreme Court concludes that school segregation denies students the equal protection of the laws. The Court orders schools to integrate "with all deliberate speed."

English literacy tests cannot ban otherwise qualified voters

1966

As citizens of the United States, Puerto Ricans who moved to New York State seek to vote, but the state requires them to pass an English-language literacy test. Some file suit on the grounds that this law violates the Voting Rights Act  of 1965. In *Katzenbach* v. *Morgan* the Supreme Court cites the Fourteenth Amendment's equal protection clause in upholding the Voting Rights Act, and stipulates that those who have achieved at least a sixth-grade education in Puerto Rico cannot be denied the right to vote.

U.S. citizens have a right to challenge being held as an enemy combatant

2004

The U.S. government believes that Yaser Esam Hamdi, an American citizen, has taken up arms to support the Taliban, the radical regime in Afghanistan. After U.S. forces overthrow the Taliban, Hamdi is seized and detained in Guantanamo Bay, and later transferred to a prison in Charleston, South Carolina. By calling Hamdi an enemy combatant, the Defense Department asserts that it can hold him indefinitely without trial. In *Hamdi* v. *Rumsfeld,* the U.S. Supreme Court disagrees, finding that due process demands that any U.S. citizen held in the United States be given a meaningful opportunity to contest the basis for that detention.

Execution of juveniles is ruled unconstitutional

2005

In a 5-to-4 decision in the case of *Roper* v. *Simmons,* the U.S. Supreme Court rules that executing juveniles who were under eighteen at the time they committed a capital crime is a violation of the Eighth and Fourteenth Amendments to the Constitution. The majority cites "evolving" social attitudes in the United States, where thirty states have banned the execution of juveniles, and around the world, where all but five other nations have also prohibited it.

Fifteenth Amendment

(1870)

WHAT IT SAYS

Section 1. The right of citizens of the United States to vote shall not be denied or abridged by the United States or by any State on account of race, color, or previous condition of servitude.

Section 2. The Congress shall have power to enforce this article by appropriate legislation.

A triumphant poster commemorates the Fifteenth Amendment with scenes depicting the advancement of African Americans since emancipation. The Fifteenth Amendment was the last of the three Reconstruction Amendments.

THE FIFTEENTH AMENDMENT.
CELEBRATED MAY 19TH 1870

WHAT IT MEANS

The Fifteenth Amendment prohibits the use of race in determining who can vote. The last of the three Reconstruction Era amendments, ratified shortly after the Civil War, the Fifteenth Amendment sought to advance the civil rights and liberties of the freed slaves and other African Americans. Section 2 of the amendment gave Congress the power to enforce it, by establishing federal legislation that ensures racial equality in voting.

The ratification of the Fifteenth Amendment in 1870 initially resulted in African Americans voting and holding office in many southern states. Later in the nineteenth century, these states imposed poll taxes, literacy tests, and other tactics to keep African Americans from voting. The ratification of the Twenty-fourth Amendment in 1964, and the passage of the Voting Rights Act of 1965, along with a number of Supreme Court decisions, have once again guaranteed voting rights as the Fifteenth Amendment envisioned.

Two college students assist a Mississippi woman in registering to vote during the "Freedom Summer" of 1965. The Fifteenth Amendment provided that the right to vote should not be restricted on account of race.

THE VOTING RIGHTS ACT OF 1965

Members of the NAACP in Detroit held a mock funeral for "Jim Crow," the symbol of racial segregation. Despite the Reconstruction Amendments, the Supreme Court had ruled in 1896 that "separate but equal" was constitutional.

By 1965, a century after the Civil War, African Americans in the South still faced barriers to the right to vote, despite the Fifteenth Amendment's guarantee. They were registered to vote in far smaller numbers than whites. When they attempted to register, discrimination and intimidation prevented them. The National Association for the Advancement of Colored People (NAACP) and the federal government pursued a strategy of suing for voting rights in individual cases, but these cases did not have as far-reaching an effect as

they had hoped. Only national legislation could achieve equality in voting rights.

President Lyndon B. Johnson was inspired to push for voting rights legislation when, in March 1965, a group of courageous African Americans marched from Selma, Alabama, to the state capital of Montgomery on behalf of voting rights. The marchers had gone only a few blocks when state troopers attacked them with clubs and tear gas. The Reverend Martin Luther King Jr. arrived to lead a much larger demonstration of African Americans and whites from across the nation determined to continue the march. A court issued an injunction that protected the right of the marchers to petition the government about their grievances. With this injunction, the marchers were allowed to cross the Pettus Bridge in Selma, in full view of television cameras from the national networks. As the marchers made their way to Montgomery their numbers swelled and the nation's attention was drawn to the struggle for voting rights in the South. Coupled with the violent murder of three civil rights workers during the previous Freedom Summer, when African American and white students from the South and North worked to register southern African

American voters, the Selma March demonstrated to the nation the unfair and unconstitutional treatment of African Americans in the South.

President Johnson told the nation that "every American citizen must have an equal right to vote. Yet the harsh fact is that in many places in this country, men and women are kept from voting simply because they are Negroes." He called on Congress to enact legislation that would strengthen the Fifteenth Amendment by allowing the federal government to supervise voting requirements and ensure that registered voters were actually allowed to cast their ballots. The Voting Rights Act ultimately won overwhelming approval in Congress, passing the House of Representatives by a vote of 333 to 48, and the Senate by a vote of 77 to 19.

Southern states asserted that the Voting Rights Act went beyond the authority of the federal government and brought lawsuits challenging its constitutionality. The Supreme Court, in *South Carolina* v. *Katzenbach* (1965), rejected those challenges and upheld the Act. As a result, African Americans are registered to vote at rates much higher than they were before the law was passed, and the promise of the Fifteenth Amendment is closer to being fulfilled.

Fifteenth Amendment

Congress passes the Enforcement Act of 1870

1870

Following ratification of the Fifteenth Amendment, Congress passes the Enforcement Act, which creates criminal penalties for those who interfere with voting rights. The next year, Congress passes the Force Act of 1871, which provides for federal oversight of elections if individual states are deemed unwilling to hold fair and open elections on their own.

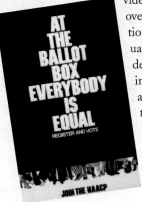

End of Reconstruction

1877

Voting by freed African Americans dramatically changes the political climate in the southern states, enabling black candidates to win seats in Congress and the state legislatures. As part of an agreement that settles the disputed election of 1876, President Rutherford B. Hayes orders the removal of troops from the states still under Reconstruction. He hopes this move will bring the North and South together. However, the withdrawal of the troops and the end of federal oversight of elections means that many southern blacks lose the voting rights they had exercised since Emancipation.

The Supreme Court upholds literacy tests

1898

Southern states also impose literacy tests for voting, on the grounds that voters need to be educated to make good decisions. Because former slaves often have little education, and because white officials administer the tests, literacy tests exclude many African Americans from voting. In *Williams* v. *Mississippi*, the Supreme Court holds that Mississippi's constitutional amendment requiring literacy tests does not violate the U.S. Constitution, as long as it is applied equally to all applicants.

Literacy tests are ruled unconstitutional

1949

Although literacy tests for voting apply to both blacks and whites, they exclude more African Americans from registration because of poor education and discriminatory administration that require African American applicants to pass more difficult tests. The U.S. Supreme Court in *Davis* v. *Schnell* hold Alabama's literacy test unconstitutional as it is clearly intended to deny the vote to African Americans and thus violates the Fifteenth Amendment.

Civil Rights Act creates a commission to investigate discrimination

1957

In response to low voter registration among African Americans, President Dwight D. Eisenhower proposes the Civil Rights Act of 1957—the first since Reconstruction. The law creates the Civil Rights Commission to investigate acts of interference with citizens' right to vote and to monitor other civil rights abuses. Civil rights leaders complain that the law is weakened because it provides for violators to be tried locally, meaning that those attempting to disenfranchise blacks would gain a sympathetic jury.

Civil Rights Act addresses racial inequities

1964

Responding to civil rights protests in the South, Congress passes the Civil Rights Act of 1964 after a lengthy filibuster by southern senators. The law prohibits discrimination in public accommodations, employment, education, and governmental services. The act also strengthens the Fifteenth Amendment by prohibiting discrimination in voting and makes voting requirements more uniform.

TIMELINE

"Grandfather clauses" are unconstitutional

1915

Some southern states have "grandfather clauses" that allow only those men to register and vote whose grandfathers had been eligible to vote in 1867, before the federal government began pressing for voting rights for blacks. This practice effectively negates the Fifteenth Amendment. In *Guinn* v. *United States,* the U.S. Supreme Court strikes down Oklahoma's "grandfather clause" as a violation of the Fifteenth Amendment. The term "grandfather clause" has since grown to mean any provision of law that exempts certain persons or preexisting conditions from the effect of a new regulation or requirement.

Poll taxes are permitted

1937

After Reconstruction, many southern states impose a poll tax on anyone who wants to vote. This tactic denies the vote to many poor African Americans and whites who cannot afford the tax. In *Breedlove* v. *Suttles,* the U.S. Supreme Court rules that Georgia's use of a poll tax violates neither the Fourteenth nor Fifteenth Amendments as they are applied to all races.

White-only primary is ruled unconstitutional

1944

The Democratic Party in several southern states limits participation to whites only in primary elections. The Supreme Court in *Grovey* v. *Townsend* (1935) upholds such restrictions, reasoning that political parties are organizations composed of voluntary members acting in a private capacity. The Court reverses itself in *Smith* v. *Allwright* (1944), concluding that even though administered by a private party, primary elections are an integral part of the election process and therefore subject to the constraints of the Fifteenth Amendment.

Poll tax amendment is ratified

1964

The Twenty-fourth Amendment makes it illegal for states to charge a poll tax in order to vote in federal elections. The tax falls hardest on poor voters, black and white, but has been upheld by the courts because it does not discriminate by race. In *Harper* v. *Virginia Board of Elections* (1966), the U.S. Supreme Court extends the poll tax ban to state elections. The Court holds that discrimination based on economic status is in violation of the equal protection clause of the Fourteenth Amendment as well as the newly adopted Twenty-fourth Amendment.

Congress passes the voting Rights Act of 1965

1965

Finding that existing federal antidiscrimination laws are not sufficient to overcome the resistance by state officials to enforce the Fifteenth Amendment, Congress adopts a comprehensive voting rights law that outlaws *any* racially discriminatory act that prevents African Americans from voting. The legislation gives the Justice Department power to oversee voting qualifications, suspend literacy tests, and ensure more uniform application of regulations. The Voting Rights Act is further extended in 1970, 1975, and 1982.

Class action suit challenges a Florida law disenfranchising convicted felons

2005

The Brennan Center for Justice and New York University's School of Law files a class action suit on behalf of 600,000 disenfranchised Florida citizens against an 1868 Florida law that permanently took away convicted felons' right to vote—only one in seven states do so. They believe that the law is discriminatory in intent because it disproportionately affects African Americans, and, therefore, it violates the Fourteenth Amendment's equal protection clause and the Fifteenth Amendment's prohibition of discriminating against voters by race. In the case of *Johnson* v. *Bush* (2005), the U.S. Court of Appeals upholds the law on the grounds that it applies to all felons regardless of race.

Sixteenth Amendment

(1913)

—

"Taxes are what we pay for civilized society."

— Justice Oliver Wendell Holmes Jr., dissenting opinion, *Compañía Generalde Tabacos de Filipinas* v. *Collector of Internal Revenue* (1927)

—

An *Internal Revenue Service poster reminds American citizens to file a tax return by March 15. (The date was later changed to April 15.) Initially only the wealthiest citizens paid income taxes, but during World War II the tax was extended to almost all wage-earning citizens.*

WHAT IT SAYS

The Congress shall have power to lay and collect taxes on incomes, from whatever source derived, without apportionment among the several States, and without regard to any census or enumeration.

TAX PROTESTS AND PROTESTORS

In 1765 colonists objected when the British government imposed stamp taxes, and American tax protests have occurred periodically ever since then. Some protests have attempted to set limits on state and local taxes. For instance, California's Proposition 13, adopted by a referendum in 1978, put a cap on the state's annual increases in property taxes. Organized groups have lobbied Congress and endorsed candidates for office who promised to lower taxes. There have also been proposals to repeal the Sixteenth Amendment. Whether one agrees with these objectives or not, their advocates have proceeded in a legal manner.

The more extreme tax protesters have been willing to break the law by refusing to pay their taxes on the grounds that the federal income tax itself is illegal. These tax resisters offer numerous reasons for their risky actions. Some of them argue that the Constitution still prohibits direct taxes like the income tax because the Sixteenth Amendment was never properly ratified. They regard the discrepancies in spelling and capitalization by the various states during the ratification process as invalidating the amendment. Other tax protesters do not accept the Internal Revenue Service's tax codes as official law. Some argue that "income" really means corporate profits, not wages. Some claim that being forced to provide information on their income tax returns violates their Fifth Amendment right against self-incrimination. Some have convinced themselves that there are no laws requiring individuals to pay taxes, that filing taxes is a voluntary act, and that people can simply choose not to pay. A few tax protesters have attempted to revoke their U.S. citizenship—and with it their obligation to pay taxes—by not accepting Social Security and other government programs.

Although asserted passionately, and often in excruciating detail, these arguments have been rejected as bogus by the federal courts. Judges accept the Sixteenth Amendment as a fully legitimate part of the Constitution that grants the federal government the ability to require all citizens to pay taxes on their earnings. Nor have the courts allowed individuals to suspend their citizenship obligations by forsaking government services. Despite these rulings, ardent tax protesters refuse to accept the opinions of judges as the final word and insist on interpreting the statutes for themselves and asserting their rights as they understand them. Those who engage in tax evasion face stiff penalties. Judges have found many of the tax protest cases to be frivolous and have set large fines for wasting the court's time. The government has prosecuted tax protesters and forced them to pay back taxes with heavy penalties, or sent them to jail. The Internal Revenue Service reminds taxpayers that while they have the right to contest their tax liabilities in court, "no one has the right to disobey the law."

TRY TO MAKE OUT MY THEORY AND YOUR INCOME TAX WORK WILL LOOK SIMPLE!

In 1929 an editorial cartoonist compared the complexity of filling out income tax forms with understanding Albert Einstein's theory of relativity.

WHAT IT MEANS

In Article I, sections 2 and 9 the U.S. Constitution said that no direct taxes could be imposed unless made in proportion to the population, as measured by the census. This meant that rather than taxing individuals directly, Congress had to levy taxes in each state based on the state's population. During the Civil War, the federal government imposed an income tax to pay for the war's expense, but in *Pollock* v. *Farmer's Loan & Trust Co.* (1895), the Supreme Court later declared federal income taxes unconstitutional because they were direct taxes. This ruling limited Congress's power to tax to a complicated formula that would be difficult to impose. Congress therefore sent to the states the Sixteenth Amendment, which specifically gives Congress the power to impose a direct income tax. This amendment greatly expanded the scope of federal taxing and spending and has been the basis for all subsequent federal income tax legislation.

TAXATION AS A FORM OF REGULATION

Early in the twentieth century, when reformers were seeking to end child labor in the United States, they had difficulty finding a solution that would meet the Supreme Court's approval. At first, Congress used the commerce clause, with its control of interstate commerce, to ban the shipment of goods made by child workers. But the Supreme Court struck this plan down in the case of *Hammer* v. *Dagenhart* (1918) for exceeding congressional authority.

Then the opponents of child labor turned to the power of taxation. Congress enacted a steep tax on the profits of any manufacturer that hired children under certain ages. The Supreme Court struck down the law in the *Child Labor Tax Case* (1922). The amount of the tax was not the issue. Instead, what the court found objectionable was that Congress was using a tax to serve as a form of regulation. Taxes cannot be substitutes for penalties or regulations, the Court decided.

In later years, however, the Supreme Court has accepted high taxes on certain items that the community wishes to control, such as drugs, gambling, and some forms of weapons. In the case of *United States* v. *Sanchez* (1950), the Court decided that "it is beyond serious question that a tax does not cease to be valid merely because it regulates, discourages, or even definitely deters the activities taxed. . . . The tax in question is a legitimate exercise in the taxing power despite its collateral regulatory purpose and effect."

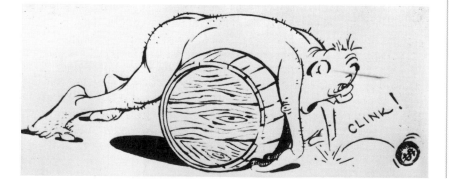

A taxpayer sent the Internal Revenue Service this cartoon suggesting that his taxes were too high. The Sixteenth Amendment permitted the federal government to levy income taxes.

Sixteenth Amendment

Congress creates an income tax to fund the Civil War

1862

Congress creates the Commissioner of Internal Revenue and enacts the first national income tax to pay war expenses. (The Confederacy also adopts an income tax.) At first, a flat 3 percent tax was set on all incomes greater than $800. This is later modified to 5 percent for incomes between $600 and $5,000, and 10 percent for incomes greater than $5,000. After the war, in 1872, Congress repeals the income tax.

Another income tax is established

1894

In an effort to reduce tariff rates, which provide the federal government with most of its revenue, Congress institutes another income tax of 2 percent on incomes greater than $4,000. Opponents decry the tax because it "takes from the wealth of the thrifty and the enterprising and gives it to the shifty and the sluggard."

The Supreme Court strikes down the federal income tax

1895

The Supreme Court rules in *Pollock* v. *Farmer's Loan & Trust Co.* that the new federal income tax is unconstitutional because it violates Article I, sections 2 and 9 of the Constitution. These sections, known as the "rule of apportionment," specify that all federal taxes must be imposed based on the population of each state, rather than directly on the people.

YOU

ARE ONE OF 50,000,000 AMERICANS WHO MUST FILL OUT AN INCOME TAX RETURN BY **MARCH 15TH**

USE YOUR WITHHOLDING RECEIPT

OR FORM 1040

You must file an income tax return if your income in 1944 was $500 or more.

FILE YOURS EARLY

UNITED STATES TREASURY DEPARTMENT
BUREAU OF INTERNAL REVENUE

Congress sets up the U.S. Tax Court

1924

Congress creates the U.S. Tax Court to give taxpayers a place to dispute decisions of the Internal Revenue Service involving payment of federal income, gift, or estate taxes. The Tax Court's decisions can be appealed to the federal courts of appeals and are subject to review by the U.S. Supreme Court. Today, there are nineteen tax court judges who are appointed by the President for terms of fifteen years.

Illegal gains are subject to the income tax

1927

In *United States* v. *Sullivan,* the Supreme Court, holds that financial gains made from illegal activities, such as drug sales or gambling, are taxable income under the Revenue Act of 1921. The Court finds that there is no reason to exclude revenues made from illegal businesses. The statute specifically requires payment from businesses of any kind and taxes are due as if the business were lawful.

TIMELINE

First income tax is levied under the Sixteenth Amendment

1913

Soon after the Sixteenth Amendment is ratified, Congress levies a 1 percent tax on personal incomes greater than $3,000 and a 6 percent tax on incomes above $500,000. These taxes affect only a very small portion of the population. At the same time, the Treasury Department devises the first Form 1040.

The Supreme Court defines "income"

1913

In *Stratton's Independence* v. *Howbert*, the Supreme Court defines income under the tax law as the "gain derived from capital, from labor, or from both combined" including both the dividends paid to corporate stockholders and the profit that is gained from selling assets.

Top tax rate hits 77 percent

1918

To raise additional taxes necessary to finance the First World War, Congress increases the top rate of the income tax to 77 percent, an all-time high. Modern federal tax rates vary between 10 and 38 percent.

Government institutes withholding taxes on wages and salaries

1943

To pay the rising costs of the World War II, Congress imposes income taxes on people with average incomes. So many people default, because they have not saved sufficiently to pay their taxes, that the government creates a new system for collecting income taxes by mandatory "withholding from wages and salaries." Employers are required to deduct the tax from employees' salaries before paying them.

The Internal Revenue Service is created

1953

The Bureau of Internal Revenue, first established in 1862, is reorganized and renamed the Internal Revenue Service (IRS). It remains the largest of the bureaus within the Department of the Treasury and is responsible for collecting federal taxes. The IRS deals directly with more Americans than any other institution, public or private.

The tax court fines "frivolous arguments"

2003

The U.S. Tax Court imposes financial penalties on taxpayers who pursue "frivolous cases" to delay the payment of their taxes. The IRS also rejects many claims raised by people who refuse to pay their taxes, such as filing returns with zeros on every line, or demanding a refund equal to the amount withheld from their earnings.

Seventeenth Amendment

(1913)

"The Senate of the United States has been both extravagantly praised and unreasonably disparaged, according to the predisposition and temper of its various critics. . . . The truth is, the Senate is just what the mode of its election and the conditions of public life in this country make it."

— Woodrow Wilson,
Congressional Government (1885)

WHAT IT SAYS

The Senate of the United States shall be composed of two Senators from each State, elected by the people thereof, for six years; and each Senator shall have one vote. The electors in each State shall have the qualifications requisite for electors of the most numerous branch of the State legislatures.

When vacancies happen in the representation of any State in the Senate, the executive authority of such State shall issue writs of election to fill such vacancies: Provided, That the legislature of any State may empower the executive thereof to make temporary appointments until the people fill the vacancies by election as the legislature may direct.

This amendment shall not be so construed as to affect the election or term of any Senator chosen before it becomes valid as part of the Constitution.

REPEAL THE SEVENTEENTH AMENDMENT?

In 2004, as his term in the Senate was ending, Georgia senator Zell Miller called for repeal of the Seventeenth Amendment. Miller thought that direct election of senators had upset the Constitution's careful balance between state and federal governments and made senators more susceptible to special interests from which they drew campaign contributions. "Make no mistake about it," said Miller, who had been appointed to the Senate by the governor to fill a vacancy and then had won a special election to finish the term. "It is the special interest groups and their fundraising power that elect U.S. senators and then hold them in bondage forever."

Ironically, the same arguments had been made a century earlier in favor of changing the means of electing senators. In 1906, the muckraking magazine writer David Graham Phillips published a series of articles in *Cosmopolitan* under the title "The Treason of the Senate." In them, Phillips argued that special interests dominated state legislatures and sent to the Senate people who would represent those special interests rather than the public interest. Progressive reformers believed that the solution to this problem was to allow the voters themselves to select their senators directly.

Some members of the House of Representatives have also suggested that the Seventeenth Amendment altered the original federalist system, in which the House would represent the people and the Senate would represent the states. They complain that the amendment severed an important link between the state legislatures and the national legislature. Regardless of such grumbling, it seems unlikely that having achieved the right to elect their own senators, the voting public would ever voluntarily give it up.

Barack Obama won a Senate seat in Illinois in 2004 by a wide margin. "I have an unusual name and exotic background," said Obama, "but my values are essentially American values. I'm rooted in the African American community, but I'm not limited by it. I think this election shows that."

WHAT IT MEANS

Initially, the legislatures of each state elected their U.S. senators. In a number of instances, disagreements between the two houses of a state legislature left Senate seats vacant for protracted periods. In addition, reformers accused special interests of corrupting the process of electing senators. The Seventeenth Amendment sought to solve these problems by having senators directly elected by the voters. This change left all the Senate's constitutional powers in place, unlike reforms that took place at the same time in other parliamentary governments, such as Great Britain's, where the power of the House of Lords, or upper chamber, was curtailed. As a result, the U.S. Senate retained equal authority over legislation with the House of Representatives.

As a result of the election of 1960 Democrats retained control of both the Senate and the House of Representatives. Since the Seventeenth Amendment was ratified in 1917, senators, like representatives, have been elected by the direct vote of the people rather than by state legislatures.

SENATE

34 SEATS AT STAKE

DEMS........ 20
REPS........ 13
UNDECIDED ... 1

HOUSE

437 SEATS AT STAKE

DEMS........ 254
REPS........ 158
UNDECIDED ... 25

Seventeenth Amendment

Congress regulates "time and procedure" for electing senators

➤ 1886

Responding to many deadlocks in state legislatures that result in U.S. Senate seats going vacant for an entire legislative session, Congress passes a federal law that sets requirements on the methods by which state legislatures elect senators. This first change in the original process for selecting senators fails to remedy the deadlocks, which only increase in frequency.

Populist Party calls for direct Senate elections

➤ 1896

In the Presidential election of 1896, the Populist Party puts into its party platform a call for the direct election of senators. This marks the first time that a political party endorses direct election, although neither the Democrats nor the Republicans pay much notice to it.

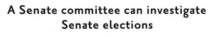

Muckrakers push for reform

➤ 1906

Muckraking magazine writers investigating corruption in government and business call for progressive reforms. Among the most notable of these is a series of articles under the title "The Treason of the Senate" that appear in William Randolph Hearst's *Cosmopolitan* magazine for several months in 1906. David Graham Phillips, author of the series, charges that senators represent special interests rather than the public interest.

Congress can regulate primary elections for Senate

➤ 1921

A Senate candidate in Michigan's primary election challenges the constitutionality of the Federal Corrupt Practices Act after he is convicted of violating federal limits on the amount of money that can be used in primary and general elections. In *Newberry* v. *United States,* the Supreme Court rules that although the Seventeenth Amendment changed who elects senators (from state legislators to voters in each state), it did not modify Article I, section 4 of the Constitution. That provision gives Congress the power to determine the time, place, and manner of holding Senate elections.

A Senate committee can investigate Senate elections

➤ 1928

In *Reed* v. *County Commissioners of Delaware County,* the U.S. Supreme Court holds that a special committee of the Senate has the power to investigate a Pennsylvania Senate election. As the Seventeenth Amendment acknowledges a federal right to elect senators, the Senate is authorized to protect these rights.

The Supreme Court requires one person, one vote

➤ 1964

The U.S. Supreme Court, in *Gray* v. *Sanders,* strikes down Georgia's "county unit" voting system as unconstitutional. Relying in part on the language of the Seventeenth Amendment, that senators are to be chosen "by the people," a voter in the primary Senate election had challenged the state system in which small rural districts are treated relatively the same as larger urban districts. In this system, rural voters have a much larger impact on the outcome of the election than urban voters. The Supreme Court rules that this violates the equal protection clause of the Fourteenth Amendment.

TIMELINE

Oregon permits voters to designate whom they want as senator

1907

An Oregon law permits voters to designate by referenda whom they want as senator and direct the legislature to support the popular choice. Nebraska soon follows Oregon's lead and other states adopt reforms that permit voters to participate in the choice of U.S. senators. Several states call for a constitutional convention to amend the federal Constitution, if Congress does not act. Between 1893 and 1911, thirty-one of the thirty-two required states submit applications for a convention to amend the Constitution and allow the popular election of senators.

The Senate agrees to support a constitutional change

1911

Although the House has long been advocating a change in the election of senators, the Senate resisted until 1911. By then at least twenty-nine states were nominating senators either in party primaries or general elections. Bowing to public demand, two-thirds of the Senate votes for an amendment sponsored by Senator Joseph Bristow of Kansas for direct election.

The first direct elections of senators are held

1914

Following ratification of the Seventeenth Amendment, the first election of senators is held, with one-third of the Senate seats up for election. To the surprise of reformers, every incumbent running wins reelection.

Residency requirements for voting are unconstitutional

1965

A district court holds that a residency requirement established by the Virginia legislature as an alternative to payment of a poll tax in federal elections is an additional qualification to voting, which violates the Seventeenth Amendment and Article I, section 2 of the Constitution. In *Harman* v. *Forssenius,* the Supreme Court agrees but bases its ruling of unconstitutionality on the Twenty-fourth Amendment (which outlawed poll taxes) rather than the Seventeenth Amendment.

Independents can be barred from voting in a party primary

1986

The Connecticut Republican Party adopts a rule that permits independent voters (those not affiliated with any party) to vote in Republican primaries for federal and statewide offices. The party then challenges a Connecticut law that requires voters to register with a party before voting in its primary. In *Tashjian* v. *Republican Party,* the Supreme Court finds that the law denies the party and its members the right to freedom of association by limiting the number of registered voters whom the party may invite to participate in the "basic function" of selecting the party's candidates. But the Court finds that the state law does not violate the Seventeenth Amendment, as the rule establishes qualifications for voting in congressional elections that differ from the qualifications for voting in primary elections for the state legislature.

Term limits for senators are unconstitutional

1995

In *U.S. Term Limits* v. *Thornton,* the Supreme Court rejects an Arkansas constitutional amendment that limits the number of times a candidate can run for the same office: two terms for U.S. senators and three terms for U.S. representatives. The Supreme Court observes that qualifications for members of Congress are determined by the U.S. Constitution and cannot be limited by the states. The Court further notes that "with the adoption of the Seventeenth Amendment, state power over the election of Senators was eliminated, and Senators, like Representatives, were to be elected directly by the people."

Eighteenth & Twenty-first Amendments

(1919 & 1933)

"Our country has deliberately undertaken a great social and economic experiment, noble in motive and far-reaching in purpose."

— Herbert Hoover, defending Prohibition during a 1928 Presidential campaign speech

WHAT IT SAYS

[Eighteenth Amendment] Section 1. After one year from the ratification of this article the manufacture, sale, or transportation of intoxicating liquors within, the importation thereof into, or the exportation thereof from the United States and all territory subject to the jurisdiction thereof for beverage purposes is hereby prohibited.

Section 2. The Congress and the several States shall have concurrent power to enforce this article by appropriate legislation.

Section 3. This article shall be inoperative unless it shall have been ratified as an amendment to the Constitution by the legislatures of the several States, as provided in the Constitution, within seven years from the date of the submission hereof to the States by the Congress.

[Twenty-first Amendment] Section 1. The eighteenth article of amendment to the Constitu-tion of the United States is hereby repealed.

Section 2. The transportation or importation into any State, Territory, or possession of the United States for delivery or use therein of intoxicating liquors, in violation of the laws thereof, is hereby prohibited.

Section 3. This article shall be inoperative unless it shall have been ratified as an amendment to the Constitution by conventions in the several States, as provided in the Constitution, within seven years from the date of the submission hereof to the States by the Congress.

Prohibition agents pour illegal liquor into a sewer. The Eighteenth Amendment made it illegal to manufacture or distribute intoxicating beverages, but Prohibition proved difficult to enforce and led to bootlegging and speakeasies that flouted the law.

WHAT IT MEANS

The Eighteenth Amendment resulted from a national effort to control the making, distribution, sale, and consumption of alcoholic beverages. Prohibition, called a "noble experiment" in a paraphrase of President Herbert Hoover's explanation of its goals, was an attempt to control reckless and destructive personal behavior. Its supporters argued that Prohibition would reduce crime, eliminate the need for poorhouses and prisons, and improve the health of all Americans.

When the Eighteenth Amendment was enacted, many of its supporters assumed that it covered only whiskeys and other hard liquor. But, when Congress passed the enforcement legislation, the Volstead Act, in 1919, it included beer and wine along with spirits. This sweeping provision made it difficult for the federal government to enforce Prohibition. Although arrests and hospitalizations related to alcoholism declined during the first years after the amendment went into effect, many negative consequences also became apparent. The amendment drove the lucrative alcohol business underground, giving rise to a large illegal market. Prohibition encouraged Americans to flout the law, resulting in a general disrespect for authority, and strengthened organized crime.

By 1932, many citizens recognized that Prohibition had failed, and organized a popular movement for its repeal. That year, the Democrats endorsed repeal, and their victory in the election demonstrated the public support for ending Prohibition. Its supporters were in such a hurry to undo the amendment that they provided for ratification by state conventions. This gave the voters in each state a say, but also avoided waiting for the state legislatures to convene. The Twenty-first Amendment repealed national Prohibition, but left it to the states to devise their own laws and restrictions on intoxicating beverages.

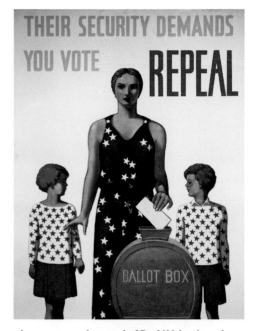

A poster urges the repeal of Prohibition in order to protect the American family. Opponents of Prohibition argued that it had encouraged lawlessness that threatened society.

FROM DRY TO WET: PUBLIC OPINION SHIFTS ON PROHIBITION

The vote in Congress for a constitutional amendment to prohibit the sale of alcoholic beverages went less along party lines than by region, ethnicity, and religion. Both Democrats and Republicans favored Prohibition, but its strongest support came from the South, the West, and rural areas of the Midwest, particularly among evangelical Protestants. Its opposition came largely from the big cities of the Northeast and Midwest, who objected that the "drys" were imposing their moral standards on the rest of society.

Most Americans complied with the Eighteenth Amendment, at first. Saloons closed and the consumption of alcoholic beverages declined sharply, as did hospitalizations for alcohol-related illnesses. But people soon began to ignore the law. Liquor was made, imported, and sold in the speakeasies that flourished during the 1920s. The notorious "rumrunner" Al Capone said: "Prohibition is a business. All I do is supply a public demand."

During the 1928 Presidential election, the Republican candidate Herbert Hoover pledged to uphold the law and prosecute offenders more effectively. His Democratic challenger, Alfred E. Smith, charged that Prohibition had bred corruption, caused a rise in crime, and encouraged disrespect for all law. Hoover won the election by a wide margin. Four years later, when the nation was suffering a major economic depression, polls showed that almost 75 percent of Americans favored the repeal of Prohibition. President Hoover would not change his position, while the Democrats made repeal a major plank in their party's platform.

That fall, the Democratic candidate, Franklin D. Roosevelt, campaigned for repeal and recovery. Across the nation, eleven states held referendums on Prohibition, and repeal won in every state by wide margins. This convinced Congress to move quickly in voting for the Twenty-first Amendment. As a consequence of the Prohibition experience, Congress became more wary of employing constitutional solutions for social and moral problems.

Eighteenth & Twenty-first Amendments

Maine becomes the first state to ban all liquor

National Prohibition Party forms

The Interstate Liquor Act prohibits shipping alcohol to dry states

1851 ── **1869** ── **1913**

Promoted by the state's temperance society, Maine passes the first law in the United States to ban alcohol except when used in medicine. Within four years, thirteen of the thirty-one states enact temperance laws. Reformers call drinking a crime against decency and against innocent women and children.

It is Time You Heard the Truth!

Temperance Rally

South End of Front Street . . . Platt Park

Hear the Facts Documented!

Demon Rum's Road to Destruction!

Broken Homes! Neglected wives and children! Lives snuffed out prematurely! Corruption in our city government!

Listen to the truth.
and
"The Truth Shall Make You Free!"

Frustrated by the failure of the major political parties to address prohibition, temperance advocates form the National Prohibition Party. The party receives little support in the general elections. Its popularity peaks in 1892 when its candidate for President receives 265,000 votes. The Prohibition Party still exists and continues to run candidates for office.

More than half of the state legislatures have passed laws declaring their states "dry." To eliminate the sale of liquor through the mail, temperance advocates successfully lobby to forbid the shipment of alcohol into these dry states.

President Hoover appoints the Wickersham Commission

The Democratic Convention advocates repeal

Prosecutions under Prohibition law cannot continue

1929 ── **1932** ── **1934**

After his election, President Herbert Hoover appoints the National Commission on Law Observance and Enforcement, popularly known as the Wickersham Commission, to examine Prohibition enforcement. While the commission concludes that Prohibition is not working, most of the commissioners believe the law should be continued anyway.

Although Presidential candidate Franklin Roosevelt draws much of his support from "dry" areas of the South and West, he accepts the Democratic Party's platform, which calls for the repeal of Prohibition. After Roosevelt's election, but before he takes the oath as President, Congress votes to repeal the Eighteenth Amendment. Within days of becoming President the following year, Roosevelt asks Congress to permit the sale of beer and wine even before the Twenty-first Amendment is ratified.

Before the states ratify the Twenty-first Amendment, the prosecution of Clause Chambers and Byrum Gibson for possessing and transporting intoxicating liquor in violation of the National Prohibition Act begins. Their prosecution continues even after Prohibition's repeal. The defendants ask the court to dismiss their case because the laws for which they have been arrested are no longer valid. In *United States* v. *Chambers*, the U.S. Supreme Court agrees that prosecution under a repealed law cannot go forward.

TIMELINE

THE AMERICAN ISSUE

A Saloonless Nation and a Stainless Flag

WESTERVILLE, OHIO, JANUARY 25, 1919

U.S. IS VOTED DRY

36th STATE RATIFIES DRY AMENDMENT JAN. 16

Congress passes the Volstead Act to enforce Prohibition

1919

Following ratification of the Eighteenth Amendment, Congress passes the National Prohibition Enforcement Act (also known as the Volstead Act), which bans any "intoxicating liquors" containing more than 0.5 percent alcohol. The Internal Revenue Service has responsibility for enforcing the Volstead Act. Its field agents, who track down illegal stills, come to be known as "revenoors."

CLOSED
FOR VIOLATION OF
NATIONAL PROHIBITION ACT
BY ORDER OF
UNITED STATES DISTRICT COURT
DISTRICT OF
All persons are forbidden to enter premises without order from the UNITED STATES MARSHAL

Efforts begin to repeal the Eighteenth Amendment

1927

State legislatures in the Northeast and Midwest pass laws preventing police from pursuing reported violations of the alcohol ban. Organized crime accounts for a large increase in illegal bars, known as speakeasies. In 1927, nine prominent New York lawyers form the "Voluntary Committee of Lawyers" to repeal the Volstead Act and the Eighteenth Amendment. They argue that the public's disregard for Prohibition threatens to undermine respect for the U.S. legal system.

Prohibition becomes an issue in the Presidential campaign

1928

Alfred E. Smith, the Democratic nominee for President, endorses the repeal of Prohibition, while the Republican candidate, Herbert Hoover, calls for more effective enforcement of the Prohibition laws. Despite Smith's loss, the campaign raises the level of debate over Prohibition and strengthens the movement for repeal.

States cannot set wine prices

1980

A wine dealer challenges California's system of setting prices for wine merchants, arguing it violates the Sherman Antitrust Act. California officials argue that the system protects small wine dealers and say that the price regulation is within the state's power to regulate alcohol granted in the Twenty-first Amendment. In *California Retail Liquor Dealers Association* v. *Midcal Aluminum, Inc.*, the U.S. Supreme Court says that while states have wide latitude to regulate alcohol under the Twenty-first Amendment, the amendment cannot be used to justify a system that violates federal antitrust laws.

Congress promotes a minimum drinking age

1987

Congress passes legislation to reduce a state's highway funding if that state does not increase the minimum drinking age to twenty-one. South Dakota challenges the law as a violation of its power to regulate alcohol under the Twenty-first Amendment. In *South Dakota* v. *Dole,* the U.S. Supreme Court holds that Congress has legitimately used its spending power to promote the public welfare and sees no conflict with the Twenty-first Amendment.

States cannot ban shipments of wine

2005

In the case of *Granholm* v. *Heald* the U.S. Supreme Court rules that the states cannot bar out-of-state shipments of wine to their residents, despite the provision of the Twenty-first Amendment, which leaves the regulation of liquor sales to the states. In this case, the Court strikes down state laws that discriminate against interstate commerce in violation of the commerce clause and concludes that such discrimination is neither authorized nor permitted by the Twenty-first Amendment.

Nineteenth Amendment

(1920)

WHAT IT SAYS

Section 1. The right of citizens of the United States to vote shall not be denied or abridged by the United States or by any State on account of sex.

Section 2. Congress shall have power to enforce this article by appropriate legislation.

On the day before Woodrow Wilson's inauguration, women staged their own parade on Pennsylvania Avenue in Washington to dramatize their demand for the right to vote. Women campaigned for a century before the Nineteenth Amendment gave them that right.

WHAT IT MEANS

Throughout the nineteenth century, most women were excluded from voting and holding elective office. Beginning in 1848, women organize a suffrage movement to win the right to vote. Some western states grant women voting rights, and Montana elects a woman to the U.S. House of Representatives in 1916. After a century of women's petitions, parades, and protests, Congress responds with the Nineteenth Amendment. Although the amendment gave Congress the authority to enact legislation to implement it, the states did not resist granting women the right to vote and hold office.

THE FIRST WOMAN IN CONGRESS

As a woman suffrage advocate in the western states, Jeannette Rankin helped persuade her home state of Montana to grant women the right to vote. She then took the next step. She successfully ran for Congress as a Republican in 1916 and became the first woman to serve in either house of the national legislature. As a representative, she focused on domestic social reforms, but as a pacifist she was also concerned about keeping the United States out of World War I in Europe. In 1917, she cast one of the fifty votes in the House against a declaration of war.

In 1918, Rankin lost the race for senator from Montana, thus failing to become the first woman senator. She retired from Congress and spent the next two decades engaged in social work, giving lectures, and ranching in Montana. In 1940, with Europe engaged in the Second World War, she ran again. In the Republican primary she challenged the incumbent congressman, Jacob Thorkelson, who was a Nazi sympathizer, and defeated him. Ironically, Rankin was serving in the House in December 1941, when Japan made a surprise attack on the U.S. naval base at Pearl Harbor, in Hawaii. Withstanding enormous pressure, Rankin cast the sole vote in Congress against going to war. She remained true to her pacifist belief, but this highly unpopular vote ended her career in politics. She chose not to run for reelection in 1942. Indeed, voters in her western Montana district replaced their isolationist Republican congresswoman with an internationalist Democrat, Mike Mansfield, who as a young man had served in all three of the existing branches of the U.S. military. (Mansfield, who rose to become majority leader of the U.S. Senate, later shared Rankin's opposition to the Vietnam War.)

Rankin resumed her social activism, devoting the rest of her life to working with the National Consumers League and the Women's International League for Peace and Freedom. In the 1960s, when she was in her eighties, she protested against the Vietnam War. After her death in 1973, the state of Montana donated a bronze statute of its first woman representative to the U.S. Capitol. "I cannot vote for war" is inscribed on its base.

"It was we, the people, not we . . . the male citizens, but we, the whole people, who formed this Union. And we formed it, not to give the blessings of liberty, but to secure them; not to half of ourselves and the half of our posterity, but to the whole people—women as well as men."

— Susan B. Anthony, 1873 speech to suffrage supporters in New York City

An editorial cartoon portrays the woman suffrage amendment as an important step upward for women, from drudgery and inequality to careers in business and law and even to the presidency.

Nineteenth Amendment

Women's rights conference is held in Seneca Falls, New York

1848

About three hundred women and men gather for a convention in Seneca Falls, New York, to discuss various ways of obtaining woman suffrage. They issue the "Declaration of Sentiments and Resolutions," modeled on the Declaration of Independence, calling for equal treatment of women and men under the law, and voting rights for women.

Woman suffrage associations are founded

1869

Differences in opinion between women activists over the relationship between woman suffrage and the movement for racial equality split the women's rights movement. Allegiances divide between two main organizations, the American Woman Suffrage Association and the National Woman Suffrage Association, which is led by Elizabeth Cady Stanton and Susan B. Anthony. Stanton and Anthony break with their abolitionist supporters and accuse them of emphasizing African American civil rights at the expense of women's rights

First woman is nominated for President

1872

The attorney Victoria Chaflin Woodhull becomes the first woman to run for President of the United States, as a candidate of the Equal Rights Party. Neither she nor any other woman is allowed to cast a vote in that election.

Wyoming gives women the right to vote

1890

Wyoming, which as a territory had allowed women to vote, joins the Union and becomes the first state to permit women to vote and hold office. In 1893, Colorado grants women the right to vote, followed by Utah, Idaho, Washington, California, Oregon, Kansas, Arizona, Illinois, Montana, Nevada, New York, Michigan, South Dakota, and Oklahoma in the years before the Nineteenth Amendment is ratified.

The National Women's Party organizes White House protests

1916

Alice Paul and Lucy Burns form the National Women's Party to lobby for a federal constitutional amendment that will allow women to vote. In 1916, the party organizes protests at the White House to dramatize their case. Police arrest the demonstrators and charge them with obstructing traffic. Some of those arrested refuse to pay their fines and are sent to prison. President Woodrow Wilson pardons the protesters in 1917.

First woman is elected to the U.S. House of Representatives

1916

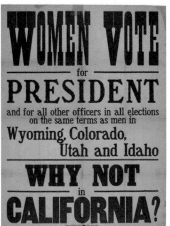

Soon after women gain the vote in Montana, Jeannette Rankin wins election as the Republican candidate for a seat in the U.S. House of Representatives. She serves one term and then loses a race for the U.S. Senate. Rankin later serves a second term in the House from 1941 to 1943. In 1932, Hattie Carraway of Arkansas becomes the first woman elected to the U.S. Senate.

TIMELINE

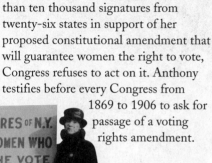

Susan B. Anthony is arrested for attempting to vote
1872

The right to vote is not a "privilege" of citizenship
1874

The Susan B. Anthony Amendment is introduced in Congress
1878

Susan B. Anthony attempts to cast her first vote to test whether the Fifteenth Amendment will be interpreted broadly enough to guarantee women the right to vote. She is arrested, tried, and found guilty of "unlawful voting" in Canandaigua, New York. Anthony refuses to pay the $100 fine, but is never jailed.

In *Minor* v. *Happersett,* the U.S. Supreme Court upholds a Missouri law limiting the right to vote to male citizens. The Court rejects Virginia Minor's claim that the state law deprives her of a "privilege or immunity" of citizenship in violation of the Fourteenth Amendment. The Court reasons that the privileges and immunities clause does not create new rights, but only guarantees the rights of citizens that were recognized at the time of the Constitution's drafting.

Although Anthony has collected more than ten thousand signatures from twenty-six states in support of her proposed constitutional amendment that will guarantee women the right to vote, Congress refuses to act on it. Anthony testifies before every Congress from 1869 to 1906 to ask for passage of a voting rights amendment.

Women vote in the 1920 elections
1920

The Nineteenth Amendment neither gives nor denies a woman's right to serve on a jury
1922

Women can be excepted from jury duty
1961

Seventy-two years after the Seneca Falls Convention first called for women's voting rights, the Nineteenth Amendment permits women to vote in the 1920 elections. Only one person who signed the Declaration of Sentiments and Resolutions, Charlotte Woodward, is still alive and able to exercise her right to vote.

The National American Woman Suffrage Association establishes the League of Women Voters to encourage women to use their newly acquired right to vote. The league promotes greater participation in the democratic process, advocates on a wide range of public policy issues, and sponsors debates between candidates for political office.

In a South Carolina murder case, the defense protests the exclusion of women from the jury following the passage of the Nineteenth Amendment. In *Mittle* v. *South Carolina,* the supreme court of South Carolina finds that the Nineteenth Amendment cannot be read to grant a right to vote or participate in jury service. It simply says that gender cannot be a basis for discrimination when determining voting qualifications. If men are allowed to vote, women are as well.

In 1961, women are eligible to serve on juries in all but three states. Florida is one of seventeen states that exempt women from jury duty unless they voluntarily register to be called. After an all-male jury convicts a Florida woman of murdering her husband when she discovered his infidelity, the woman argues that the jury's verdict might have been different if the jury had included women, who were more likely to be sympathetic with her. She notes that in 1957, when the trial took place, only 220 women had registered for jury duty, out of 46,000 registered women voters in the county. In *Hoyt* v. *Florida* (1961) the Supreme Court rules that the Florida statute is based on a reasonable assumption that women are "still regarded as the center and home of family life," and so can be excused from mandatory civic duties.

Twentieth Amendment

(1933)

"No longer would a new Congress need to wait a year between its election and its first meeting. No longer would lame-duck members remain in office so long after their defeat. No longer would four-month interregnums exist between the election and inauguration of a president."

— Senator Robert C. Byrd, describing the impact of the Twentieth Amendment in *The Senate, 1789–1989: Addresses on the History of the Senate* (1989)

WHAT IT SAYS

Section 1. The terms of the President and Vice-President shall end at noon on the 20th day of January, and the terms of Senators and Representatives at noon on the 3d day of January, of the years in which such terms would have ended if this article had not been ratified; and the terms of their successors shall then begin.

Section 2. The Congress shall assemble at least once in every year, and such meeting shall begin at noon on the 3d day of January, unless they shall by law appoint a different day.

Section 3. If, at the time fixed for the beginning of the term of the President, the President elect shall have died, the Vice-President elect shall become President. If a President shall not have been chosen before the time fixed for the beginning of his term, or if the President elect shall have failed to qualify, then the Vice-President elect shall act as President until a President shall have qualified; and the Congress may by law provide for the case wherein neither a President elect nor a Vice-President elect shall have qualified, declaring who shall then act as President, or the manner in which one who is to act shall be selected, and such person shall act accordingly until a President or Vice-President shall have qualified.

Section 4. The Congress may by law provide for the case of the death of any of the persons from whom the House of Representatives may choose a President whenever the right of choice shall have devolved upon them, and for the case of the death of any of the persons from whom the Senate may choose a Vice-President whenever the right of choice shall have devolved upon them.

Section 5. Sections 1 and 2 shall take effect on the 15th day of October following the ratification of this article.

Section 6. This article shall be inoperative unless it shall have been ratified as an amendment to the Constitution by the legislatures of three-fourths of the several States within seven years from the date of its submission.

Uncle Sam considers it more important to aim at the "quack remedies" proposed by members of Congress than the lame duck sessions of Congress in this cartoon, which casts doubt on the need for a constitutional amendment. The Twentieth Amendment changed the congressional calendar to lessen the need for lame duck session.

WHAT IT MEANS

March 4 was initially chosen as the date a new President, Vice President, and Congress took office, because there needed to be time to travel to the capital and for the new representatives and senators to settle their affairs at home before sitting as a Congress. As transportation and communications improved, this meant that the departing Congress and President remained in office for an unnecessarily long time. By moving the beginning of the new term from March 4 to January 20 (and in the case of Congress to January 3) proponents of the Twentieth Amendment hoped to put an end to the "lame duck" syndrome. Lame ducks, incumbents who had been defeated or had not stood for reelection, were perceived to be able to accomplish little of value, and Congress and these Presidents were less likely to support each other's initiatives.

This shortened interval between the election and the convening of a new Congress on January 3 and the Presidential inauguration on January 20 allows the outgoing President time to consider the outgoing Congress's legislation for signature or veto while enabling the government to be passed swiftly to the new administration.

The Twentieth Amendment also provides for succession plans if the newly elected President or Vice President is unable to assume his or her position. If the President is not able to hold office, either because of death or failure to qualify, the Vice President will act as President. If the Vice President is also not able to carry out the Presidential duties, Congress may select someone to act as President.

LAME DUCK SESSIONS HELD SINCE THE PASSAGE OF THE TWENTIETH AMENDMENT

CONGRESS (YEAR)	SENATE DATES	HOUSE DATES
76th (1940–1941)	Nov. 7–Jan. 3	Nov. 7–Jan. 2
77th (1942)	Nov. 5–Dec. 16	Nov. 5–Dec. 16
78th (1944)	Nov. 14–Dec. 19	Nov. 14–Dec.19
80th (1948)	Dec. 31	Dec. 31
81st (1950–1951)	Nov. 27–Dec. 22	Nov. 27–Dec. 22
	Dec. 26–29	Did not meet
83rd (1954)	Nov. 8–17	Did not meet
	Nov. 29–Dec. 2	Did not meet
91st (1970–1971)	Nov. 16–Jan. 2	Nov. 16–Jan. 2
93rd (1974)	Nov. 18–26	Nov. 18–26
	Dec. 2–20	Dec. 2–20
96th (1980)	Nov. 12–25	Nov. 12–24
	Dec. 1–16	Dec. 1–16
97th (1982)	Nov. 29–Dec. 23	Nov. 29–Dec. 21
103rd (1994)	Nov. 30, Dec. 1	Nov. 29
105th (1998)	Did not meet	Dec. 17–19
106th (2000)	Nov. 14	Nov. 13–14
	Dec. 5–15	Dec. 4–15
107th (2002)	Nov. 7–8	Nov. 7–8
	Nov. 12–20	Nov. 12–22
108th (2004)	Nov. 16–24	Nov. 16–24

SENATOR NORRIS TARGETS THE LAME DUCK SESSIONS

Originally applied to businessmen who went bankrupt, the term "lame duck" has transferred to politicians who continue in office after they have been defeated, have chosen not to run for reelection, or have been legally barred from seeking another term. (In the federal government, only the President is limited to two terms. Some states have set term limits for their own state legislators, but the Constitution does not permit them to place limits on the terms of U.S. senators and representatives.) The Twentieth Amendment is called the Lame Duck Amendment because it was designed to reduce the chances of legislators meeting and casting votes after failing to win reelection.

As chairman of the Senate Judiciary Committee, Senator George W. Norris (above) sponsored the Twentieth Amendment. A Republican from Nebraska, Norris had earned a reputation as a progressive reformer in the House of Representatives, where he led a revolt against the powerful Speaker Joseph Cannon to make the House operate more democratically. Serving in the Senate during the conservative 1920s, Norris forged alliances with liberals and progressives in both parties to promote his reforms. The author of much legislation, he is remembered primarily as the author of the legislation that created the Tennessee Valley Authority, which brought electrical power to vast areas of the rural South.

Twentieth Amendment

The Confederation Congress sets the beginning of the new government

1788

With the ratification of the Constitution, the outgoing Congress under the Articles of Confederation sets March 4, 1789, as the date on which the new federal government will begin. The House of Representatives is unable to establish a quorum to conduct business until April 1, and the Senate does not get its first quorum until April 6. George Washington is inaugurated as the first President on April 30, 1789.

First lame duck session of Congress

1790

The Constitution provides that the Congress will begin each session on the first Monday in December. The first session of each two-year Congress therefore begins thirteen months after the congressional elections are held. The second session begins a month after the next election, and continues until March 3. Some of the members who serve during that second session might have been defeated or chosen not to run for reelection in the last election. They are known as "lame ducks," and any session held after an election is a "lame duck session."

Congress establishes a line of Presidential succession

1792

Congress passes the Presidential Succession Act, which provides that should both the President and Vice President be unable to serve, the president pro tempore of the Senate (selected to preside over the Senate when the Vice President is absent) will serve as President. Next in line of succession are the Speaker of the House of Representatives, followed by the members of the cabinet in the order in which departments were created.

First Congress to convene in January

1935

Under the Twentieth Amendment, the Seventy-fourth Congress, elected in November 1934, meets in January 1935, rather than waiting until the following December, as had been the previous practice. As a result, the outgoing Seventy-third Congress has no "lame duck session." In later years, Congress only rarely holds lame duck sessions.

Franklin Roosevelt is the first President inaugurated on January 20

1937

President Roosevelt's first term, which began on March 4, 1933, ends at noon on January 20, 1937, when he becomes the first President to be inaugurated under the Twentieth Amendment.

Threat of war deeps Congress in a lame duck session

1940

Europe goes to war in September 1939, and, while the United States struggles to remain out of the war, the constant threat of hostilities keeps Congress in session throughout 1940, even during the months after the November election. This is the first lame duck session held after the Twentieth Amendment was ratified. Congress also holds lame duck sessions in 1942 and 1944, while the United States is engaged in World War II.

TIMELINE

John Tyler becomes the first Vice President to assume the Presidency

1841

William Henry Harrison died of pneumonia within a month of becoming President. Vice President John Tyler then assumes the Presidency. Some members of Congress refer to Tyler as the "acting President," and suggest that a special election should be held to fill the post. However, Tyler claims the full rights of the Presidency and serves out all of the nearly four years remaining in Harrison's term.

Congress changes the order of succession to the Presidency

1886

In 1886, Congress passes a new Presidential Succession Act that removes the president pro tempore of the Senate and the Speaker of the House of Representatives from the line of succession. After 1886, cabinet officers, in the order their departments were created, are next in line for the Presidency. In 1948, Congress reinstates the Speaker of the House and president pro tempore of the Senate in that order in the line of succession.

Franklin Roosevelt is the last President inaugurated on March 4

1933

The Twentieth Amendment is ratified in 1933, but not in time to change the date of the inauguration. As a result there is a five-month interval between Roosevelt's election in November 1932 and his inauguration in March. The economy slips to the lowest level of the depression, with widespread bank failures, foreclosures, and unemployment. Neither the outgoing President Herbert Hoover nor the incoming President Roosevelt feels he has authority to confront those issues during the interregnum.

Censure of Senator Joe McCarthy

1954

The Senate returns in a lame duck session following the election of 1954 to consider the censure of Joseph R. McCarthy, a Wisconsin Republican accused of conduct unbecoming a senator. McCarthy gained national publicity for his controversial hearings into Communist subversion of the government and assailed anyone who criticized his tactics, including other senators. In a lame duck session in December 1954, the Senate votes 67 to 22 to condemn McCarthy's conduct.

Speaker O'Neill denounces lame duck sessions

1982

After the elections in November 1982 the House of Representatives returns to a lame duck session to deal with unresolved budget and appropriations issues. The session is so frustrating and unproductive that House Speaker Tip O'Neill vows never to hold another lame duck session while he is in office. He keeps his word, but after O'Neill retires Congress resumes occasional lame duck sessions to wrap up unfinished work.

A lame duck House of Representatives impeaches President Clinton

1998

With President Bill Clinton being investigated for lying to a grand jury about his relationship with a White House intern, Republicans in the House of Representatives move toward voting to impeach the President prior to the 1998 election. House Speaker Newt Gingrich predicts that his party will increase its numbers in the House in 1998, but instead the party loses seats and Gingrich resigns. Despite polls showing that public opposes impeachment, a lame duck session of the House votes almost entirely along party lines to impeach the President. Clinton is acquitted in a Senate trial the next year.

Twenty-second Amendment

(1951)

WHAT IT SAYS

Section 1. No person shall be elected to the office of the President more than twice, and no person who has held the office of President, or acted as President, for more than two years of a term to which some other person was elected President shall be elected to the office of the President more than once. But this Article shall not apply to any person holding the office of President, when this Article was proposed by the Congress, and shall not prevent any person who may be holding the office of President, or acting as President, during the term within which this Article becomes operative from holding the office of President or acting as President during the remainder of such term.

Section 2. This article shall be inoperative unless it shall have been ratified as an amendment to the Constitution by the legislatures of three-fourths of the several States within seven years from the date of its submission to the States by the Congress.

NO THIRD TERM: FRANKLIN D. ROOSEVELT CONFRONTS A TRADITION

Franklin Delano Roosevelt, or FDR as he was commonly known, was the only U.S. President to have been elected to four terms. He came into office during the Great Depression in 1932. By March 1933 more than 13 million people were unemployed; banks were closing, homes were being foreclosed, families were starving, and the nation's economy was in a complete shambles.

During his first hundred days in office, Roosevelt pledged relief to business, agriculture, and the unemployed in what he called the New Deal. By the 1936 election, the nation was on the road to recovery and Roosevelt won reelection by a landslide, carrying all but two states. In his second term, Roosevelt stumbled politically when he tried to increase the number of justices on the U. S. Supreme Court so that he could appoint justices who would be sympathetic to his programs. This "court packing" scheme divided the Democratic Party and hindered the passage of much new domestic legislation.

Then, in 1939, Europe went to war and Americans fixed their attention on foreign policy. Roosevelt agreed to let his party nominate him for an unprecedented third term. His popularity and public unease about the growing threat of war carried him to another victory in 1940. The United States entered the war after the Japanese attacked Pearl Harbor in 1941, and it was still at war as the Presidential election of 1944 approached. Rather than change leaders in the middle of the war, voters chose Roosevelt for a another term, despite increasing concerns about his health. Just months after his fourth inauguration, Roosevelt died from a cerebral hemor-

rhage. The possibility of an unlimited number of Presidential terms died with him. As soon as the Republicans regained the majority in Congress they passed a constitutional amendment limiting future Presidents to two terms.

Ships lie in ruin following the Japanese surprise attack on Pearl Harbor in 1941. Congress immediately declared war on Japan.

WHAT IT MEANS

Nothing in the original Constitution limited the number of terms that a President could serve, but the nation's first President, George Washington, set a precedent by declining to run for a third term, suggesting that two four-year terms were enough for any President. Washington's precedent survived until 1940, when Franklin D. Roosevelt, a Democrat who had steered the nation through the Great Depression, ran for a third term on the eve of the Second World War. Roosevelt won a third term in 1940 and a fourth term in 1944.

Following Roosevelt's death in April 1945, just months into his fourth term, Republicans in Congress took the lead in proposing a limit of two terms for future Presidents. The amendment specified that if a Vice President took over for a President but served less than two years of the of the former President's term, the new president could serve for two full four-year terms. If more than two years of the Presidential term remain when the Vice President assumes office, the new President may serve only one additional term.

The bull moose served as the symbol of the Progressive Party, which nominated former President Theodore Roosevelt as its Presidential candidate in 1912, meaning that Roosevelt was running for an unprecedented third term. The popular Roosevelt came in second in that election, ahead of the Republicans but losing to the Democrats.

> *"I had made plans for myself, plans for a private life [but] my conscience will not let me turn my back on a call to service."*

— Franklin D. Roosevelt, explaining his decision to run for a third term, in his acceptance speech to the Democratic Convention in 1940

An editorial cartoon opposed Franklin Roosevelt's campaign for an unprecedented fourth term by suggesting that his tenure was turning the President into a king. The Twenty-second Amendment banned Presidents from serving for more than two terms.

Twenty-second Amendment

First President steps down after two terms

1797

President George Washington is still widely admired when he completes his second term as President, and many hope that he will run for a third term. Washington declines on the grounds that an orderly transition of authority is necessary to prevent rule by a king-like power. Washington also grew sensitive to the increased partisanship and resulting newspaper attacks on his administration during his second term, which made him anxious to retire to Mount Vernon.

Thomas Jefferson steps down after two terms

1809

After defeating John Adams in his run for reelection, Thomas Jefferson goes on to serve two terms as President. Jefferson then steps down voluntarily, solidifying the tradition of Presidents serving only two terms.

THOMAS JEFFERSON.

Grant considers a third term

1875

As President Ulysses S. Grant, a Republican, nears the end of his second term in the White House, he contemplates running for a third term. The House of Representative, where the Democrats hold the majority, pass a resolution denouncing a third term as a violation of American political tradition. Grant chooses not to be a formal candidate, but stands ready to be drafted in 1876 and 1880. His party chooses other candidates.

FDR elected for a fourth term

1944

In the midst of the Second World War, Franklin Delano Roosevelt runs for an unprecedented fourth term. His Republican opponent, New York governor Thomas Dewey, chooses not to criticize the President's handling of the war, but instead questions his ability to lead the nation given his age and health, calling Roosevelt "a tired old man." The strategy fails and Roosevelt is returned to office one last time, but he dies only four months into this fourth term, in April 1945.

Republicans win control of Congress and change the constitution

1946

For the first time since the beginning of the depression, Republicans win control of both the Senate and House of Representatives in 1946. Among the party's chief objectives is a constitutional amendment that will prevent another President from running for more than two terms. With the support of President Harry Truman, who took office in 1945 after Franklin Roosevelt's death, Congress approves the Twenty-second Amendment and sends it to the states, with a seven-year deadline for ratification.

Truman chooses not to run for a third term

1952

The Twenty-second Amendment specifically exempts the incumbent President, Harry Truman. As Vice President, he had become President just four months into Franklin Roosevelt's fourth term. Few people believe that Truman has a chance of being elected in 1948, when all the polls show the Republican candidate, Thomas E. Dewey, winning easily. Instead, Truman fights a scrappy campaign and pulls off a stunning victory. The Korean War, which begins during Truman's second term, makes him increasingly unpopular. Although Truman is eligible to run for a third term in 1952, he chooses to retire from the Presidency.

TIMELINE

Theodore Roosevelt runs for a third term

1912

Theodore Roosevelt comes to the Presidency after the assassination of President William McKinley in 1901. He serves out the remainder of McKinley's term and is reelected in 1905. After his reelection, he announces that he will honor the two-term tradition and not seek a third term in 1909. However, by 1912, he has fallen out with his successor President William Taft and challenges him for the Republican Presidential nomination. Roosevelt sweeps the primaries but is denied the nomination. He runs instead on the Progressive (Bull Moose) Party ticket. Although Roosevelt receives more votes than Taft, the split he causes within the Republican ranks hands the election to the Democratic candidate, Woodrow Wilson.

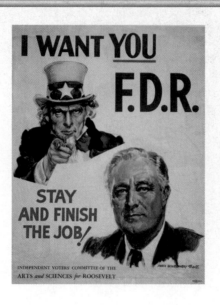

FDR elected for a third term

1940

Having served two terms in which he guided the nation through the depression, Franklin Delano Roosevelt remains popular among the voting public. With war looming in Europe, he breaks with tradition and runs for a third term in 1940. His Republican opponent, Wendell Wilkie, attacks Roosevelt's New Deal programs, and accuses the President of seeking to lead the nation into another war. Three-quarters of the nation's newspapers endorse Wilkie and oppose another term for Roosevelt. Despite this opposition, Roosevelt becomes the first President ever elected to a third term.

Eisenhower is the first President restricted to two terms

1960

While Republicans pressed for a two-term limit to the Presidency, it is a Republican President, Dwight D. Eisenhower, who is the first to fall under the amendment's restriction. Eisenhower remains popular after serving two terms, and observers believe he could have won a third term had he been able to run.

Repeal of Twenty-second Amendment is proposed

1986

With Ronald Reagan in his second term as President and limited from running again, Republican representative Guy Vander Jagt introduces a bill to repeal the Twenty-second Amendment, but Congress does not act upon it. Similarly, during President Bill Clinton's second term, several Democrats introduce bills to repeal the amendment. In 2003, a bipartisan bill to repeal the Presidential term limit is submitted. Congress does not approve any of these bills.

Twenty-third Amendment

(1961)

A cartoonist for the Washington Star *portrayed the "voteless" city of Washington welcoming the new President, Calvin Coolidge, for his inauguration in 1925. In 1961, the Twenty-third Amendment finally allowed residents of the District to vote in Presidential elections.*

The District of Columbia proudly sent delegates to the Republican national convention in 2004. (Their banner is at bottom right.) The Twenty-third Amendment gave the District three electoral votes.

WHAT IT SAYS

Section 1. The District constituting the seat of Government of the United States shall appoint in such manner as the Congress may direct:

A number of electors of President and Vice President equal to the whole number of Senators and Representatives in Congress to which the District would be entitled if it were a State, but in no event more than the least populous State; they shall be in addition to those appointed by the States, but they shall be considered, for the purposes of the election of President and Vice President, to be electors appointed by a State; and they shall meet in the District and perform such duties as provided by the twelfth article of amendment.

Section 2. The Congress shall have power to enforce this article by appropriate legislation.

The Constitution allowed Congress to select an area ten miles square to serve as the permanent seat of the federal government. Since 1800, the government has operated out of the District of Columbia. There were few permanent residents of the district at first, but by 1960 its population exceeded three-quarters of a million people. As a federal district, the capital had neither an elected local governor nor the right to vote in national elections. At the same time, District residents had all the responsibilities of citizenship.

The Twenty-third Amendment did not make Washington, D.C., a state, but did grant its citizens the right to vote in Presidential elections and it allotted the District the number of electors it would have had if it were a state. The amendment did not provide the District with representation in Congress, but subsequently the District gained a nonvoting delegate in the House of Representatives and an elected local government.

Let Washington Speak.

Congressional Voting Rights for D.C.

George Washington is gagged in this political advertisement to symbolize the fact that residents of Washington, D.C., cannot elect senators and representatives. The District elects only a non-voting delegate to the House of Representatives.

THE FAILED D.C. STATEHOOD AMENDMENT

For more than two centuries the residents of Washington, D.C., have sought home rule and representation in the national government. After ratification of the Twenty-third Amendment, which gave the District of Columbia's voting-age population the right to participate in Presidential elections, the District's supporters in Congress began a campaign to turn the District into a state.

In the 1970s, Massachusetts senator Edward M. Kennedy led an unsuccessful movement to pass a law that would grant the district representation in the House and Senate. In 1971, the district obtained a nonvoting delegate in the House of Representatives, but it failed to gain entry into the Senate. Opponents of statehood argued that the district was different from other states. It had been formed out of land donated by Maryland and Virginia, and the Constitution assigned its jurisdiction to Congress. Supporters concluded that their only hope was to enact a constitutional amendment giving the district full voting rights in Congress. If the amendment passed, Washington, D.C., would become the equivalent of a state. Although it would be tiny geographically in comparison to even the smallest state, its population was actually greater and paid more in federal taxes than several of the states. Supporters in Congress appealed to civil rights sentiments, arguing that voting and representation, among the most important of all civil rights, were being denied in the nation's capital.

In 1978, Congress sent a constitutional amendment to the states that would have repealed the Twenty-third Amendment and given the District four electors (rather than three), which reflected its population size, as well as voting members of the Senate and House of Representatives. The proposed amendment encountered significant opposition. Rural states objected that the intensely urban District differed radically from all the other states. Others argued that Article V of the Constitution specified that no state would be deprived of its equal representation in the Senate, and that adding two senators for the District would dilute their own votes. Republicans also worried that congressional races in the District, with its high proportion of Democrats, would not be competitive. A growing national mood against big government in Washington also worked to the district's disadvantage, and only sixteen states ratified the statehood amendment before its seven-year time limit expired.

"I have always felt that the District of Columbia should be the model of perfection in municipal government, and showplace for our Nation for all who visit the National Capital to see. . . . As a result of ratification of the 23rd Amendment, the people of the District are now able to vote for President and Vice President. This is not enough. They should also be entitled to representation in the Congress."

— Connecticut Senator Prescott Bush (father of President George H. W. Bush and grandfather of President George W. Bush), speaking in the Senate in 1961

Twenty-third Amendment

Virginia and Maryland donate land for a federal capital

1790

Article I, section 8, clause 17 of the Constitution authorizes Congress to create a seat of government ten miles square and grants exclusive jurisdiction over it. The states of Virginia and Maryland donate the land for a District of Columbia, and construction soon begins on the White House, Capitol, and other federal buildings.

The federal government moves to the District of Columbia

1800

Meeting first in New York City, and then in Philadelphia, officials of the federal government move to the Washington, D.C., in 1800. Congress convenes there in December. When established, the District has a population of only five thousand residents, far fewer than the thirty thousand speci-fied for the size of congressional districts. Many are tem-porary residents, living in the district only for the few months the Congress is in session and returning to their home states to vote.

The Organic Acts are passed

1801

After Congress takes up residence in the new capital, it passes the Organic Acts of 1801, taking direct control of the District. Under the law, people living in the District are denied the right to vote in either Maryland or Virginia, the states from which the District has been created.

Local board of elections is established

1955

Congress directs the appointment of a three-member board of elections to oversee the District's election of local political party officers, party committee members, and delegates to political parties' national conventions.

The District votes for President

1964

For the first time, under the new Twenty-third Amendment, residents of the District of Columbia vote in a Presidential election. The District overwhelmingly supports President Lyndon Johnson over his Republican challenger, Arizona senator Barry Goldwater.

President Johnson appoints Mayor Washington

1967

In 1967, President Lyndon Johnson appoints Walter Washington to fill the new post of mayor commissioner of the District of Columbia. Washington accepts the post as a first step toward home rule for the District. The follow-ing year, rioting and looting erupt in the capital following the assassination of Martin Luther King Jr., making the need for a stable local government all the more urgent.

TIMELINE

Alexandria returns to Virginia

First D.C. local government is formed

Congress takes over the District government

1846   1871   1878

The original government buildings constructed are all on the Maryland side of the Potomac River. People living in the portion of the District on the other side of the Potomac seek to rejoin Virginia. In 1846, Congress votes to give back to Virginia thirty-two square miles of land that Virginia donated to the government in 1790. Residents of Alexandria and Arlington counties again become Virginia citizens and are entitled to vote in that state.

The District of Columbia receives its first democratically elected government, which consists of a governor, a bicameral legislature with an appointed eleven-member upper house, and an elected twenty-two-member lower house. District residents also elect a nonvoting delegate to the U.S. House of Representatives after Congress establishes this territorial government.

In response to charges that the District government is corrupt and nearing bankruptcy, Congress creates a commission form of government to run the city. For the next century, three Presidentially appointed commissioners run the district. The position of the nonvoting delegate is abolished.

The District gains a nonvoting delegate to the House of Representatives

Home rule is achieved

A statehood amendment fails

1970   1973   1985

The U.S. House of Representatives restores the position of nonvoting delegate from the District of Columbia. The Honorable Walter Fauntroy is elected to the position in 1971.

Congress passes the District of Columbia Self-Government Reorganization Act, which provides for an elected mayor and city council for Washington, D.C. Walter E. Washington becomes the city's first elected mayor under the new system.

Although it receives overwhelming bi-partisan support in Congress, a constitutional amendment granting voting rights to residents of the District of Columbia is approved by only sixteen of the thirty-eight states necessary for ratification. After seven years, the amendment expires.

Twenty-fourth Amendment

(1964)

Section 1. The right of citizens of the United States to vote in any primary or other election for President or Vice President for electors for President or Vice President, or for Senator or Representative in Congress, shall not be denied or abridged by the United States or any State by reason of failure to pay any poll tax or other tax.

Section 2. The Congress shall have power to enforce this article by appropriate legislation.

A 1964 cartoon portrays the poll tax being added to a museum of historical relics, along with slavery and Prohibition. That year the Twenty-fourth Amendment abolished the poll tax.

WHAT IT MEANS:

Although the Fifteenth Amendment prohibited voting discrimination on account of race, many southern states enacted laws to make it difficult for African Americans to vote. The Twenty-fourth Amendment was designed to address one particular injustice, the poll tax. The requirement to pay a fee in order to vote kept low-income citizens, both white and black, from taking part in elections. The Twenty-fourth Amendment made it illegal to charge any voter for the right to cast a ballot in any federal election.

"I'm as much a Southerner as anyone, but this is a moderate proposal. It seems to me the South can help its own cause by taking an affirmative position on this."

— Florida Senator Spessard L. Holland, defending the constitutional amendment to outlaw the poll tax, speaking in the Senate in 1962

A COMPLEX LEGISLATIVE SCHEME IS THWARTED

In 1965, African American citizens of Virginia had hope that the recently passed Voting Rights Act would finally guarantee them the right to vote. Literacy tests were now illegal, and the Twenty-fourth Amendment had eliminated the poll tax as a voting requirement. Virginia was one of the last five states to maintain the poll tax as late as 1964. But the Virginia legislature had anticipated the amendment. The legislature eliminated the poll tax as a prerequisite to voting in federal elections, but it introduced a requirement that voters either pay the customary poll tax or file a certificate of residence six months before the election. Filing a certificate was cumbersome and time-consuming.

Disgruntled citizens filed two class-action suits against this complicated and discriminatory procedure, claiming that the statute violated the Fourteenth, Seventeenth, and Twenty-fourth Amendments. The courts were on their side. In *Harman* v. *Forssenius* (1965), the U.S. Supreme Court found the Virginia statute to be in violation of the Twenty-fourth Amendment. "The State may not

Officials in Arlington, Virginia, verify that residents have paid their poll taxes before they can vote in 1944. The Twenty-fourth Amendment banned the poll tax, which tended to discriminate against poor people and minorities.

impose a penalty upon those who exercise a right guaranteed by the Constitution," the Court stated, especially considering that "the Virginia poll tax was born of a desire to disenfranchise the Negro." The residency requirement was too burdensome as an alternative to the poll tax, especially as the Twenty-fourth Amendment had ruled out the poll tax.

The Supreme Court's decision marked a definite shift in thinking from previous years. Before the Twenty-fourth Amendment, the Supreme Court and other federal courts upheld poll taxes as the right of the states to impose, so long as they applied to all citizens equally. Passage of the amendment shifted the legal emphasis to protecting vulnerable groups' right to vote. The Court sought to remove the threat of complex legislative schemes established to disenfranchise certain voters.

Twenty-fourth Amendment

New Hampshire eliminates property requirement

1792

New Hampshire is the first state to eliminate the rule that only property owners and taxpayers can vote. Following New Hampshire's lead, other states begin to shift away from such restrictions in an effort to open the electorate to all white males over age twenty-one. In 1856, North Carolina becomes the last state to eliminate property holding as a requirement for voting.

The Supreme Court upholds literacy tests for voting

1898

In *Williams* v. *Mississippi*, the U.S. Supreme Court held that literacy tests for voting did not violate the Fourteenth Amendment's equal protection clause so long as there was no proof that they were being given in a discriminatory fashion to exclude voters because of their race.

"Grandfather clause" is struck down

1915

In *Guinn* v. *United States*, the U.S. Supreme Court declares unconstitutional the "grandfather clause" in the Oklahoma Constitution, which allows illiterate men to vote if they can prove that their grandfathers had held the right. This provision allows illiterate white men to vote, but not illiterate blacks, as most of their grandfathers had been slaves.

Congress passes the Civil Rights Act of 1964

1964

In a sweeping move, Congress passes the Civil Rights Act of 1964, which bars discrimination on the basis of race, national origin, religion, and gender in voting, pu blic accommodations (such as restaurants and hotels), the work- place, and schools.

The Voting Rights Act of 1965 is adopted

1965

Believing the social gains that African Americans achieved by the Civil Rights Act of 1964 can best be protected by exercising the right to vote, Congress writes a comprehensive voting rights law. It temporarily suspends literacy tests and provides for the appointment of federal examiners with the power to register qualified citizens to vote. Under this law, *any* racially discriminatory act that prevents Americans from voting is prohibited.

The Supreme Court strikes down Virginia's residency requirement

1965

Following ratification of the Twenty-fourth Amendment, Virginia amends its poll tax law. Voters can either pay the poll tax or file a "certificate of residency" prov- ing they lived in the state six months prior to the election. In *Harman* v. *Forssenius*, the Supreme Court rules that the burden of proving residency so far in advance of an election violates the Twenty-fourth Amendment.

TIMELINE

Poll taxes are upheld as constitutional

1937

Many southern states adopt the policy of charging voters a poll tax. This tactic denies the right to vote to both black and white voters who cannot afford the tax. In *Breedlove* v. *Suttles,* Breedlove, a twenty-eight-year-old white male, seeks to have Georgia's poll tax declared unconstitutional. The Supreme Court holds that the statute does not violate the Constitution, as it does not discriminate arbitrarily.

Alabama literacy tests are found unconstitutional

1949

In *Davis* v. *Schnell,* the U.S. Supreme Court finds that an Alabama constitutional amendment that requires citizens to pass a test demonstrating their understanding of an article of the federal Constitution in order to vote violates that very document. The legislative history of the Amendment discloses that the tests are intended to disenfranchise African Americans.

for full employment after the war
REGISTER ‹TO› VOTE
CIO POLITICAL ACTION COMMITTEE

North Carolina's literacy tests are upheld

1959

In *Lassiter* v. *Northampton County Board of Elections,* the U.S. Supreme Court rules that the state of North Carolina's requirement that all voters pass a literacy test in order to vote is constitutional. The Court finds that the policy is not inconsistent with the Fourteenth and Fifteenth Amendments' standards of fairness.

Poll taxes are ruled unconstitutional

1966

In *Harper* v. *Virginia Board of Elections,* the U.S. Supreme Court overrules its earlier decision in *Breedlove* v. *Suttles* (1937) and declares that the use of a poll tax at state elections is unconstitutional. The Court holds that discrimination based on economic status is in violation of the equal protection clause of the Fourteenth Amendment. As a result of this ruling and the passage of the Twenty-fourth Amendment, poll taxes can no longer be used in federal or state elections.

"Durational residency" rule is found unconstitutional

1972

Tennessee passes a "durational residency" rule for citizens to qualify to vote. Under this rule, voters must live in the state for one year and in the county for ninety days before being allowed to vote. In *Dunn* v. *Blumstein,* the U.S. Supreme Court strikes down the residency rule as an unconstitutional restriction on the right to vote. The Court notes that there are other ways to achieve the state's goals of deterring voter fraud and ensuring that voters are knowledgeable without blocking otherwise eligible voters from participating in elections.

Congress strengthens the Voting Rights Act

1982

Renewing its commitment to voting rights for another twenty-five years, Congress extends the authority of the Justice Department to review legislative redistricting in some southern states. In *Mobile* v. *Bolden* (1980), the Supreme Court rejects a class action suit by African Americans who argue that electing the Mobile, Alabama, city council on an at-large basis—meaning that council members were elected by the city population as a whole rather than in neighborhood-based districts—dilutes the black vote. The Court finds that at-large elections are racially neutral. In response to this ruling, Congress amends the Voting Rights Act to permit a finding of racial discrimination without proof that the state specifically intends to discriminate.

Twenty-fifth Amendment

(1965)

"When a stunned nation mourned the tragedy of President Kennedy's assassination in 1963, questions were again raised about presidential succession and national stability. What if the Vice President had also been struck down?"

— Senator Birch Bayh, chair of the Senate subcommittee that drafted the amendment, in *American Roulette: The History and Dilemma of the Vice Presidency* (1965)

President Gerald R. Ford (right) in the Oval Office with National Security Adviser Henry Kissinger (left) and Vice President Nelson Rockefeller (center). Ford and Rockefeller came to office by appointment instead of election.

WHAT IT SAYS

Section 1. In case of the removal of the President from office or of his death or resignation, the Vice President shall become President.

Section 2. Whenever there is a vacancy in the office of the Vice President, the President shall nominate a Vice President who shall take office upon confirmation by a majority vote of both Houses of Congress.

Section 3. Whenever the President transmits to the President pro tempore of the Senate and the Speaker of the House of Representatives his written declaration that he is unable to discharge the powers and duties of his office, and until he transmits to them a written declaration to the contrary, such powers and duties shall be discharged by the Vice President as Acting President.

Section 4. Whenever the Vice President and a majority of either the principal officers of the executive departments or of such other body as Congress may by law provide, transmit to the President pro tempore of the Senate and the Speaker of the House of Representatives their written declaration that the President is unable to discharge the powers and duties of his office, the Vice President shall immediately assume the powers and duties of the office as Acting President.

Thereafter, when the President transmits to the President pro tempore of the Senate and the Speaker of the House of Representatives his written declaration that no inability exists, he shall resume the powers and duties of his office unless the Vice President and a majority of either the principal officers of the executive department or of such other body as Congress may by law provide, transmit within four days to the President pro tempore of the Senate and the Speaker of the House of Representatives their written declaration that the President is unable to discharge the powers and duties of his office. Thereupon Congress shall decide the issue, assembling within forty-eight hours for that purpose if not in session. If the Congress, within twenty-one days after receipt of the latter written declaration, or, if Congress is not in session, within twenty-one days after Congress is required to assemble, determines by two-thirds vote of both Houses that the President is unable to discharge the powers and duties of his office, the Vice President shall continue to discharge the same as Acting President; otherwise, the President shall resume the powers and duties of his office.

WHAT IT MEANS

Following the assassination of President John F. Kennedy in November 1963, Vice President Lyndon B. Johnson became President, and the office of Vice President sat vacant for more than a year until the next election. The Twenty-fifth Amendment was then passed to allow the President to appoint a Vice President if that office becomes vacant, subject to a vote of approval by the House and Senate. The Twenty-fifth Amendment also clarifies what happens upon the death, resignation, or temporary incapacity of the President.

The Twenty-fifth Amendment went into effect in 1967 and was first applied in 1973 upon the resignation of Vice President Spiro Agnew, who was facing charges of bribery and corruption. President Richard Nixon then appointed House Republican minority leader Gerald R. Ford as the new Vice President. Less than a year later, Nixon resigned the Presidency as a result of the Watergate scandal. Ford became President and appointed former New York governor Nelson Rockefeller as Vice President. Ford and Rockefeller thus became the nation's first unelected team of President and Vice President.

If a President should fall seriously ill or for some other reason must temporarily step down, the amendment provides that the President give notice of the disability to the president pro tempore of the Senate (the presiding officer of the Senate) and the Speaker of the House. The Vice President is then authorized to serve as acting President to carry on the President's duties. The President can resume the duties of office upon giving appropriate notice to the congressional leadership. The Vice President and the cabinet can ask for a vote of Congress should they doubt the President's fitness to resume office. A vote of two-thirds of each house is required to prevent a President's return.

The "acting President" provision of the Twenty-fifth Amendment was first invoked on July 13, 1985, when President Ronald Reagan underwent cancer surgery. He signed a letter transferring power to Vice President George H. W. Bush and sent another letter to the Speaker of the House and president pro tempore of the Senate, as the amendment required. Following his surgery, Reagan notified them that he was fit to resume his Presidential duties. In 2002, President George W. Bush signed similar letters to transfer power temporarily to Vice President Dick Cheney, while Bush was sedated briefly during a medical procedure known as a colonoscopy.

THE NATION'S FIRST UNELECTED PRESIDENT

In October 1973, Spiro Agnew resigned as Vice President after pleading no contest to charges of having taken bribes. President Richard Nixon recognized that under the Twenty-fifth Amendment his choice to replace Agnew would require confirmation by both the Senate and House. The Republican congressional leaders favored former governors Nelson Rockefeller and Ronald Reagan (who tied), Treasury Secretary John Connally, and House Republican leader Gerald Ford, in that order. When Nixon discussed the candidates with the Democratic leaders in Congress, Ford topped their list. Ford accepted Nixon's offer to become Vice President, and both houses easily confirmed him. At the time, President Nixon was being investigated for his role in the break-in at the Democratic Party headquarters in the Watergate building, and tapes he had secretly made of his conversations in the White House provided evidence of his participation in a cover-up of the crime. As the House moved toward impeaching him, he resigned in August 1974. The vacancy made Ford the nation's first unelected President, and demonstrated the value of the Twenty-fifth Amendment. The Presidency changed hands, but not party. Although unelected, Ford had risen to the office through legitimate constitutional means and his assumption of Presidential power went unquestioned. One of Ford's first acts as President was to appoint former New York governor Nelson Rockefeller as Vice President, so that by the end of 1974 both of the top executive posts had been filled.

Twenty-fifth Amendment

Vice President John Tyler becomes President

1841

On the morning of April 5, 1841, Vice President John Tyler is informed that President William Henry Harrison had died of pneumonia the previous day. Some members of Harrison's cabinet view Tyler as "Vice President, acting as President," but Tyler is determined to be President in his own right. He rejects calls for a Presidential election, and serves for the remainder of Harrison's term. Although Tyler asserts the full powers of the Presidency, there are many who continue to call him "His Accidency."

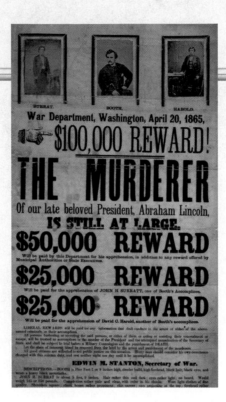

A plot against the President and Vice President

1865

When John Wilkes Booth shoots President Abraham Lincoln on April 14, 1865, other conspirators working with him are sent to kill the Vice President and Secretary of State, who are next in line to succeed to the Presidency. The conspirators believe that this will destabilize the Union government. Although President Lincoln died, conspirator George Atzerodt lost his nerve and fled without assailing Vice President Andrew Johnson, and Lewis Powell is able only to wound Secretary of State William Seward. Johnson takes the oath of office as President and the federal government continues to function despite the tragedy.

President Ford chooses his own Vice President

1974

President Ford nominates former New York governor Nelson A. Rockefeller to become Vice President, filling the vacancy his own elevation to the Presidency has created. Congress conducts lengthy hearings on Rockefeller but eventually confirms him several months later. For the first time, the voters have elected neither the President nor the Vice President in a national election.

The Twenty-fifth Amendment is considered after the President is shot

1981

A deranged man shoots President Ronald Reagan outside a hotel in Washington, D.C. While the President is undergoing surgery, his advisers discuss invoking the Twenty-fifth Amendment, but reject the idea. Secretary of State Alexander Haig claims, contrary to the constitutional line of succession, that he was "in charge" until Vice President George H. W. Bush returns to Washington.

TIMELINE

President Kennedy is assassinated
1963

While riding in a motorcade in Dallas, Texas, President John F. Kennedy is shot and killed. Vice President Lyndon Johnson takes the oath as President, but the Vice Presidency then remains vacant for more than a year until the next election. Johnson had suffered a heart attack several years earlier, and the Speaker of the House and president pro tempore of the Senate, next in line of succession, are both elderly men. Congress acts to rectify this situation by sending to the states the Twenty-fifth Amendment.

Vice President Agnew resigns
1973

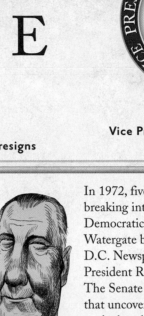

Charged with tax fraud and bribery, Vice President Spiro Agnew resigns from office. Two months later, President Richard Nixon nominates the House Republican minority leader, Gerald R. Ford, to become Vice President, the first time that the Twenty-fifth Amendment is invoked. Ford is confirmed by the Senate and House.

Vice President Ford becomes President
1974

In 1972, five burglars are arrested while breaking into the offices of the National Democratic Committee located at the Watergate building in Washington, D.C. Newspaper accounts soon link President Richard Nixon to the incident. The Senate holds a lengthy investigation that uncovers evidence that links Nixon to the burglary and subsequent cover-up. As the House Judiciary Committee moves toward recommending Nixon's impeachment, he resigns the Presidency. Vice President Gerald Ford is then sworn in as President.

The Vice President serves as "Acting President"
1985

President Ronald Reagan undergoes an operation to remove cancerous tissue from his colon. Before undergoing the procedure, Reagan sends a letter to the House and Senate, indicating that Vice President Bush will serve as acting President during the eight hours that Reagan is under anesthesia. However, the President does not expressly invoke the Twenty-fifth Amendment.

President Bush makes plans to turn over power
1991

Upon learning that he has an irregular heartbeat, President George H.W. Bush announces that Vice President Dan Quayle will be acting President if the President requires electric shock therapy. As the treatment is never required, power is never transferred. Like President Bush, President Bill Clinton plans for the possibility of a disabling illness, including how and when power will be turned over to the Vice President. These plans are never needed.

First formal use of disability clause
2002

When President George W. Bush undergoes a medical treatment that requires anesthesia, he transfers power to Vice President Dick Cheney for the hour that he will be sedated. This is the first formal use of the disability clause.

Twenty-sixth Amendment

(1971)

A grim cartoon reminded Americans that soldiers who were old enough to fight and die for their country were not old enough to vote for their leaders. The Twenty-sixth Amendment extended the right to vote in all local, state, and federal elections to eighteen-year-olds.

WHAT IT SAYS

Section 1. The right of citizens of the United States, who are eighteen years of age or older, to vote shall not be denied or abridged by the United States or by any State on account of age.

Section 2. The Congress shall have power to enforce this article by appropriate legislation.

THE YOUTH VOTE IN THEIR FIRST ELECTION

The first election following the ratification of the Twenty-sixth Amendment took place in 1972, when President Richard M. Nixon ran for reelection against Democratic senator George McGovern of South Dakota. The Vietnam War continued that year, despite Nixon's earlier promise that he had a plan to end the war. Senator McGovern campaigned on the slogan "Come Home, America," pledging to withdraw all American combat troops.

During the course of the war, the military draft had grown increasingly unpopular. Some students burned their draft cards, some refused to be inducted, and some left the country to avoid the draft. Other young men were drafted or volunteered. As the antiwar movement grew, with large rallies and demonstrations, a consensus developed that those old enough to fight for their country should have the right to participate in the democratic process and elect those who would set the policies that would affect their lives.

As the election approached, the Census Bureau estimated that there could be 25 million possible new votes in the election with the lowered voting age. On Election Day, however, fewer than half of the potential voters between eighteen and twenty-one came to the polls. This reflected an overall decline in voting, with only 55.6 percent of the eligible voters participating. Those between the ages of forty-five and sixty-four had the highest participation, with 71 percent voting.

The turnout disappointed Senator McGovern, who had aimed much of his campaign at the youth vote, especially among students. Polls showed that those students who did vote cast their ballots about evenly between McGovern and Nixon. President Nixon won reelection in a landslide, and on election night he declared that he had accomplished what most people had considered impossible: "We won a majority of the votes of young Americans."

Although the youth vote often trailed behind older voters, it rose significantly in the Presidential election of 2004, when more than half of all registered voters between ages eighteen and thirty went to the polls. Younger voters favored the Democratic candidate, John Kerry, by a margin of 54 to 44 percent over President George W. Bush.

During the Vietnam War, President Richard Nixon signed the Twenty-sixth Amendment, which extended the vote to those citizens between the ages of eighteen and twenty-one. Supporters of the Amendment argued that those who fought the war should have a role in the election of their leaders.

WHAT IT MEANS

The unpopularity of the military draft during the Vietnam War raised questions about why young men between eighteen and twenty-one should be qualified to fight for their country but not to vote for the leaders who made decisions about war and peace. The Twenty-sixth Amendment lowered the voting age to eighteen. It was a continuation of a movement toward democratization that began with efforts to remove property qualifications for voting, and expanded to include African Americans and women. Along the way other obstacles such as poll taxes, literary tests, and residency requirements also fell to constitutional challenges and change.

"*The failure to vote is a national disgrace. You wonder how the high schools and colleges fail to put an emphasis on voting. The 18-year-olds are not voting, and their mothers and fathers are not doing much better. This worries me. If the decline continues, we will elect a president by a majority of the minority outvoting the rest of the minority.*"

— West Virginia Senator Jennings Randolph, the chief sponsor of the Twenty-sixth Amendment, in a *Washington Post* interview, October 14, 1984

Twenty-seventh Amendment

(1992)

"We can eradicate the aura of privilege that has hung over the chamber for two hundred years. James Madison saw something wrong with members of Congress increasing their own salaries, unchecked by their constituencies. Adoption of this much-delayed amendment to the Constitution will prevent a future Congress from raising its own pay until a recorded vote has been held and an election has intervened. This is progress, after 200 years of delay."

— Oregon Representative Peter A. DeFazio, speaking in the House of Representatives on May 19, 1992

WHAT IT SAYS

No law varying the compensation for the services of the Senators and Representatives shall take effect, until an election of Representatives shall have intervened.

TWO HUNDRED YEARS: THE DATES ON WHICH STATES RATIFIED THE TWENTY-SEVENTH AMENDMENT

Maryland	December 19, 1789	Connecticut	May 13, 1987
North Carolina	December 22, 1789	Wisconsin	July 15, 1987
South Carolina	January 19, 1790	Georgia	February 2, 1988
Delaware,	January 28, 1790	West Virginia	March 10, 1988
Vermont	November 3, 1791	Louisiana	July 7, 1988
Virginia	December 15, 1791	Iowa	February 9, 1989
Ohio	May 6, 1873	Idaho	March 23, 1989
Wyoming	March 6, 1978	Nevada	April 26, 1989
Maine	April 27, 1983	Alaska	May 6, 1989
Colorado	April 22, 1984	Oregon	May 19, 1989
South Dakota	February 21, 1985	Minnesota	May 22, 1989
New Hampshire	March 7, 1985	Texas	May 25, 1989
Arizona	April 3, 1985	Kansas	April 5, 1989
Oklahoma	July 10, 1985	Florida	May 31, 1990
New Mexico	February 14, 1986	North Dakota	March 25, 1991
Indiana	February 24, 1986	Alabama	May 5, 1992
Utah	February 25, 1986	Michigan	May 7, 1992
Arkansas	March 13, 1987	New Jersey	May 7, 1992
Montana	March 17, 1987	Illinois	May 12, 1992

Ratification was completed on May 7, 1992, when the thirty-eighth and thirty-ninth states approved the amendment, providing the three-quarters of the states necessary to add the amendment to the Constitution. The archivist of the United States declared the amendment valid on May 18, 1992.

The only one of the original twelve amendments that Congress passed in 1789 that the states did not ratify would have set the number of people in each congressional district at 50,000. Following the 2000 census, the average apportionment of congressional districts was 646,952, meaning that each of the current districts would need to be divided into thirteen had that amendment been adopted.

WHAT IT MEANS

The Twenty-seventh Amendment prevents any congressional pay raise from going into effect until after the voters have been able to cast ballots in the next election, registering their approval or disapproval. With the voters in mind, legislators were likely to be more cautious about increasing their own salaries. James Madison introduced the Amendment in 1789 and it was sent to the states with the Bill of Rights. An insufficient number of states ratified it and the amendment lay dormant until 1982, when public outrage over a large boost in congressional salaries encouraged the states to revive the amendment. Unlike modern amendments, the Twenty-seventh had no time limit for ratification, so that some state legislatures ratified it more than two hundred years apart. In 1992, the Michigan state legislature passed the amendment, and it was finally ratified.

CONGRESSIONAL SALARIES PRIOR TO RATIFICATION OF THE TWENTY-SEVENTH AMENDMENT		
1789		$1,500
1817		$2,000
1855		$3,000
1865		$5,000
1871		$7,500
1874		$5,000*
1907		$7,500
1925		$10,000
1932		$9,000**
1933		$8,500
1934		$9,500
1935		$10,000
1947		$12,500
1955		$22,500
1965		$30,000
1969		$42,500
1975		$44,600
1977		$57,500
1979		$60,663
1983		$69,800
1984		$72,600
1985		$75,100
1987		$89,500
1990	Senate:	$98,400
	House:	$96,600
1991	Senate:	$101,900***
	House:	$125,100
1991		$125,100****

* After an unpopular increase known as the Salary Grab, Congress reduced its salary

** As an economic move during the Great Depression, government salaries were cut

*** The Senate chose not to raise its salary as high as the House, but allowed senators to accept honoraria for giving speeches away from the Senate

**** The Senate raised its salary to the House level, but banned honoraria for outside activities

When members of Congress voted to increase their own salaries, a furniture store ran an advertisement offering its products at a reasonable price "Because not everyone can vote themselves a raise." Public unhappiness with the pay raise led to passage of the Twenty-seventh Amendment.

Twenty-sixth Amendment

Wartime service raises calls to lower the voting age	Jennings Randolph introduces a proposal to lower the voting age	Georgia becomes the first state to lower its voting age
1941	1942	1943

As America enters World War II, the phrase, "old enough to fight, old enough to vote" becomes a popular slogan among those seeking to lower the voting age to eighteen, the same age that men can be drafted into the military.

Jennings Randolph, a Democratic representative from West Virginia, introduces an amendment to lower the voting age to eighteen. He continues to propose this amendment repeatedly during the course of his four decades in the House and the Senate until it eventually passes in 1971.

Georgia passes a law to lower the voting age to eighteen for state and local, but not federal, elections.

Twenty-seventh Amendment

Congress sends the amendment to the states as part of the Bill of Rights	Unless Congress sets a date for terminating ratification, amendments are valid	Wyoming revives the pay raise amendment
1789	1939	1978

Congress sends the states twelve amendments to the Constitution, but only ten of the amendments—known as the Bill of Rights—are ratified. The two that are not adopted deal with congressional pay raises and the size of districts for the House of Representatives. The pay raise amendment is approved by only six of the eleven states needed for ratification, and rejected by five states.

Under a ruling of the U.S. Supreme Court in the landmark case of *Coleman* v. *Miller,* any proposed amendment for which Congress has not specified a ratification deadline remains in play. The Court says that states may continue to consider an amendment regardless of how long it has been since it was first proposed.

A century after the last state, Ohio, ratified the salary amendment, the Wyoming legislature adds its ratification. This act is part of a general dissatisfaction with the directions of the federal government on matters of taxing and spending expressed by western states in what became known as the Sagebrush Rebellion.

TIMELINE

President Johnson gradually escalates the war in Vietnam

1965

Following a reelection campaign in which he pledges not to send Americans to fight a war in Asia, President Johnson gradually escalates American troop strength in South Vietnam, until more than a half million American soldiers, sailors, and marines are engaged in combat. The government uses the draft to build its military strength.

Congress can lower the voting age in federal, but not state, elections

1970

Following the passage of a five-year extension of the Voting Rights Act of 1965, the U.S. government files suits against the states of Arizona and Idaho to seek compliance with the law. Texas and Oregon file lawsuits claiming Congress has overstepped its authority when it passed the law. In the U.S. Supreme Court, the four cases are combined into one, *Oregon* v. *United States.* The Court upholds the federal prohibitions on literacy tests and residency requirements and certain rules on absentee balloting. The Court also rules that Congress can lower the voting age in federal elections, but not in state and local elections.

Young voters turn out in high numbers

1972

In the first election in which they are eligible to vote, 50 percent of Americans between eighteen and twenty-one go to the polls on Election Day. However, in Presidential election years between 1972 and 2000, the national voter turnout rate declines among younger voters, much more sharply than among older voters.

A student researches the issue

1982

In 1982, while looking for a research paper topic, University of Texas graduate student Gregory Watson discovers that in addition to the ten amendments that became the Bill of Rights, there were two other amendments that the First Congress had proposed and submitted to the states for ratification. In a paper, he argues that those amendments, though not ratified at the time, are still viable because they do not contain a "sunset provision" limiting the time for ratification. His professor is not impressed with his argument and gives him a C on his paper. Convinced that the amendment is still pending, Watson then begins a campaign to lobby state legislatures to ratify the forgotten amendments. When Congress votes itself a large pay increase, the campaign gains momentum.

Michigan ratifies Twenty-seventh Amendment

1992

Between 1983 and 1992, thirty-three additional states ratify the pay raise amendment. On May 7, 1992, 203 years after its submission to the states, the Twenty-seventh Amendment is ratified with its passage by the Michigan State Legislature. The U.S. Senate and House of Representatives adopt concurrent resolutions agreeing that the Twenty-seventh Amendment has been validly ratified, despite the unorthodox lapse between its submission and completion.

Members of Congress are not harmed by pay increases

2001

Representative Bob Schaffer and three others challenge the cost-of-living increases in the Ethics Reform Act of 1989, arguing that such automatic increases grant legislators raises before a new Congressional session begins. In *Schaffer* v. *Clinton,* the district court dismisses three of the plaintiffs (a state legislator, a taxpayer, and a voter), on the ground that they have no standing to bring the case. The court dismisses case finding that the cost-of-living raises accomplish the goal of the Twenty-seventh Amendment because they "eliminate the possibility that Congress will grant itself a new pay raise during its current session." The court of appeals dismisses the appeal because Schaffer, by receiving the pay increase, has not suffered any real injury.

Delegates to the Constitutional Convention

CONNECTICUT

Oliver Ellsworth (1745–1807) was born in Windsor, Connecticut. He attended Yale, graduated from the College of New Jersey (which later became Princeton), and studied law. He served in the Connecticut General Assembly, and the Continental Congress. After becoming a judge of the Connecticut Superior Court, Ellsworth was elected to the U.S. Senate as a Federalist from 1789 to 1796. There, he sponsored the Judiciary Act of 1789. He resigned from the Senate to become chief justice of the United States from 1796 until 1800, when he retired. He did not sign the Constitution.

William Samuel Johnson (1727–1819) was born in Stratford, Connecticut. He graduated from both Yale and Harvard and studied law. He served in the colonial legislature and as a delegate to the Stamp Act Congress in 1765. Connecticut sent him as agent extraordinary to the court of England to determine the colony's title to Indian lands from 1767 to 1771. He was then a judge of the Connecticut Supreme Court, and a member of the Continental Congress. Johnson was the first president of Columbia College of New York City, from 1787 to 1800; and as a Federalist served as a U.S. senator from Connecticut from 1789 to 1791. He signed the Constitution.

Roger Sherman (1721–1793) was born in Newton, Massachusetts. After working as a surveyor of New Haven County in Connecticut, he studied law and became a member of the Connecticut legislature for various terms between 1755 and 1785. He was a judge of the state's superior court, a member of the executive committee that ran the colony's day-to-day functions during the American Revolution called the council of safety, and a member of the Continental Congress. Sherman signed the Declaration of Independence and was a member of the committee that prepared the Articles of Confederation. He was mayor of New Haven and served as a Federalist in the U.S. House of Representatives from 1789 to 1791, and in the U.S. Senate from 1791 until his death. Signed.

DELAWARE

Richard Bassett (1745–1815) was born in Cecil County, Maryland. He studied law and practiced in Delaware. He was a captain of a Delaware troop during the Revolutionary War and a member of Delaware's constitutional conventions in 1776 and 1792. He also served in the state legislature. He was elected to the U.S. Senate and served from 1789 to 1793, when he became chief justice of the state's court of common pleas. A Federalist, Bassett served as governor of Delaware from 1799 to 1801. Signed.

Gunning Bedford (1742–1797) was born in Philadelphia, Pennsylvania. He was serving as a lieutenant colonel in the Continental Army when he was wounded in the Battle of White Plains. He studied law and became a member of the Delaware General Assembly. He was elected to the Continental Congress but declined to serve. Bedford served as governor of Delaware from 1796 until he died the following year. Signed.

Jacob Broom (1752–1810) was born in Wilmington, Delaware. He prepared George Washington's maps for the Battle of Brandywine, in 1776. He served as burgess (or mayor) of Wilmington and as a member of the state legislature. Broom became the first postmaster of Wilmington, from 1790 to 1792, and devoted himself to diverse business interests, among them operating a machine shop and cotton mill. Signed.

John Dickinson (1732–1808) was born in Talbot County, Maryland, and moved as a child to Dover, Delaware. He studied law in Philadelphia and London and practiced in Philadelphia. He was a member of both the Delaware and Pennsylvania legislatures, a delegate to the Stamp Act Congress of 1765, and a member of the Continental Congress from both Pennsylvania and Delaware. Dickinson was a brigadier general of Pennsylvania militia, governor of Delaware in 1781, and governor of Pennsylvania from 1782 to 1785. Signed.

George Read (1733–1798) was born in Cecil County, Maryland. He studied law and practiced in New Castle, Delaware. He served as attorney general for lower Delaware, as a member of the colonial legislature, and as a member of the Continental Congress, where he signed the Declaration of Independence. He served in the Delaware legislature and as a judge of the U.S. Court of Appeals. Read represented Delaware at the Annapolis Convention in 1786, and served in the U.S. Senate as a Federalist from 1789 until 1793, when he became chief justice of Delaware. Signed.

GEORGIA

Abraham Baldwin (1754–1807) was born in North Guilford, Connecticut. He graduated from Yale and became a minister and a teacher at Yale. During the Revolutionary War he served as a chaplain. He later studied law and moved to Augusta, Georgia, where he became a member of the Georgia House of Representatives and became president of the University of Georgia. A member of the Continental Congress, Baldwin was elected as a Democratic-Republican to the U.S. House of Representatives, where he served from 1789 to 1799, and then to the U.S. Senate from 1799 to 1807. The Senate elected Baldwin its president pro tempore. Signed.

William Few (1748–1828) was born near Baltimore, Maryland, and moved as a child to North Carolina. He studied law and practiced in Augusta, Georgia. He served in the state legislature and as a lieutenant colonel in the Georgia militia. After serving as a member of the Continental Congress, he was elected to the U.S. Senate and served from 1789 to 1793, when he was defeated in his run for reelection. Few became a judge of the circuit court of Georgia from 1794 to 1797 and then moved to New York City, where he served in the New York State assembly from 1802 to 1805, as well as state prison inspector and as a city alderman from 1813 to 1814. Signed.

William Houston (1755–1813) was born in Savannah, Georgia, and studied law in London. Although Houston's father had been a member of the royal government of Georgia, the son joined the movement for independence. He served in the Continental Congress from 1783 to 1786. Did not sign.

William Pierce (1740–1789) was born in Georgia. During the Revolutionary War he served as an aide-de-camp to General Nathanael Greene. He became a merchant in Savannah, Georgia, a member of the Georgia House of Representatives, and a member of the Continental Congress. Did not sign.

MARYLAND

Daniel Carroll (1730–1796) was born in Upper Marlboro, Maryland. He attended Jesuit School in Maryland and St. Omer's College in France. In the Continental Congress, he signed the Articles of Confederation. Carroll later was elected to the Maryland state senate and to the U.S. House of Representatives, where he served from 1789 to 1791. President George Washington appointed him as one of the commissioners for the new District of Columbia. Signed.

Daniel of St. Thomas Jenifer (1723–1790) was born in Charles County, Maryland. He served as an agent for the last two proprietors of Maryland, became a member of the colonial court, and sat on the Maryland royal governor's council until 1776. He then joined the state's council of safety and was president of the first state senate. He was also a member of the Continental Congress and represented Maryland at the Mount Vernon Conference in 1785. Signed.

Luther Martin (1748–1826) was born in Brunswick, New Jersey, and graduated from the College of New Jersey (later Princeton). He moved to Maryland, where he taught and also studied law. He became attorney general of Maryland and joined the Baltimore Light Dragoons. Elected to the Continental Congress, he declined to serve. He led the fight against ratification of the Constitution by Maryland. He later became a defense lawyer for Supreme Court Justice Samuel Chase during his impeachment trial, in 1805, and for former Vice President Aaron Burr during his treason trial, in

1807. Once again becoming Maryland's attorney general, he argued the losing side in the Supreme Court case of *McCulloch* v. *Maryland*. Did not sign.

James McHenry (1753–1816) was born in Ballymena, Ireland, and immigrated to Philadelphia around 1771. He studied medicine, and during the Revolutionary War was surgeon in the Fifth Pennsylvania Battalion and secretary to General Washington. He became a member of the Maryland state senate, and later a member of the Continental Congress. He then served as secretary of war in the cabinets of George Washington and John Adams. Signed.

John Francis Mercer (1759–1821) was born in Stafford County, Virginia. He graduated from the College of William and Mary, studied law, and practiced in Williamsburg, Virginia. During the Revolutionary War he rose to lieutenant colonel of the Virginia cavalry. He was a delegate from Virginia to the Continental Congress before moving to Anne Arundel County, Maryland. There, he served in the Maryland House of Delegates and was elected to the U.S. House of Representatives, where he served from 1792 to 1794. He was governor of Maryland from 1801 to 1803. Did not sign.

MASSACHUSETTS

Elbridge Gerry (1744–1814) was born in Marblehead, Massachusetts, and graduated from Harvard. He served in the colonial House of Representatives and in the Continental Congress, becoming a signer of the Declaration of Independence. Elected to the U.S. House of Representatives from 1789 to 1793, he was sent on a diplomatic mission to France in 1797. He became governor of Massachusetts from 1810 to 1811, and as a Democratic-Republican was elected Vice President of the United States with President James Madison, serving from 1813 until his death. When he died in 1814, he was on his way to preside over the U.S. Senate. Did not sign.

Nathaniel Gorham (1738–1796) was born in Charlestown, Massachusetts. He served in the colonial legislature and in the Continental Congress, becoming its president from 1786 to 1787. He was later a judge of the Massachusetts Court of Common Pleas. Signed.

Rufus King (1755–1827) was born in Scarboro, Maine (then part of Massachusetts). He graduated from Harvard, served in the Revolutionary War, studied law, and practiced in Newburyport, Massachusetts. King served in the Massachusetts legislature and the Continental Congress. He moved to New York City and became a member of the New York State assembly. He was elected to the U.S. Senate in 1789 and served until 1796, when he became U.S. minister to Great Britain. He later returned to serve in the Senate from 1813 to 1825, chairing the Foreign Relations Committee. King ran unsuccessfully as the Federalist candidate for Vice President in 1804, for governor of New York in 1816, and for President in 1816. Signed.

Caleb Strong (1745–1819) was born in Northampton, Massachusetts, and graduated from Harvard. He studied law and practiced in Northampton. During the Revolution he was a member of a committee of correspondence and safety, and served in the Massachusetts state legislature. He was elected to the Continental Congress, although he did not serve. He served in the U.S. Senate as a Federalist from 1789 to 1796, and was governor of Massachusetts from 1800 to1807, and again from 1812 to 1816. Did not sign.

NEW HAMPSHIRE

Nicholas Gilman (1755–1814) was born in Exeter, New Hampshire. He served in the Continental Army during the Revolutionary War, and in the Continental Congress. He was elected to the U.S. House of Representatives, where he served from 1789 to 1797, chairing the Committee on Revisal and Unfinished Business. He then served as a Democratic-Republican in the U.S. Senate from 1805 until his death in 1814. Signed.

John Langdon (1741–1819) was born in Portsmouth, New Hampshire. After going to sea as a young man, he became a merchant. He served in the New Hampshire state legislature and in the Continental Congress. During the Revolutionary War he was in charge of the construction of several ships of war, equipped an expedition against the British, and commanded a company of soldiers at Saratoga. He served in the U.S. Senate from 1789 to 1801, and was elected the Senate's first president pro tempore. During those years, his politics shifted from Federalist to Democratic-Republican. He returned to New Hampshire to serve again in the state legislature and as governor from 1805 to 1811. Signed.

NEW JERSEY

David Brearly (1745–1790) was born near Trenton, New Jersey, and graduated from the College of New Jersey (later Princeton). He studied law and practiced in Allentown, New Jersey. During the Revolutionary War he rose to colonel in the state militia. He was elected chief justice of the New Jersey Supreme Court and served as an elector in the first Presidential election. President Washington appointed him to be a federal district judge. Signed.

Jonathan Dayton (1760–1824) was born in Elizabeth, New Jersey, graduated from the College of New Jersey (later Princeton), and studied law. In the Revolutionary War he served in two New Jersey regiments, rising to the rank of captain. He was Speaker of the New Jersey General Assembly. Elected to the U.S. House of Representatives, he served from 1791 to 1799, and became Speaker of the House and chairman of the Committee on Elections. He was then elected to the U.S. Senate as a Federalist, serving from 1799 to 1805. Dayton was arrested in 1807, charged with treasonous conspiracy with Vice President Aaron Burr, but he was released and never stood trial. He later served again in the New Jersey assembly. Signed.

William C. Houston (1746–1788) was born in Sumter District, South Carolina. He graduated from Princeton College and became a professor there until he resigned to serve as captain in the Somerset militia during the Revolutionary War. He was deputy secretary of the Continental Congress, member of the New Jersey colonial legislature, the council of safety in 1778, and the Continental Congress. After the war he studied law and practiced in Trenton, New Jersey. He was a delegate to the Annapolis Convention in 1786. Did not sign.

William Livingston (1723–1790) was born in Albany, New York. He graduated from Yale and studied law. He served in the New York State legislature before moving to Elizabeth, New Jersey. He served on the New Jersey Committee of Correspondence and in the Continental Congress. He commanded a New Jersey militia during the Revolution until he was elected governor of New Jersey. Active in the antislavery movement, he chaired the committee at the Constitutional Convention that reached a compromise on slavery. Signed.

William Paterson (1745–1806) was born in County Antrim, Ireland, and immigrated to Pennsylvania with his parents in 1747. He graduated from the College of New Jersey (later Princeton), studied law, and practiced in New Bromley, New Jersey. He was a member of the New Jersey legislature and state attorney general. Elected to the Continental Congress, he declined the office. He served in the U.S. Senate as a Federalist from 1789 to 1790, resigning to become governor of New Jersey. In 1793 he became an associate justice of the U.S. Supreme Court, where he served until his death. Signed.

NEW YORK

Alexander Hamilton (1757–1804) was born on Nevis in the British West Indies and immigrated to New Jersey in 1772. He graduated from King's College (later Columbia), and became an aide-de-camp to General Washington during the Revolutionary War. He was a member of the Continental Congress, a delegate to the Annapolis Convention of 1786, and served in the New York State assembly. Hamilton was an author of *The Federalist*, in support of the Constitution's ratification. He later studied and practiced law in New York City. He served as secretary of the treasury under President George Washington from 1789 to 1795. In 1804, he was mortally wounded in a duel with Vice President Aaron Burr. Signed.

John Lansing Jr. (1754–1829) was born in Albany, New York. He studied law and practiced in Albany. He became a member and Speaker of the New York State assembly, a member of the Continental Congress, and a justice of the New York State Supreme Court. In 1829 he disappeared after leaving his hotel to mail a letter. Did not sign.

Robert Yates (1738–1801) was born in Schenectady, New York. He studied law and practiced in Albany, where he was a member of the board of aldermen. During the Revolution, he served on the Albany committee of safety and the colonial legislature, and helped draft the first constitution for New York State. He was chief justice of the New York Supreme Court. Yates became an Anti-Federalist leader in New York. Did not sign.

NORTH CAROLINA

William Blount (1749–1800) was born in Bertie County, North Carolina. He served as paymaster for the Continental troops in North Carolina, as a member of the state legislature, and a member of the Continental Congress. President Washington appointed Blount to be governor of the Territory South of the Ohio. He also served as superintendent of Indian affairs and chairman of the convention that wrote Tennessee's first state constitution. He was then elected a U.S. senator from Tennessee and served from 1796 until the House voted to impeach him for a plan to incite the Creeks and Cherokees to aid the British in conquering the Spanish territory of West Florida. He was expelled from the Senate in 1797, but was elected to the Tennessee state senate. Signed.

William R. Davie (1756–1820) was born in Egremont, England, and migrated to South Carolina as a child. He attended Queen's Museum College in Charlotte, North Carolina, and graduated from the College of New Jersey (later Princeton). He studied law and practiced in North Carolina. During the Revolutionary War, he was a colonel in a cavalry troop and was wounded in action. He later became commissary-general for the Carolina campaign. Although he left the convention without signing the Constitution, he was a leader in supporting its ratification in North Carolina. He became a founder of the University of North Carolina, and the state governor. In 1799, President John Adams appointed Davie a brigadier general in the U.S. Army and a peace commissioner to France. He was defeated when he ran for Congress in 1803. Did not sign.

Alexander Martin (1740–1807) was born in Hunterdon County, New Jersey, and graduated from the College of New Jersey (later Princeton). In 1756, he moved to Salisbury, North Carolina, where he became a merchant and a judge, and served in the state legislature. He was an officer during the Revolutionary War, and later became governor of North Carolina. He was elected to the Continental Congress but declined to serve. Martin served in the U.S. Senate from 1793 to 1799. When he was not reelected, he returned to the state senate. Did not sign.

Richard Dobbs Spaight (1758–1802) was born in New Bern, North Carolina. He attended the University of Glasgow in Scotland before returning to North Carolina in 1778. He joined the Continental Army and was a member of the state legislature and the Continental Congress. Spaight became governor of North Carolina and was elected to the U.S. House of Representatives as a Democratic-Republican, serving from 1798 to 1801. He was later mortally wounded in a duel with John Stanly, the man who succeeded him in Congress. Signed.

Hugh Williamson (1735–1819) was born in West Nottingham Township, Pennsylvania. He graduated from the University of Pennsylvania as a student in theology but became a professor of mathematics. After studying medicine in Scotland and Holland, he returned to practice medicine in Philadelphia. During the Revolutionary War he became surgeon general of the North Carolina troops. He served in the North Carolina legislature and the Continental Congress. Elected as a Federalist, he served in the U.S. House of Representatives from 1790 to 1793. He spent his last years as a writer in New York City. Signed.

PENNSYLVANIA

George Clymer (1739–1813) was born in Philadelphia, Pennsylvania. A merchant, he was captain of a volunteer company in the Revolutionary War, a member of the committee of safety, a member of the Continental Congress, and a signer of the Declaration of Independence. Clymer was also elected to the Pennsylvania legislature. He served in the U.S. House of Representatives from 1789 to 1791 and chaired the Committee on Election. When he left Congress he was appointed collector of excise duties, but resigned after the Whiskey Rebellion. Signed.

Thomas Fitzsimons (1741–1811) was born in Ireland and immigrated to Philadelphia, where he was clerk in a countinghouse. He commanded a company of volunteer home guards during the Revolutionary War and was a member of the Continental Congress and the state legislature. He served in the U.S. House of Representatives from 1789 to 1795, until he lost his election for a fourth term. He became president of the Philadelphia Chamber of Commerce and a founder and director of the Bank of North America. Signed.

Benjamin Franklin (1706–1790) was born in Boston, Massachusetts, where he learned the printing trade. He moved to Philadelphia and founded the *Pennsylvania Gazette* and published *Poor Richard's Almanac*. Franklin served as postmaster of Philadelphia and a member of the colonial legislature. Pennsylvania sent him as its agent to London from 1757 to 1762 and 1764 to 1775. As a member of the Continental Congress he signed the Declaration of Independence. The Continental Congress sent him as a diplomatic commissioner and later minister to France, where he helped negotiate the treaty of peace with Great Britain. Signed.

Jared Ingersoll (1749–1822) was born in New Haven, Connecticut, and graduated from Yale. He received a legal education in London and practiced law in Philadelphia. He was a member of the Continental Congress in 1780, the first attorney general of Pennsylvania, and U.S. district attorney for the eastern district of Pennsylvania. After he lost his race as the Federalist candidate for Vice President in 1812, Ingersoll became presiding judge of the district court of Philadelphia County. Signed.

Thomas Mifflin (1744–1800) was born in Philadelphia, Pennsylvania, and graduated from the University of Pennsylvania. He served in the colonial legislature and the Continental Congress. During the Revolutionary War he was an aide-de-camp to General Washington and quartermaster general of the Continental Army. He served as Speaker of the Pennsylvania House of Representatives, president of its Supreme Executive Council, and governor of Pennsylvania. He was president of the state constitutional convention in 1790. Signed.

Gouverneur Morris (1752–1816) was born in New York City and graduated from King's College (later Columbia University). He studied law and practiced in New York City. After serving in the New York colonial legislature, he became a lieutenant colonel in the state militia, a member of the first council of safety, the state legislature, and the Continental Congress, where he signed the Articles of Confederation. In 1779 he moved to Philadelphia, where he became assistant superintendent of finance. He moved back to New York and then went to France as minister plenipotentiary. In 1800, he was elected as a Federalist to the U.S. Senate from New York, and served until 1803, when he lost his race for reelection. He was later chairman of the Erie Canal Commission. Signed.

Robert Morris (1734–1806) was born in Liverpool, England, and immigrated to Maryland as a child. He became a merchant in Philadelphia, a member of the Pennsylvania council of safety, and a member of the Continental Congress, where he signed the Declaration of Independence. During the Revolutionary War, Morris was national superintendent of finance. He also established the Bank of North America and served in the Pennsylvania state legislature. As a Federalist he served in the U.S. Senate from 1789 to 1795. Morris was imprisoned for debt resulting from his unsuccessful land speculations from 1798 to 1801. Signed.

James Wilson (1742–1798) was born in Carskerdo, Scotland, and attended the universities of St. Andrews, Glasgow, and Edinburgh. He immigrated to New York City in 1765 and then to Philadelphia, where he studied law; he practiced in Reading and Carlisle, Pennsylvania. He was a member of the Continental Congress, where he signed the Declaration of Independence. He also served as a brigadier general in the Pennsylvania state militia. Wilson later became an associate justice of the U.S. Supreme Court, from 1789 to 1798, and a professor of law at the University of Pennsylvania. Signed.

SOUTH CAROLINA

Pierce Butler (1744–1822) was born in County Carlow, Ireland, and came to America in 1758 as an officer in the British Army. After resigning his commission, he became a planter near Charleston, South Carolina. He served in the Continental Congress and was elected to the U.S. Senate, where he served from 1789 to 1796 and again from 1802 to 1804, as a Democratic-Republican. Signed.

Charles Pinckney (1757–1824) was born in Charleston, South Carolina, where he later practiced law. He served in the state House of Representatives, and fought in the Revolutionary War. After the war he was a member of the Continental Congress. He served several terms as governor of South Carolina and served in the U.S. Senate as a Democratic-Republican, from 1798 to 1801, when he became minister to Spain. He later returned to again serve in the state general assembly and as governor. Signed.

Charles Cotesworth Pinckney (1746–1825) was born in Charleston, South Carolina, a second cousin of Charles Pickney. As a child he went to England with his father, the colonial agent for South Carolina. He graduated from Christ Church College, Oxford, and studied law in London. Pinckney returned to South Carolina in 1769 and was elected to the colonial legislature. He chaired the local committee of safety, and became a colonel in the First South Carolina Regiment. When Charleston fell to the British in 1780, he was held prisoner until 1782. Pinckney later served in the South Carolina state legislature. From 1796 to 1798 he was minister to France. In 1800 he ran unsuccessfully for Vice President on the Federalist ticket. In 1804 and 1808 he was the Federalist candidate for President, but lost both elections. Signed.

John Rutledge (1739–1800) was born in Christ Church Parish, South Carolina. He studied law in London and practiced in Charleston, South Carolina. He was a member of the colonial legislature, a delegate to the Stamp Act Congress in 1765, and a member of the Continental Congress. He then became governor of South Carolina. Rutledge received the electoral vote of South Carolina for Vice President in 1789. He served as associate justice of the U.S. Supreme Court from 1789 to 1791 and chief justice of South Carolina from 1791 to 1795. President Washington nominated him to be chief justice of the United States in 1795. He served briefly, but the Senate declined to confirm him, citing his intemperate political speeches. Signed.

VIRGINIA

John Blair (1732–1800) was born in Virginia and graduated from the College of William and Mary. He studied law in London and practiced in Williamsburg, Virginia. Blair was a member of the Virginia House of Burgesses, served in the Virginia constitutional convention, and became a judge in the Virginia circuit courts. President Washington later appointed him an associate justice of the U.S. Supreme Court, where he served from 1789 until his death in 1800. Signed.

James Madison (1751–1836) was born in Port Conway, Virginia, and graduated from the College of New Jersey (later Princeton University). He was a member of a committee of safety, a member of the first state legislature of Virginia, and a member of the Continental Congress. He was one of the authors of *The Federalist,* in defense of the Constitution. From 1789 to 1797 he served in the U.S. House of Representatives, where he was the principal sponsor of the Bill of Rights. As a Democratic-Republican, he became secretary of state under President Thomas Jefferson from 1801 to 1809, and then was elected President, serving from 1809 to 1817. During his Presidency, British troops invaded and burned much of Washington, D.C. Signed.

George Mason (1725–1792) was born in Fairfax County, Virginia. Mason managed his family's plantation, Gunston Hall, and became an officer in the Ohio Company, which speculated in land west of the Appalachians. His neighbor, George Washington, was a member of the company. When Washington was appointed commander in chief of the Continental Army, Mason took his seat in the Virginia legislature. There he took the lead in writing Virginia's constitution and bill of rights. Mason also took part in the Mount Vernon Conference that negotiated a navigation agreement between Virginia and Maryland regarding the Potomac River. He opposed the Constitution because it lacked a bill of rights, and he declined to serve in the federal government. Did not sign.

James McClurg (1746–1823) was born near Hampton, Virginia, and graduated from the College of William and Mary. He studied medicine at the University of Edinburgh, and in London and Paris. McClurg returned to Williamsburg, Virginia, to be a professor of anatomy and medicine at William and Mary. He later served on Virginia's executive council. Did not sign.

Edmund Randolph (1753–1813) was born in Williamsburg, Virginia, and graduated from the College of William and Mary. He studied law and practiced in Williamsburg. During the Revolutionary War he was an aide-de-camp to General Washington and attorney general of Virginia. He became a member of the Continental Congress and governor of Virginia. President Washington appointed Randolph to be the first attorney general. He held that post from 1789 until 1794, when he became secretary of state. Randolph was later a counsel for Vice President Aaron Burr during his treason trial. Did not sign.

George Washington (1732–1799) was born in Westmoreland County, Virginia. As a land surveyor and an officer in the Virginia militia, Washington became a lieutenant colonel and an aide-de-camp to General Edward Braddock during the French and Indian War. He went from the Virginia House of Burgesses to the Continental Congresses, which chose him as commander in chief of the Continental Army during the American Revolution. After the war, he resigned his commission and returned to his estate, Mount Vernon. Washington presided over the Constitutional Contention and was unanimously elected as the nation's first President, serving from 1789 until 1797. Following his Presidency, he was re-appointed lieutenant general and commander of the U.S. Army. Signed

George Wythe (1726–1806) was born in Elizabeth City County, Virginia, and attended the College of William and Mary. He studied law and practiced in Williamsburg, Virginia. He served in the colonial House of Burgesses, was a member of the Committee of Correspondence, and a member of the Continental Congress, where he signed the Declaration of Independence. He was also a professor of law at William and Mary and later led a private school in Richmond, Virginia. Did not sign.

APPENDIX 2
Supreme Court Decisions that Shaped the Constitution

Judicial Review: *Marbury* v. *Madison* (1803). On the last night of his Presidency, John Adams appointed a number of Federalists to office, just before Thomas Jefferson and the Democratic-Republicans assumed power. Among these, Adams appointed William Marbury of Maryland to be a justice of the peace in the District of Columbia. When James Madison took over as the new secretary of state, he declined to deliver Marbury's commission to him. Marbury sued directly to the Supreme Court, as was permitted under existing law. Chief Justice John Marshall was a Federalist who had also been one of Adams's late appointees. Although Marshall sympathized with Marbury, he knew that the Court had no power to enforce its decision against Jefferson's will and would look weak. Instead, Marshall wrote an opinion that the law under which Marbury brought suit had been unconstitutional. Rather than weakening the Court, the ruling strengthened it, as this marked the first time that it had expressed the right of judicial review.

The Constitution and State Authority: *Trustees of Dartmouth College* v. *Woodward* (1819). In 1814 the board of trustees of Dartmouth College voted to remove the school's president, John Wheelock. The state legislature responded by voting to lift the private college's old royal charter and to restore Wheelock as president. The board of trustees appealed to the U.S. Supreme Court. Defending them in court was an alumnus of the college, the American statesman Daniel Webster. He argued eloquently that the state legislature had violated the constitutional ban on states passing laws that would break contracts. Writing for the Court, Chief Justice John Marshall agreed that a charter was a contract and the state legislature therefore lacked the power to void it. This ruling boosted the authority of the federal Constitution over the states.

Federal Supremacy: *McCulloch* v. *Maryland* (1819). A Maryland law required the federally chartered Bank of the United States to pay a state tax. Joseph McCulloch, the cashier in the bank's Maryland branch, refused to pay the tax or any penalty. The bank sued in Maryland courts and eventually the case went to the U.S. Supreme Court, where Daniel Webster defended the bank. Chief Justice John Marshall wrote the Court's opinion in favor of the bank based on the supremacy clause. The Court found that allowing a state to tax an institution of the federal government violated the concept of federal supremacy. Later, Joseph McCulloch was caught embezzling money from his bank, and this news emboldened the state of Ohio to enact its own taxes against the bank. In the case of *Osborn* v. *Bank of the United States* (1824), the Supreme Court upheld its earlier reasoning, once again asserting the national government's primacy over the states.

Regulating Interstate Commerce: *Gibbons* v. *Ogden* (1824). A New Jersey steamboat operator, Aaron Ogden, purchased monopoly rights on the Hudson River, the state of New York. His former partner, Thomas Gibbons, who had a federal license, challenged the state monopoly. Ogden then sued Gibbons. The case made its way to the Supreme Court, where Daniel Webster, who defended Gibbons, argued that the Constitution gave Congress the power to regulate interstate commerce, regardless of laws enacted by individual states. Chief Justice John Marshall, writing for the Court, agreed that federal law was superior to state law. The ruling furthered future interstate transportation and commerce.

Permitting State Improvements: *Charles River Bridge* v. *Warren Bridge* (1837). In 1785 the state of Massachusetts incorporated a group of businessmen to build a toll bridge over the Charles River, replacing an earlier ferry service that had operated as a monopoly. As Boston grew so did the need for new bridges, but the owners of the Charles River Bridge argued that such competition would diminish the value of their property. The Charles River Bridge proprietors sued the builders of the Warren Bridge, and hired Daniel Webster as their attorney. Before the case reached the Supreme Court, John Marshall died and Roger B. Taney became chief justice. In contrast to the earlier *Dartmouth College* case, which had upheld original contracts, the Supreme Court now voted 7 to 2 against the Charles River Bridge, finding that the contract did not create an "exclusive privilege" and that signing additional contracts was within the state's authority.

Claiming Freedom: *Dred Scott* v. *Sandford* (1857). When Dr. John Emerson, an army surgeon, left St. Louis for service in Illinois and Wisconsin, he took with him as a servant Dred Scott, a slave who belonged to the Emerson family. Scott lived in free territory for five years before returning to Missouri, where slavery was permitted. After Dr. Emerson died, his widow moved to New York and left Scott with Henry Blow, who personally opposed slavery. Seeking to set a precedent, Henry Blow arranged for Dred Scott to sue for his freedom on the grounds that he became free when he left the slaveholding South. The case was appealed to the Supreme Court at a time when the nation was divided over whether to permit slavery in the new western territories. The case was filed by John F. A. Sanford, the legal administrator for the woman who owned Dred Scott. Due to a clerical error, the court recorded his name as Sandford. Seeking to settle this contentious issue, Chief Justice Roger Taney and a majority of the justices ruled that, as a slave, Scott was not a citizen and could not use the federal courts. The majority then went further and declared the Missouri Compromise unconstitutional because Congress had no right to limit the spread of slavery. Rather than restore harmony, the ruling inflamed antislavery passions. Having lost the case, Henry Blow granted Dred Scott his freedom.

Trying Civilians in Military Courts: *Ex Parte Milligan* (1866). Lambdin P. Milligan was a Northern Democrat who opposed the Civil War—a faction labeled by their opponents as Copperheads. In 1862, President Abraham Lincoln issued a proclamation declaring that anyone who discouraged others from enlisting in the Union Army would be subject to martial law. When Milligan urged men not to enlist, he was arrested by the military, charged with treason, and sentenced to be hanged. When the war ended President Andrew Johnson reduced his sentence to life imprisonment. *Ex Parte* (in the case of) *Milligan* went to the Supreme Court, which ruled that it had been wrong to try Milligan in a military court when the civilian courts were open and operating.

Striking Down State Regulation of Interstate Commerce: *Munn* v. *Illinois* (1877). In response to persistent complaints of corrupt business practices, particularly in connection with the railroads, the state of Illinois sought to regulate both the warehouses and the railroads. Having lost in the legislature, business interests turned to the courts for relief from state regulation. The company of Munn & Scott, which operated grain elevators and warehouses, brought suit against the state. To their dismay, the Supreme Court ruled that the Constitution permitted regulation in the public interest. The warehouse operators resigned themselves to accepting state regulation, although by then Munn & Scott had gone out of business.

Separate but Equal: *Plessy* v. *Ferguson* (1896). Homer Plessy purchased a first-class train ticket in New Orleans, but he was arrested when he refused to leave the first-class car and sit in a car reserved for African Americans. Like other southern states, Louisiana law required racial segregation. Plessy's case was argued before Judge John Ferguson, who ruled against him. The case was appealed and eventually reached the Supreme Court, which ruled that "separate but equal" facilities did not violate the Fourteenth Amendment's requirement of equal protection of the laws. Justice John Marshall Harlan strongly dissented, arguing that arbitrary separation of citizens by race was "a badge of servitude wholly inconsistent with the civil freedom and the equality before the law established by the constitution."

Congress Has the Authority to Enact Antitrust Laws: *Northern Securities Co.* v. *United States* (1904). After competing against each other, the Union Pacific Railroad, Great Northern Railroad, and Northern Pacific Railroad were united through a holding company called Northern Securities Co. President Theodore Roosevelt believed that this arrangement violated federal antitrust laws, and the federal government sued Northern Securities. The majority of the Supreme Court agreed with Roosevelt and held that Northern Securities was an illegal combination. The decision confirmed Congress's authority to enact antitrust laws and gave a boost to the antitrust movement in the Progressive era.

Protecting Women Workers: *Muller* v. *Oregon* (1908). Portland laundry owner Curt Muller was convicted of violating an Oregon law that prohibited requiring women to work longer than a ten-hour day. Muller appealed his conviction to the U.S. Supreme Court. Attorney Louis Brandeis, known as the People's Attorney for his advocacy of public welfare cases, appeared on behalf of Oregon. Brandeis argued that the state had a right to regulate labor policy to cure social ills. He offered statistics and social evidence concerning the benefits of a shorter workday. The Court accepted this evidence and ruled in favor of the protective legislation.

Delegation of Federal Power: *Schechter* v. *United States* (1935). In response to the Great Depression, President Franklin D. Roosevelt proposed and Congress adopted a National Recovery Administration (NRA) to regulate various businesses and promote fair wages and hours. Those who participated used its logo, a Blue Eagle with the slogan "We Do Our Part." Despite the agency's popularity, not everyone wanted to participate. The four Schechter brothers who ran a poultry market in Brooklyn objected to federal regulation on the grounds that none of their product was sold outside of New York State. The Supreme Court unanimously agreed with them, ruling that it was unconstitutional for Congress to delegate so much of its power over interstate commerce to the President, and that the federal government could not regulate business that did not cross state lines. President Roosevelt complied by shutting down the NRA, but Congress passed other laws to preserve some of the functions and goals of that agency.

Saluting the Flag: *Minersville School District* v. *Gobitis* (1940). In 1936 the principal of the Minersville public school sent twelve-year-old Lillian and ten-year-old William Gobitis home until they agreed to salute the flag each morning with the other children in their classes. The Gobitises were Jehovah's Witnesses, for whom saluting the flag ran contrary to their faith. They sued and a lower federal court ruled in their favor. The case then went to the Supreme Court. Writing for the majority, Justice Felix Frankfurter called it a lamentable "clash of rights, not the clash of wrongs." The majority found that the school was within its rights to compel all students to participate in the flag salute. This decision stirred so much controversy that several justices had second thoughts. Three years later, in the case of *West Virginia State Board of Education* v. *Barnette* (1943), the Supreme Court reversed itself and ruled that governments cannot coerce schoolchildren and other citizens into participating in patriotic rituals that violate their religious beliefs.

Equality in Education: *Brown* v. *Board of Education of Topeka, Kansas* (1954). Although separate schools for racial minorities were supposedly equal with schools for white students, those for minorities rarely received the same funding, books, and equipment. Even if the facilities were equal, critics argued that separating students on racial grounds stigmatized the minority students. Lawyers for the National Association for the Advancement of Colored People (NAACP) filed suit on behalf of a number of African American students, among them Louise Brown of Topeka, Kansas. Under Chief Justice Earl Warren, the Supreme Court unanimously ruled that school segregation was unconstitutional because it violated the equal protection clause of the Fourteenth Amendment, thereby reversing the earlier decision in *Plessy* v. *Ferguson*.

One Person, One Vote: *Baker* v. *Carr* (1962). For the first time, in 1920, the U.S. census showed that a majority of Americans lived in urban rather than rural areas. Despite the increasing movement of people from farms to cities, state legislative districts remained locked in place. Sparsely populated rural districts outweighed more heavily populated urban and suburban districts in most state legislatures. Ruling on a case from Tennessee, the Supreme Court held that these unequal districts violated the equal protection clause of the Fourteenth Amendment. The resulting one person, one vote doctrine soon affected all legislative bodies, from local governments to the U.S. House of Representatives.

Right to Counsel: *Gideon* v. *Wainwright* (1963). Writing from a Florida prison, Clarence Earl Gideon petitioned the Supreme Court that he had been unjustly convicted of breaking into a pool hall, because he was too poor to hire a lawyer. He argued that this absence of counsel violated due process of the law and was a denial of fundamental fairness. The Supreme Court declared that the right of anyone charged with a crime, even the poorest defendant, to have counsel was fundamental and essential to a fair trial. Gideon stood trial again, this time with a court-appointed lawyer, and was found not guilty.

A Free Press: New York Times v. *United States* (1971). In 1971, the *New York Times* obtained a set of classified documents from Daniel Ellsberg, a former Pentagon employee who had turned against the Vietnam War. The Pentagon Papers documented how the United States had become involved in the war. President Richard Nixon obtained an injunction from the federal courts to prevent the *Times* and other newspapers from publishing these still secret documents. The papers argued that such "prior restraint" would violate the freedom of the press and the public's right to know. The Supreme Court ruled that the government had failed to prove its argument that publication of the documents would jeopardize national security. Justice Hugo Black observed that "The press was to serve the governed, not the governors."

Abortion Rights: *Roe* v. *Wade* (1973). In 1970, Norma McCorvey, a pregnant twenty-one-year-old single woman sued to overturn a Texas state law that made abortions illegal. The suit was filed under the name "Jane Roe." The legal issue was whether individual privacy rights covered a woman's decision to seek an abortion, even though privacy is not explicitly mentioned in the Constitution. The Supreme Court concluded that personal privacy could be found implicitly in the First, Fourth, Fifth, Ninth, and Fourteenth Amendments, and therefore struck down all state laws that banned abortions. Writing for the majority, Justice Harry Blackmun outlined a situation in which a state could not interfere with a woman's right to choose an abortion in the first three months of a pregnancy, but that in later stages of pregnancy the state could set regulations.

The Limits of Executive Privilege: *United States* v. *Richard Nixon* (1974). When a Senate committee investigated connections between the White House and the burglary of the Democratic Party headquarters at the Watergate building, it discovered that President Richard Nixon had been secretly tape-recording all his conversations in the Oval Office. The committee subpoenaed certain tapes to determine whether the President had been involved in either the burglary or later efforts at a cover-up. Nixon released selected transcripts but refused to comply with everything the committee requested, citing executive privilege. The Supreme Court ruled unanimously that the President must surrender evidence that might be used in a criminal case. The President turned over the material, and the release of a tape made on June 23, 1972 implicated him in the cover-up and led to his resignation.

Reverse Discrimination: *Regents of the University of California* v. *Bakke* (1978). Allen Bakke was rejected when he applied to the medical school at the University of California, Davis. The medical school had established a special admissions program to ensure the racial diversity of its student body, and some of the minority students admitted had lower scores on the Medical College Admission Test than had Bakke, who was white. Bakke sued on the grounds that the admissions program constituted a racial quota and reverse discrimination. The Supreme Court ruled in Bakke's favor, striking down racial quotas. The Court agreed that race could be used as one of many criteria in determining admission, so long as it was not the sole criterion.

Gender Equality: *United States* v. *Virginia* (1996). As a state school the Virginia Military Institute (VMI) could not bar women students. The institute had been founded in 1839 and had a long history as an all-male academy. Virginia argued the benefits of single-sex education and offered to create a Virginia Women's Institute for Leadership. But this plan did not convince the Supreme Court that the two schools would be equally rigorous in their training. The Court ruled that barring women violated the equal protection clause of the Fourteenth Amendment. Following this decision, VMI admitted women as cadets in 1997.

Constitutional Glossary

advice and consent: Article II provides that Presidents may nominate judges and high-level executive branch officers and negotiate treaties with the "Advice and Consent of the Senate." The Constitution is clear about what constitutes "consent" (it requires a majority of the Senate to approve a nominee and two-thirds of the Senate to consent to a treaty) but ambiguous on "advice," leading to frequent quarrels with Presidents who acted without consulting with the Senate. The House plays no role in the advice and consent process.

Articles of Confederation: Before the Constitution was ratified, the thirteen states joined in a loose confederation from 1781 until 1789. The Articles of Confederation established a single legislative branch, without an executive or legislature. This national government depended on the states for funding and any changes in the Articles required the unanimous approval of the states.

Bill of Rights: The first ten amendments to the Constitution, which were proposed and approved by the First Congress. They offer specific guarantees of liberty to citizens and restrictions on the powers of government. Originally, the Bill of Rights applied only to the federal government. Since the adoption of the Fourteenth Amendment, however, the courts have gradually extended these rights and restrictions to the states as well.

checks and balances: Power is divided among the three branches of the federal government and the states, each of which checks— that is, restrains—and balances the others. By dividing power, the Constitution pitted the ambitions of one branch against the others to keep any one part of the government from becoming all-powerful and tyrannical. The branches share certain powers but also exercise some exclusive powers.

civil liberties: The basic individual rights of all citizens, as expressed in the Bill of Rights and reinforced by the Fourteenth Amendment. These include the right to freedom of speech, press, religion, and assembly; the right to petition; as well as freedom from unreasonable search and seizure.

civil rights: Freedom from discrimination, particularly by race, but also by gender, religion, age, ethnicity, and physical ability. The constitutionality of civil rights is centered in the Thirteenth, Fourteenth, and Fifteen Amendments.

commerce clause: Article I, section 8, which grants Congress the power to regulate commerce between the states, with Indian tribes, and with foreign nations. Congress and the courts have broadly interpreted this clause to cover almost any endeavor that crosses state lines, from transportation and other economic issues to equal accommodations and other such civil rights issues.

common law: The accumulated precedents set by court rulings in Britain and the United States, usually involving civil cases. The Seventh Amendment addresses suits rising from the common law.

cruel and unusual punishment: The Eighth Amendment prohibits "cruel and unusual punishment," in a measure designed to prevent torture and the deliberately painful systems of execution that had existed in the past. Definitions of "cruel and unusual" have been left to statutes and to court decisions. In recent years, some have argued that the death penalty itself constitutes cruel and unusual punishment.

double jeopardy: The Fifth Amendment protects people from being tried again on charges for which they have been acquitted. It does not prevent a second trial if there is a hung jury—one unable to render a verdict—or if a convicted person seeks a retrial based on new evidence.

due process of the law: The Fifth and Fourteenth Amendments guarantee that governments cannot deprive people of their lives, liberty, or property without "due process," that is, appropriate legal proceedings.

elastic clause: After providing Congress with a long list of specific powers, Article I, section 8 granted Congress authority to make all laws that are "necessary and proper" to implement those powers. Because this broad phrase covers such an extensive sweep of activities, it has been called the "elastic clause."

Electoral College: When people vote for President of the United States they are actually choosing representatives who will then form the Electoral College that goes on to elect the President. Each party puts forward a slate of electors who are pledged to vote for the party's candidate—although occasionally an "unfaithful" elector will vote for another candidate as an act of protest against the party's choice. Each state has the number of electors that equals the total of its senators and representatives, so that no state will have fewer than three electors. The electors vote in their individual states and the ballots are then sent to Congress, which counts the ballots in a joint session and officially declares a victor. On a few occasions, the candidate who has won the greatest number of popular votes has lost the Electoral College and the Presidency.

emoluments: The Constitution gives Congress the power to set salaries, or emoluments, for the other branches of government, but prohibits it from cutting the salary of Presidents or judges as a form of punishment or intimidation. The Twenty-seventh Amendment also requires that any increase in congressional salary be delayed until after the next election, to give the voters a chance to react.

enumerated powers: The Constitution grants specific powers to the government, particularly to the Congress, which are known as the enumerated powers. They are the opposite of implied powers, which are known as unenumerated.

equal protection of the law: The Fourteenth Amendment guarantees all citizens equal protection of the law. This provision prevents the government from discriminating against any particular group, and ensures citizens' civil rights.

ex post facto law: A law that is passed after an action has occurred to make that action illegal. Congress and the courts are prohibited from passing any such law by Article I, section 9.

federalism: This broad term, not mentioned in the Constitution, describes the constitutional relationship between the states and the national government, in which power is distributed between the central authority and the states.

full faith and credit: Article IV, section 1 provides that all states governments and courts must respect the laws, records, and court rulings of other states, giving them "Full Faith and Credit."

habeas corpus: From the Latin for "let us have the body," habeas corpus is a legal requirement that those arrested for a crime cannot be detained for a long period without judicial proceedings. During wartime or periods of civil insurrection, Presidents can suspend habeas corpus.

impeachment: A form of accusation or indictment by the House of Representatives, requiring a majority vote, used to bring charges against a federal officer. The Senate then holds a trial and if two-thirds of the senators vote to convict, the official is removed from office. Sometimes Congress votes to prohibit an official who has been impeached and convicted from holding any further office. Otherwise, conviction carries no penalties than removal, although an impeached official can also be tried in civil and criminal courts.

implied powers: The Constitution suggests, rather than specifies, some powers, particularly in considering what might be "necessary and proper" to implement them. Implied powers are the opposite of enumerated powers.

judicial review: Since 1803, the Supreme Court has interpreted the Constitution as giving it the final authority to review the constitutionality of the acts of the legislative and executive branch. The process by which the courts examine the laws is known as judicial review.

lame duck sessions: Throughout the nineteenth century, the second session of every Congress was held after the most recent election, when some members either had been defeated or did not run for reelection. When they returned for the second session, they were called "lame ducks" (a slang term the British had originally used for someone who went bankrupt). Out of concern that lame ducks were not likely to promote the public interest, the Twentieth Amendment moved up the opening date of Congress to eliminate most lame duck sessions.

oath of office: Article II provides an oath of office for Presidential inaugurations. All other federal officers take a different oath, created by statute rather than by the Constitution. Those who take a federal oath of office swear (or affirm, if for religious reasons they cannot swear) that they will uphold the Constitution of the United States.

original intent: The effort to determine precisely what the authors and ratifiers of the Constitution and its amendments had in mind is called the search for "original intent." As the delegates to the Constitutional Convention left little in the way of official minutes, this search has usually involved reading the notes of the individual delegates, *The Federalist,* and the records of Congress. Those who believe in finding "original intent" usually prefer a stricter rather than a flexible interpretation of the Constitution.

other persons: The Constitution deliberately did not mention "slaves," even though enslaved African Americans constituted a large percentage of the young nation's population. For purposes of taxation and counting for congressional apportionment, the Constitution referred euphemistically to "other persons."

pocket veto: Presidents can veto a bill and send it back to Congress with an explanation, but a two-thirds vote in both houses of Congress can override a President's veto. However, if Congress adjourns within ten days of sending a bill to the White House, the President can simply not sign the bill. This is called a "pocket veto" (suggesting that the bill has been slipped into a pocket). In such cases, Congress has no opportunity to attempt to override the veto.

power of the purse: The federal government can neither receive nor spend any money that Congress has not authorized and appropriated. Known as the "power of the purse," the ability to provide or withhold funds is Congress's ultimate weapon against the other branches of the government and the state governments. In both the Senate and House the Appropriations Committees are among the most powerful and prestigious committees.

Presidential succession: If a President dies, resigns, or becomes incapacitated, the Constitution provides that the Vice President will step into the Presidency. By statute, Congress determines who will follow next after the Vice President. The current order of Presidential succession is the Speaker of the House, the president pro tempore of the Senate, and the members of the cabinet, in the order in which their departments were created. The Twenty-fifth Amendment also permits Presidents to appoint a Vice President, if that post becomes vacant. Both the Senate and House must confirm such a Vice Presidential appointment.

privacy: The Constitution does not specifically include a right to privacy, but the Supreme Court has found that it is implied in the Bill of Rights, particularly in the Fourth Amendment's protection against unreasonable searches of a person's property. The Ninth Amendment also specifies that rights are not void because they are not enumerated.

qualifications of office: Presidents must be at least thirty-five and natural-born citizens—born in the United States or of American parents elsewhere—and are limited to two terms in office. Senators must be at least thirty and representatives must be at least twenty five and reside in the state they represent. States cannot add qualifications, other than those specified in the Constitution.

ratification: The Constitution established that it would be confirmed when ratified, or approved, by nine of the thirteen states, and that all amendments must be ratified by two-thirds of the Senate and House and three-quarters of the states. Amendments can be ratified by the state legislatures or by elected state conventions.

reapportionment: Every ten years, after each census is taken, the House of Representatives is reapportioned to make congressional districts contain as mathematically equal a number of residents as possible. Originally, the House expanded in size to reflect population growth, but once the number of seats was fixed at 435, each reapportionment has required some states to gain seats and some to lose them. Each state must have at least one representative.

recess appointments: An appointment for a federal office made by a President when the Senate is not meeting. Recess appointments can serve until the end of the next session of the Senate. The President may nominate them again, but if they are not confirmed they must give up the post. In the nineteenth century, this process enabled Presidents to keep the government functioning during the many months that Congress stood adjourned. In modern times, congressional recesses are much shorter and Presidents have used recess appointments mostly for controversial nominees whose confirmations have been stalled.

search and seizure: The Fourth Amendment prohibits authorities from conducting a "search and seizure" of anyone's house, papers, or other property without a warrant issued by the courts on just cause—reasonable suspicion that evidence of a crime will be located there.

self-incrimination: Witnesses in criminal trials, or those whose testimony before Congress might result in a criminal indictment, are not required to give testimony against themselves. As this protection against self-incrimination is specified in the Fifth Amendment, declining to testify is sometimes called "taking the Fifth."

separation of powers: The Constitution assigns specific powers to each branch of the federal government. Some powers belong exclusively to a single branch, others are shared among the branches. No one can serve in more than one branch simultaneously. This system differs from a parliamentary government, where officials with executive powers, such as the prime minister and members of the cabinet, are members of the parliament or legislature.

states' rights: The Tenth Amendment reserved for the states all rights not granted to the federal government. This has led to numerous political and judicial disagreements between the states and the federal government over where the line should be drawn.

supremacy clause: The clause of Article VI that makes the Constitution "the supreme law of the land," elevating federal laws and federal court decisions over those of the states.

treason: This extreme crime against the state involves "levying war" against the United States or giving "aid and comfort" to its enemies. A person can be convicted of treason only if he or she confesses, or if there are two witnesses to the act of treason.

treaty-making power: The President negotiates treaties with foreign nations, but the treaty cannot go into effect until it is approved by a two-thirds vote of the Senate. Senators can amend a treaty (change its wording) or enact reservations (change its interpretation) by a simple majority, which enables them to build a consensus to achieve a two-thirds vote.

veto: After Congress passes a bill, the President may veto, or reject it, sending the reasons for the objection back to Congress, which may amend the bill to meet the President's objections or override the veto by a two-thirds vote of each house. If a President does not sign a bill within ten days, and the Congress adjourns during that period, it is known as a "pocket veto," which Congress cannot override.

war powers: Among the more ambiguous provisions of the Constitution are the war powers. Only Congress can declare a war and appropriate the funds necessary to fight it, but the President as commander in chief of the military has considerable latitude in sending American troops into combat. Congress has not formally declared war since World War II, although the United States has fought many wars since then.

Further Reading

Creating the Constitution

Benton, Wilbourn E. *1787: Drafting the Constitution.* College Station: Texas A&M University Press, 1986. A collection, in two volumes, of the delegates' notes and draft texts.

Bowen, Catherine Drinker. *Miracle at Philadelphia: The Story of the Constitutional Convention, May to September, 1787.* Boston: Little, Brown, 1966. A classic study of the delegates to the Constitutional Convention.

Bradford, M. E. *Original Intentions: On the Making and Ratification of the United States Constitution.* Athens: University of Georgia Press, 1993. A skeptical analysis of the framers' "idealism."

Butzner, Jane, ed. *Constitutional Chaff: Rejected Suggestions of the Constitutional Convention of 1787, with Explanatory Argument.* 1941. Reprint, Port Washington, N.Y.: Kennikat, 1970. Proposals that did not make it into the Constitution.

Collier, Christopher, and James Lincoln Collier. *Decision in Philadelphia: The Constitutional Convention of 1787.* New York: Random House, 1986. A study of the Constitutional Convention with an emphasis on the Connecticut Compromise.

Faber, Doris and Harold Faber. *We the People: The Story of the United States Constitution* (New York: Scribner's, 1987). A basic history of the Constitution.

Kurland, Philip B., and Ralph Lerner, eds. *The Founders' Constitution.* 4 vols. Chicago: University of Chicago Press, 1987. A collection of the thoughts, opinions, and arguments of the framers of the Constitution. Also accessible online at http://press-pubs.uchicago.edu/founders/

National Archives. *Our Documents: 100 Milestone Documents from the National Archives.* New York: Oxford University Press, 2003. The Constitution and other basic documents of American democracy.

Rakove, Jack. *James Madison and the Creation of the American Republic.* New York: Longman, 2002. A biography of the principal author of the Constitution.

Rakove, Jack. *Original Meanings: Politics and Ideas in the Making of the Constitution.* New York: Knopf, 1996. A rebuttal of the doctrine of "original intent."

Rodell, Fred. *55 Men: The Story of the Constitution, Based on the Day-by-Day Notes of James Madison.* 1936. Reprint, Harrisburg, Pa.: Stackpole, 1986. The story of the delegates and their debates at the Constitutional Convention.

Rossiter, Clinton. *1787: The Grand Convention.* 1966. Reprint, New York: W.W. Norton, 1987. A perceptive retelling of the Constitutional Convention.

Ratifying the Constitution

Alexander, John. *The Selling of the Constitutional Convention: A History of News Coverage.* Madison, Wis.: Madison House, 1990. How the press covered the Constitution.

Cornell, Samuel. *The Other Founders: Anti-Federalism and the Dissenting Tradition in America, 1788–1828.* Chapel Hill: University of North Carolina Press, 1999. The loyal opposition's viewpoint.

Cooke, Jacob E., ed. *The Federalist.* Middletown, Conn.: Wesleyan University Press, 1961. An authoritative text of the essays that helped win ratification of the Constitution. *The Federalist* is also accessible online at: http://thomas.loc.gov/home/histdox/fedpapers.html

Jensen, Merrill. *The New Nation: A History of the United States during the Confederation, 1781–1789.* 1950. Reprint, Boston: Northeastern University Press, 1981. The tumultuous years leading to the Constitutional Convention.

Kaminski, John P., and Richard Leffler, eds. *Federalists and Antifederalists: The Debate over the Ratification of the Constitution.* Madison, Wis.: Madison House, 1989. The arguments on both sides of the ratification fight.

Ketchum, Ralph, ed. *The Anti-Federalist Papers; and, The Constitutional Convention Debates.* New York: New American Library, 1986. Arguments of the opponents of the Constitution.

Morris, Richard B. *Witnesses at the Creation: Hamilton, Madison, Jay, and the Constitution.* New York: Holt, Rinehart, and Winston, 1985. The story of the authors of *The Federalist.*

Sheehan, Colleen A., and Gary L. McDowell, eds. *Friends of the Constitution: Writings of the "Other" Federalists, 1787–1788.* Indianapolis: Liberty Fund, 1998. Other defenders of the Constitution beyond the authors of *The Federalist.*

Wills, Gary. *Explaining America: The Federalist.* Garden City, N.Y.: Doubleday, 1981. An analysis of the writings of Madison, Hamilton, and Jay.

Amending the Constitution

American Political Science Association and American Historical Association. *This Constitution: From Ratification to the Bill of Rights.* Washington: Congressional Quarterly, 1998. Historical essays on the writing, ratification, and early amending of the Constitution.

Berger, Raoul. *The Fourteenth Amendment and the Bill of Rights.* Norman: University of Oklahoma Press, 1989. How one amendment changed the others.

Bernstein, Richard B., with Jerome Agel. *Amending America: If We Love the Constitution So Much, Why Do We Keep Trying to Change It?* New York: Times Books, 1993. A survey and analysis of the many proposed amendments to the Constitution.

Cortner, Richard C. *The Iron Horse and the Constitution: The Railroads and the Transformation of the Fourteenth Amendment.* Westport, Conn.: Greenwood, 1993. How the railroads changed a Reconstruction Era amendment.

Flexner, Eleanor, and Ellen Fitzpatrick. *Century of Struggle: The Woman's Rights Movement in the United States.* Enlarged ed. Cambridge, Mass.: Harvard University Press, 1996. A history of the long protest movement leading to the Nineteenth Amendment.

Kyvig, David E. *Explicit and Authentic Act: Amending the U.S. Constitution.* Lawrence: University Press of Kansas, 1996. An authoritative study of the substance and process of amending the Constitution.

Meyer, Howard N. *The Amendment that Refused to Die: Equality and Justice Deferred: The History of the Fourteenth Amendment.* Updated ed. Lanham, Md.: Madison Books, 2000. The tortuous history of defining the Fourteenth Amendment.

Monk, Linda R. *The Words We Live By: Your Annotated Guide to the Constitution.* New York: Hyperion, 2004. A guided tour of the Constitution's various parts and their historical impact.

Patrick, John J. *The Bill of Rights: A History in Documents.* New York: Oxford University Press, 2003. Key documents relating to the first ten amendments to the Constitution.

Veit, Helen E., Kenneth R. Bowling, and Charlene Bangs Bickford, eds. *Creating the Bill of Rights: The Documentary Record of the First Federal Congress.* Baltimore: Johns Hopkins University Press, 1991. Documents how Congress enacted the Bill of Rights.

Zacharias, Gary, and Jared Zacharias, eds. *The Bill of Rights.* San Diego, Calif.: Greenhaven, 2003. Aspects of civil rights and civil liberties under the Bill of Rights.

Implementing the Constitution

Abraham, Henry J. *Justices and Presidents: A Political History of Appointments to the Supreme Court.* 3rd ed. New York: Oxford University Press, 1992. Two centuries of struggle between the executive and the legislature over the judiciary.

Amar, Akhil Reed. *America's Constitution: A Biography.* New York: Random House, 2005. Reviews the long life and changing times of the Constitution as a legal and political document.

Beth, Loren P. *The Development of the American Constitution, 1877–1917.* New York: Harper & Row, 1971. Constitutional law in the Gilded Age.

Crabb, Cecil W., Jr., and Pat M. Holt. *Invitation to Struggle: Congress, the President, and Foreign Policy.* Washington, D.C.: Congressional Quarterly Press, 1992. How the Constitution inspires constant struggle between the White House and Capitol Hill over foreign policy.

Cunliffe, Marcus. *The Nation Takes Shape: 1789–1837.* Chicago: University of Chicago Press, 1959. A compact history of the early years of constitutional government.

Currie, David P. *The Constitution in Congress: The Federalist Period, 1789–1801.* Chicago: University of Chicago Press, 1997. How Congress initially implemented the Constitution.

Dahl, Robert A. *How Democratic Is the American Constitution?* New Haven, Conn.: Yale University Press, 2001. An essay on the lapses of democracy in the Constitution.

Fisher, Louis. *The Politics of Shared Power: Congress and the Executive.* College Station: Texas A&M University Press, 1998. The overlapping areas of responsibility resulting from the separation of powers.

Foner, Eric. *Reconstruction: America's Unfinished Revolution, 1863–1877.* New York; Harper & Row, 1988. Includes the history of the Thirteenth, Fourteenth, and Fifteenth Amendments and related laws and court cases, as well as the struggle between the President and Congress over Reconstruction policy.

Foner, Eric. *The Story of American Freedom.* New York: W. W. Norton, 1998. An analysis of how well the Constitution secured the "blessings of liberty."

Garraty, John A. *Quarrels that Have Shaped the Constitution.* Rev. ed. New York: Harper & Row, 1987. Historical case studies of landmark Supreme Court decisions.

Greenberg, Jack. *Crusaders in the Courts: How a Dedicated Band of Lawyers Fought for the Civil Rights Revolution.* New York: Basic Books, 1994. The story of the lawyers for the NAACP and their efforts to convince the courts to reinterpret the Constitution.

Hall, Kermit L., ed. *The Oxford Companion to the Supreme Court of the United States.* 2nd ed. New York: Oxford University Press, 2005. Entries on the functioning and decisions of the Supreme Court.

Hobson, Charles F. *The Great Chief Justice: John Marshall and the Rule of Law.* Lawrence: University Press of Kansas, 1996. The long-lasting impact of Chief Justice Marshall.

Hyman, Harold M., and William M. Wiecek. *Equal Justice under Law: Constitutional Development, 1835–1875.* New York: Harper & Row, 1982. The Constitution from slavery to freedom, through the Civil War and Reconstruction.

Kammen, Michael G. *A Machine that Would Go of Itself: The Constitution in American Culture.* New York: St. Martin's, 1994. A social and cultural history of the Constitution.

Klarman, Michael J. *From Jim Crow to Civil Rights: The Supreme Court and the Struggle for Racial Equality.* New York: Oxford University Press, 2004. The evolution of judicial thinking on civil rights.

Levy, Leonard W., Kenneth L. Karst, and Dennis J. Mahoney, eds. *Encyclopedia of the American Constitution.* 6 vols. New York: Macmillan, 2000. Interpretive essays on every aspect of the Constitution.

Morris, Richard B. *The Forging of the Union, 1781–1789.* New York: Harper & Row, 1987. The United States under the Articles of Confederation.

Murphy, Paul L. *The Constitution in Crisis Times, 1918–1969.* New York: Harper & Row, 1972. A history of the Constitution in the critical years of the twentieth century.

Patrick, John J. *The Supreme Court of the United States: A Student Companion.* 2nd ed. New York: Oxford University Press, 2001. Entries on how the Supreme Court operates, including constitutional case law.

Patrick, John J., and Gerald P. Long, eds. *Constitutional Debates on Freedom of Religion: A Documentary History.* Westport, Conn.: Greenwood, 1999. Understanding the First Amendment.

Pious, Richard M. *The Presidency.* Boston: Allyn and Bacon, 1996. The evolution of the office of President of the United States.

Pious, Richard M. *The Presidency of the United States: A Student Companion.* 2nd ed. New York: Oxford University Press, 2001. Entries on the operations of the American Presidency.

Rehnquist, William H. *All the Laws but One: Civil Liberties in Wartime.* New York: Knopf, 1998. A chief justice reviews the history of civil liberties in wartime.

Rehnquist, William H. *The Supreme Court.* New York: Knopf, 2001. A chief justice examines the evolution of the Supreme Court.

Ritchie, Donald A. *The Congress of the United States: A Student Companion.* 2nd ed. New York: Oxford University Press, 2001. Entries on aspects of how Congress operates.

Ritchie, Donald A. *The U.S. Constitution.* New York: Chelsea House, 1988. A bicentennial summary of constitutional history.

Schlesinger, Arthur M., Jr. *The Imperial Presidency.* Boston: Houghton Mifflin, 1973. The growth of Presidential power from the founders to Watergate.

Simon, James F. *What Kind of a Nation? Thomas Jefferson, John Marshall, and the Epic Struggle to Create the United States.* New York: Simon & Schuster, 2002. Two polar opposites in the interpretation and implementation of the U.S. Constitution.

Stone, Geoffrey R. *Perilous Times: Free Speech in Wartime from the Sedition Act of 1798 to the War on Terror.* New York: Norton, 2004. Wartime tests to the First Amendment.

Warren, Earl. *The Memoirs of Earl Warren.* Garden City, N.Y.: Doubleday, 1977. A major twentieth-century chief justice explains how the Court changed under his leadership.

White, G. Edward. *The Marshall Court and Cultural Change, 1815–1835.* New York: Oxford University Press, 1991. How the Supreme Court applied the Constitution to an evolving nation.

Websites

The American Presidency   http://ap.grolier.com/
Sponsored by Grolier Online, an educational portal drawing from Grolier's various encyclopedias, this site provides information about American Presidents, Vice Presidents, Presidential candidates, and Presidential elections.

The American President   http://www.americanpresident.org/
Sponsored by the Miller Center of the University of Virginia, this site examines the history and function of the American Presidency, drawing in part on the Miller Center's oral histories with members of various Presidential administrations.

American Presidents   http://www.americanpresidents.org/
Based on C-SPAN's television series, this site provides extensive material on each President, featuring video interviews with historians, visits to Presidential sites, and extensive background information.

The Articles of Confederation
http://www.yale.edu/lawweb/avalon/artconf.htm
Sponsored by the Avalon Project at Yale Law School, this site offers the text of the Articles of Confederation and other documents relating to it and the road to the U.S. Constitution.

Bill of Rights Institute   http://www.billofrightsinstitute.org
The Bill of Rights Institute's mission is to educate high school students and teachers about the Constitution and Bill of Rights through the words and ideas of the framers. It examines the liberties and freedoms guaranteed in these founding documents and how they have affected and shaped a free society. The site includes classroom lessons and other materials for teachers, landmark Supreme Court cases, and historical documents.

Center for Civil Education   http://www.civiced.org/index.php
The Center for Civil Education specializes in civic and law-related education and international educational exchange programs for developing democracies. Its programs focus on the U.S. Constitution and Bill of Rights; American political institutions at the federal, state, and local levels; and the rights and responsibilities of citizens. This site offers lessons for students from kindergarten up to 12th grade regarding Constitution Day and Citizenship Day, and other resources for teachers and school coordinators. It also includes an online newsletter and various speeches, articles, and papers relating to the Constitution and to the annual "We the People" competition for students, which is sponsored by the center.

CongressLink   http://www.congresslink.org/
Sponsored by the Everett McKinley Dirksen Center, in Pekin, Illinois, CongressLink offers information about the U.S. Congress—its operations, its members, its leaders, and its public policies, with a mix of current and historical information.

Constitutional Rights Center   http://www.crf-usa.org/
The Los Angeles–based Constitution Rights Center provides technical assistance and training to teachers; coordinates civic participation projects in schools and communities; organizes student conferences, competitions, and mock trials; and develops publications on law and government. Through its civic participation programs it educates on the rights and responsibilities of active citizenship. The site features online lessons on the Constitution and constitutional law and information about available educational programs.

The Constitution Project   http://www.constitutionproject.org
An organization that seeks consensus on controversial legal and constitutional issues through a unique combination of scholarship and activism, the Constitution Project has produced a number of books and other material as resources for reporters, lawmakers, and students. The site contains information about the project's many initiatives, announcements of public programs, and various free publications.

Famous Trials
http://www.law.umkc.edu/faculty/projects/ftrials/ftrials.htm
A plethora of information about famous trials in the United States and other nations, offering essays, transcripts, and evidence.

The Federal Judiciacy   http://www.uscourts.gov
An official website maintained by the Administrative Office of the U.S. Courts that offers information from and about the judicial branch, including the Supreme Court, appeals courts, district courts, and bankruptcy courts.

The Federalist
http://www.law.emory.edu/FEDERAL/federalist/
This site offers the entire text of *The Federalist* essays by James Madison, Alexander Hamilton, and John Jay, written to explain and promote the ratification of the Constitution

First Amendment Center   http://www.fac.org
The First Amendment Center, based at Vanderbilt University and in Arlington, Virginia, offers research tools on key First Amendment issues and topics, a First Amendment Library, and guest analyses by legal specialists. The site offers research material on free-

dom of speech, press, religion, assembly, and petition, and provides a digest of ongoing cases involving these freedoms.

First Federal Congress Project

http://www.gwu.edu/~ffcp/exhibit/

A massive publication project on the First Congress, its members, and its output, the First Federal Congress Project also offers online exhibits related to the First Congress, which passed the Bill of Rights and otherwise implemented the Constitution.

Founders' Constitution

http://press-pubs.uchicago.edu/founders/

An authoritative account of the writings and arguments of the delegates to the convention.

The Freedom Forum

http://www.freedomforum.org/

A nonpartisan foundation dedicated to free press, free speech, and free spirit for all people, the Freedom Forum operates the Newseum in Washington, D.C. (http://www.newseum.org/).

Its website includes the Freedom Library, an online library that serves as a clearinghouse for information concerning the five freedoms guaranteed by the First Amendment: speech, press, assembly, petition, and religion. It offers an array of judicial, legislative, historical, analytical, journalistic, editorial, and other materials.

History Matters

http://historymatters.gmu.edu/

This massive site serves as a U.S. history survey on the Internet. Among its many offerings is an abundance of information relating to the Constitution, the Bill of Rights, and the many political events and judicial decisions that have shaped the United States.

Justice Learning

http://www.justicelearning.org/

An innovative, issue-based approach for engaging in informed political discourse, sponsored by the Annenberg Foundation. This website uses audio from the Justice Talking radio show and articles from the *New York Times* to teach students about reasoned debate and the often-conflicting values inherent in our democracy. It includes articles, editorials, and oral debate from journalists and advocates. The material is supported by summaries and additional links, with curricular material for high school teachers and detailed information about how the courts, the Congress, the Presidency, the press, and the schools affect the issue. The site includes Justice Learning's Guide to the Constitution.

Landmark Supreme Court Cases

http://www.landmarkcases.org/

Sponsored by Street Law and the Supreme Court Historical Society, this site provides a full range of resources and activities to support the teaching of landmark Supreme Court cases, helping students explore the key issues of each case. Its "resources" section features background summaries and excerpts of opinions. The "activities" section contains a range of exercises.

Library of Congress, American Memory

http://memory.loc.gov/ammem/help/constRedir.html

This massive site includes a compilation of documents related to the Constitutional Convention and the evolution of Congress. Its Thomas site also provides extensive information on the current activities of Congress (http://thomas.loc.gov/).

National Archives and Records Administration

http://www.archives.gov/

The records of the entire federal government are housed in the National Archives. This site provides find aids and other information about those records, and a National Archives Digital Classroom (http://www.archives.gov/digital_classroom/) geared toward teaching with documents, including the Constitution.

The National Constitution Center

http://www.constitutioncenter.org/

An impressive museum dedicated to the Constitution, the National Constitution Center is located in Philadelphia, within sight of Independence Hall, where the Constitution was drafted. The center aims to increase public understanding of, and appreciation for, the Constitution, its history, and its contemporary relevance. This website provides information about the museum and its changing exhibits, with other materials related to the Constitution.

Our Documents

http://www.ourdocuments.gov

A joint project of the National Archives, the History Channel, National History Day, and the USA Freedom Corps, this site helps people think, talk, and teach about the rights and responsibilities of citizens. It offers 100 milestone documents of American history that reflect the nation's diversity and unity, and the commitment to strive to "form a more perfect union."

United States House of Representatives

http://www.house.gov/

The official website of the House of Representatives offers information about current members, committees, floor proceedings, and legislation. It also contains historical information about the House (http://clerk.house.gov/histHigh/index.html).

United States Senate

http://www.senate.gov

The official website of the Senate, gives similar information about the current senators, and committees, as well as extensive reference information on the history of the institution and the U.S. Capitol.

United States Supreme Court

http://www.supremecourtus.gov/

The official website of the Supreme Court provides information about the current justices and the Court's most recent cases.

White House

http://www.whitehouse.gov/

The official website of the White House provides information about the recent activities of the president and first lady, as well as life in the White House.

Museums and Historic Sites
Related to the Constitution

Federal Hall

26 Wall Street, New York, NY 10005

212-825-6990

http://www.nps.gov/feha/

On this site stood Federal Hall, when the Congress under the Articles of Confederation met in 1787, while the Constitution was being written in Philadelphia. The First Congress met here from 1789 to 1790, and George Washington was inaugurated as the first President on its balcony. It was in this hall that the first Congress debated and passed the amendments that became the Bill of Rights. Federal Hall was demolished in 1812. The current building opened in 1842 as the U. S. Customs House. In 1920, it became a Federal Reserve Bank. The museum includes a video and exhibits that highlight the events that occurred in Federal Hall.

Gunston Hall, George Mason's home

10709 Gunston Road, Mason Neck, VA 22079

http://www.gunstonhall.org/

Although he served as a delegate to the Constitutional Convention, George Mason did not sign the Constitution because it lacked a bill of rights. Mason, the author of Virginia's Declaration of Rights, lived in Gunston Hall, a plantation twenty miles south of Washington, D.C. Today, you can visit this Georgian house, constructed between 1755 and 1760, on a 550-acre site in Fairfax County, Virginia.

Independence Hall

6th and Market Streets, Philadelphia, PA 19106

215-965-2305 (Visitor Center)

http://www.nps.gov/inde

Located in Center City Philadelphia, Independence National Historical Park is the birthplace of the United States, the location of the signing of the Declaration of Independence and the drafting of the U.S. Constitution. The park also interprets events and the lives of the diverse population of Philadelphia during the years from 1790 to 1800, when the city was the capital of the United States. A section of the park where Benjamin Franklin's home once stood is dedicated to teaching about Franklin's life and accomplishments. Spanning approximately forty-five acres, the park has about twenty buildings open to the public.

Manzanar National Historic Site

P.O. Box 426, Independence, CA 93526-0426

760-878-2194 ext. 10

http://www.nps.gov/manz/

At the foot of the Sierra Nevada Mountains in California's Owens Valley, during World War II, the Manzanar War Relocation Center served as one of ten camps in which Japanese American citizens and resident Japanese aliens were interned. Today it stands as a monument to a lapse in our constitutional civil liberties. Its interpretive center offers exhibits and a twenty-minute introductory film.

Montpelier, James Madison's home

11407 Constitution Highway, Montpelier Station, VA 22957

540-672-2728

http://www.montpelier.org/

In Orange County, Virginia, about midway between Washington, D.C., and Charlottesville, stands the home of James and Dolley Madison. Montpelier is a 2,750-acre estate that includes farmland, racecourses, a terraced 2-acre formal garden, a panoramic landscape, a National Landmark Forest, active archaeological sites, and more than 130 buildings, including the main house. The Montpelier Education Center features exhibits on Madison's life and his role as an architect of the Constitution and Bill of Rights.

Mount Vernon, home of George Washington

3200 Mount Vernon Memorial Highway

Mount Vernon, VA 22121

703-780-2000

http://www.mountvernon.org

At Mount Vernon, representatives from Maryland and Virginia met in 1785 to discuss navigation rights on the Potomac River. This meeting set in motion a chain of events that culminated with the Constitutional Convention in 1787, over which Washington presided. The farm where Washington lived and is buried was called the Mansion House Farm. Today about five hundred acres remain of the original eight thousand. It stands on the shore of the Potomac River, south of Washington, D.C.

National Archives and Records Administration

700 Constitution Avenue, NW, Washington, DC 20408
202-501-5000
http://www.archives.gov/
The Constitution and other original documents are on display in the Rotunda of the National Archives. There are also interactive exhibits on the "Treasures of the Vault," featuring samples of the records of the United States government housed in the Archives.

National Constitution Center

525 Arch Street, Independence Mall, Philadelphia, PA 19106
866-917-1787
http://www.constitutioncenter.org/index.shtml
Established by the Constitution Heritage Act of 1988, the National Constitution Center opened on July 4, 2003. Located on Independence Mall in Philadelphia, it stands within sight of Independence Hall. The center tells the story of the U.S. Constitution through interactive and multimedia exhibits, photographs, texts, films, and artifacts. A striking feature is its Hall of Signers, where visitors can wander among life-size bronze statutes of the framers of the Constitution.

National Underground Railroad Freedom Center

50 East Freedom Way, Cincinnati, OH 45202
877-648-4838
http://www.freedomcenter.org
The National Underground Railroad Freedom Center brings to life the struggles for freedom around the world and throughout history. Made up of three buildings that symbolize the cornerstones of freedom—courage, cooperation, and perseverance—the Freedom Center directly addresses the most contentious issue of the Constitution and the early republic, the existence of human slavery.

The Newseum

Pennsylvania Avenue and Sixth Street, NW
Washington, DC 20001
888-NEWSEUM or 703-284-3544
http://www.newseum.org
Scheduled to open in 2007, this interactive museum of news seeks to further public understanding of the news media. It is dedicated to the First Amendment rights of a free press, free speech, freedom to worship, freedom to assemble, and freedom to petition the government for redress of grievances.

The United States Capitol

First Street, Washington, DC, 20001
202-225-6827
http://www.aoc.gov
The United States Capitol is a magnificent monument, but it is also a working legislative building where the Senate and House meet to debate and vote on legislation. Among the historic rooms open to visitors are the original Supreme Court room, where Chief Justices John Marshall and Roger B. Taney presided over the Court; the Old Senate Chamber, where Henry Clay, Daniel Webster, and John C. Calhoun debated; and Statuary Hall, the old chamber of the House of Representatives, where John Quincy Adams and Abraham Lincoln once served.

The United States Supreme Court

One First Street, NE, Washington, DC 20543
202-479-3211
http://www.supremecourtus.gov
Located on Capitol Hill, across from the U.S. Capitol, is the building the Supreme Court has occupied since 1935. In its chamber the Court hears oral arguments and renders decisions. The Supreme Court also offers a variety of educational programs, exhibits, and a theater, where a film on the Supreme Court is shown.

The White House

1600 Pennsylvania Avenue, NW, Washington, DC 20500
202-456-7041
http://www.whitehouse.gov/history/tours
The White House has been home to every President since John Adams. Tours focus on the elegant state rooms on the first floor, where Presidential meetings, press conferences, and formal entertainments take place. Tours do not include the family quarters on the upper floors, or the West Wing, where the Oval Office is located and where the President, Vice President, and high-level presidential aides work, making it literally the hub of the executive branch of government.

Women's Rights National Park

136 Fall Street, Seneca Falls, NY 13148
315-568-2991
http://nps.gov/wori/
In 1848 women's rights advocates met in Seneca Falls, New York, where they called for equal rights for women, including the right to vote. This was the beginning of the movement toward passage of the Nineteenth Amendment. The Women's Rights National Historical Park consists of four major historical properties: the Wesleyan Chapel, where the First Women's Rights Convention took place, and the homes of several people active in the movement, Elizabeth Cady Stanton, Thomas and Mary Ann M'Clintock, and Richard and Jane Hunt. A visitor center offers a film and exhibits.

Index

Pictures and their captions are indicated by page numbers in **bold**.

Picture Credits

akg-images, London: 231 (1956); Courtesy, American Antiquarian Society: 128; AP: 83 (bottom), 152; Architect of the Capitol: 73; Architect of the Capitol, National Statuary Hall: 83 (top); Architect of the Capitol, Senate Wing of the U.S. Capitol: 129; Courtesy of the Atwater Kent Museum of Philadelphia: 90; The Authentic History Center: 200 (1929, 1934) 201 (1919), 204 (1890), 213 (1940); bpk Berlin / Photo: Erich Salomon: 118; © British Library / HIP / Art Resource, NY: 19; Courtesy of the Bronx County Historical Society Collections. The Bronx, New York: 153; George Bush Presidential Library: 55, 224 (1981); Center for legislative archives, National Archives: 61, 60, 89 (bottom), 108; Center for the Study of Complex Systems, University of Michigan: 175 (1952); Chicago Historical Society ICHi-26257: 211 (top); Citizens Committee for the Right to Keep and Bear Arms: 144; William J. Clinton Presidential Library: 89 (top); Corocan Gallery of Art, Washington, D.C.: 72; DCVote.org: 215; Courtesy Death with Dignity National Center: 164; Department of Defense: 99, 102, 115 (199); Jeffrey D. Allred, Deseret Morning News: 159; Feinmore Art Museum, Cooperstown, NY / Richard Walker: 58; Courtesy Gerald R. Ford Library: 222; © Gilcrease Museum: 14; The Granger Collection, New York: 28; Image Select / Art Resource, NY: 143 (head); Courtesy, Independence National Historical Park: 12 (top), 16 (top), 139, 196 (1928); © Inter-IKEA Systems B.V., 1990 / U.S. Senate Historical Office: 229; Lyndon Baines Johnson Library, National Archives and Records Admninistration: 110; Kansas State Historical Society: 92; Courtesy Abraham Katz, Private Collection: 213 (1986, Both); Collection of James C. Kelly / Virginia Historical Society: 32; U.S. Army Signal Corps/John Fitzgerald Kennedy Library, Boston: 209 (head); Courtesy of Kent State University Press: 199; Kiplinger Washington Collection.: 21; Edward Kuekes © 11/9/1952 The Plain Dealer. Reprinted with Permission: 226; Lester S. Levy Collection / Johns Hopkins University: 2; Library of Congress, American Memory:177 (top), 203 (bottom); Library of Congress, Geography and Maps Division 59, 100; Library of Congress, Manuscript Division 49, 85 (bottom); Library of Congress, Prints and

Photographs Division: 10, 22, 40, 43, 45, 46, 47, 48, 62, 70, 71 right, 81, 82, 85 top, 91 (bottom), 94, 97 (1898), 106, 111, 113, 114 (1798), 114 (1795), 115 (1815), 117 (top), 120, 122 (top), 124 (1795), 131, 132, 133, 135 (top), 142 (1918), 142 (1836), 142 (1962), 143 (1989), 145, 147 (2000), 154 (1943), 154 (1876), 155 (1924), 158 (1968), 158 (1930), 158 (1948), 159 (head), 159 (1971), 159 (1954), 160, 162 (1890), 162 (1910), 163 (head), 166 (1819), 166 (1918), 166 (1973), 167 (head), 167 (1935), 167 (1941), 167 (1936), 171 (head), 174 (1787), 174 (1828), 177 (bottom), 178 (1863), 179 (head), 179 (1914), 180, 185 (head), 185 (1966), 185 (1954), 185 (1896), 186, 187 (bottom), 187 (top), 188 (1870), 189 (head), 189 (1964), 196 (1896), 197 (1965), 198, 202, 201 (1927), 204 (1872), 204 (1916), 205 (1872), 204 (1848), 205 (head), 205 (1874), 205 (1922), 206, 208 (1788), 208 (1940), 208 (1937), 209 (1954), 209 (1841), 212 (1809), 212 (1946), 213 (1960), 213 (1912), 215 (1800), 216 (1790), 217 (1970), 218, 219, 220 (1965), 220 (1964), 221 (head), 221 (1949), 221 (1966), 224 (1841), 224 (1974), 225 (1991), 225 (1973), 230 (1941), 231 (1972); Library of Congress, Prints and Photographs / New York World-Telegram and Sun Collection: 7, 23, 27, 35, 37, 38, 39, 51 (top &bottom), 53, 95, 98, 105, 109, 116, 119 (bottom), 123, 136, 141 (top), 172, 183, 191 (bottom), 195 (bottom), 210; Library of Congress/ Alexandria Szyk Bracie / Arthur Szyk Society www.szyk.org: 68 (bottom); Library of Congress, Prints and Photographs Division / © 1925, The Washington Post: 214 (left); Library of Congress, Prints and Photographs Division © 1929, The Washington Post: 191 (top); Library of Congress, U.S. Copyright Archives 93 (bottom); The Mariner's Museum, Newport News, VA: 103; Mary Evans Picture Library: 115 (head), 170 (1821), 188 (1877), 212 (1875); Minnesota Historical Society: 97 (1861); Minnesota Public Radio / Lorna Benson (127); Montana Historical Society, Helena, PAc 87-103: 203 (top); The Museum of American Political Life, University of Hartford: 50, 57,174 (1797), 175 (1888); NARA/ General Records of the United States Government; Record Group 11: 33, 228, 230 (1789); NARA, Louisiana Purchase Treaty, April 30, 1803; General Records of the U.S. Government; Record

Group 11: 114 (1803); NARA, Old Military and Civil Records: 112, 121 (bottom); NARA: Records of the Continental and Confederation Congresses and the Constitutional Convention, 1774-1789, Record Group 360; Old Military and Civil Records: Cover, 13, 17, 68-69 (top); NARA / Records of the United States Senate: 173; NARA, 306-PS-176-S-51-141: 156; NARA, 306-SSM-4C(46)14: 36; NARA, 48-CP-121: 15; NARA, 64-NA-113A: 9; NARA, 67-49-9a: 224; NARA, 69-RP-8-113: 26; NARA, E3397C-05A: 65; NARA, NAIL: NWDNS-111-C-CC45804: 52; NARA, NWDNS-148-CC-13(3): 31; NARA, NWDNS-179-WP-165: 193 (1943); NARA, NWDNS-44-PA-2474: 192 (1924); NARA, NWDNS-44-PA-2474A: 190; NARA, NWDNS-4-P-224: 91 (top); National Constitution Center, groundbreaking ceremony, September 17, 2000: 56; A View of Mount Vernon, Gift of Edgar William and Bernice Chrysler Garbisch Image © 2005 Board of Trustees, National Gallery of Art, Washington: 11; © National Maritime Museum: 169; National Museum of American History, Smithsonian Institution: 188 (1957), 220, (1898); Courtesy of the National Museum of the U.S. Army, Army Art Collection: 78; Courtesy National Numismatic Collection, Smithsonian Institution / Photography by Richard Doty: 107; Photograph by Ted Polumbaum / Newseum: 187; Collection of the New-York Historical Society negative number 1176, accession number 1903.12: 18; Collection of the New-York Historical Society negative number 1372, accession number 1864.17: 16 (bottom); Collection of the New-York Historical Society, negative number 50758: 104; Courtesy of JP Morgan and Chase Archives / Collection of the New-York Historical Society: 122 (bottom); Photography Collection, Miriam and Ira D. Wallach Division of Art, Prints and Photographs, The New York Public Library, Astor, Lenox and Tilden Foundations: 197 (1914); Picture Collection, The Branch Libraries, The New York Public Library, Astor, Lenox and Tilden Foundations: 76, 181; © 1958, The Washington Post / General Research Division, the New York Public Library, Astor, Lenox, and Tilden Foundations: 63; Courtesy of the New York State Museum: 42; Nevada Historical Society: 126 (left and right); Barack Obama for Illinois: 195 (top);

Onemileup.com: 71, (left and middle), 147 (1968), 193 (1953); 197 (head), 225 (head); Planned Parenthood® Federation of America, Inc © 2005 PPFA, All Rights Reserved: 165; Princeton University Library, Political Cartoon Collection. Public Policy Papers. Department of Rare Books and Special Collections. Princeton University Library: 211 (bottom); Courtesy Ronald Reagan Library: 117 (bottom); Reflections Photography / Washington D.C.: 214 (right); Courtesy of the Franklin Delano Roosevelt Library: 24; Mary Scullion Collection, photo: Nora Wertz: 225 (1963); Shutterstock: 96 (1812), 96 (1941), 96 (1801), 97 (1991), 97 (Head), 114 (1848), 124 (1798), 125 (head), 125 (1970), 125 (1980), 142 (1966), 146 (1934), 146 (1939), 146 (1994), 147 (1987), 147 (1996), 150 (1914), 150 (1949), 150 (1984), 151 (1965), 151 (1968), 151 (2001), 151 (2003), 151 (head), 154 (1857), 155 (1922), 155 (head), 162 (1977), 163 (1943), 163 (1998), 167 (1995), 170 (1974), 171 (1892), 171 (1908), 171 (2002), 175 (head), 178 (1918), 178 (1949), 179 (1972), 179 (1993), 179 (2003), 184 (1873), 184 (1964), 185 (2005), 192 (1894 both), 192 (1927), 193 (2003), 193 (head), 200 (1913), 201 (2005), 201 (1987), 216 (1964), 217 (1871), 230 (1978), 231 (1982); Shutterstock.com / Jason Maehl: 119 (top); Shutterstock.com / Stanislav Khrapov: 12 bottom; Vic Boswell / *Collection of the Supreme Court of the United States:* 121 (top), 168; Collection, The Supreme Court Historical Society: 148; Supreme Court Historical Society (Lester Sloan / Woodfin Camp and Associates): 54; Courtesy of the State Preservation Board, Austin, Texas. CHA 1989.685, Photographer Eric Beggs, 6/4/97, post conservation: 34; Jim Steinhart of TravelPhotoBase.com: 130; Edward Lewis Bartlett Papers, UAF-1969-95-115, Archives, Alaska and Polar Regions Collections, Rasmuson Library, University of Alaska Fairbanks: 79; Doonesbury © 1987 G. B. Trudeau. Reprinted with permission of Universal Press Syndicate: 135 (bottom); United States Court of Appeals for the Federal Circuit: 124 (1891); United States Patent Office: 93 (top); U.S. Senate Collection: 75, U.S. Senate Historical Office: 66, 80, 207, 196, (1906); Westerville Public Library: 201 (head); Jeff White: 200 (1851); Wisconsin Historical Society, Whi-30131: 86; Quill Logo: Getty images

ABOUT THE AUTHOR

Donald A. Ritchie is associate historian of the U.S. Senate. He is the author of *Reporting from Washington: The History of the Washington Press Corps*; *Press Gallery: Congress and the Washington Correspondents* (which won the Organization of American Historians' Richard Leopold Prize); *American Journalists: Getting the Story*; *Doing Oral History: A Practical Guide*; *James M. Landis: Dean of the Regulators*; and *The Congress of the United States: A Student Companion*. He is the coauthor of *The Oxford Guide to the United States Government* and of several high school textbooks, including *The American Vision* and *The American Republic*. Dr. Ritchie has served on the editorial board of *The Public Historian*, edited the Twayne oral history series, and prepared for publication the previously closed hearings of Senator Joseph R. McCarthy. A former president of the Oral History Association, he has served on the councils of the American Historical Association, the Society for History in the Federal Government, and the International Oral History Association, and has taught in the Cornell in Washington program.

ABOUT JUSTICE LEARNING

Justice Learning is an innovative, issue-based approach for engaging high school students in informed political discourse. The web site uses audio from the *Justice Talking* radio show and articles from *The New York Times* to teach students about reasoned debate and the often-conflicting values inherent in our democracy. The web site includes articles, editorials, and oral debate from the nation's finest journalists and advocates. All of the material is supported by age-appropriate summaries and additional links. In addition, for each covered issue, the site includes curricular material from *The New York Times* Learning Network for high school teachers and detailed information about how each of the institutions of democracy (the courts, the Congress, the presidency, the press, and the schools) affect the issue.